SAMUEL DAVIES

Apostle of Dissent in Colonial Virginia

SAMUEL DAVIES

Apostle of Dissent in Colonial Virginia

GEORGE WILLIAM PILCHER

THE UNIVERSITY OF TENNESSEE PRESS

Knoxville

LIBRARY OF CONGRESS CATALOG CARD NUMBER 77–134737
INTERNATIONAL STANDARD BOOK NUMBER 87049–121–0

Copyright © 1971 by The University of Tennessee Press
Printed in the United States of America
All Rights Reserved. First Edition

Frontispiece: Samuel Davies. A line conversion from
the original in the collections of the
Presbyterian Historical Society, Philadelphia

For Jean

Preface

SAMUEL DAVIES was convinced that God had pulled him from
death's door to send him on his three-hundred-mile errand into
the wilderness of Virginia. Had Divine Providence not intervened,
the young pastor, in poor health and painfully unsure of himself,
most certainly would not have left home and friends in Delaware to
set out for his first pastorate in frontier Hanover. In fact, just a year
earlier in the spring of 1747, Samuel had turned down the same
position, and the mental and physical state that had prompted the
refusal had only worsened since that time. The year had been one
of long hours of study and almost constant travel on horseback to
increasingly numerous preaching assignments, further damaging
his health to the point that his concerned parents were now accompanying him. Even more serious personally had been the recent loss of his wife and abortive son. It had truly been a bleak
winter for Samuel. Furthermore, he was acutely aware of the
hostile forces awaiting him in Virginia, not only the opposition of
the Anglican Church toward dissenting preachers, but also the
antagonism of the conservative faction within his own Presbyterian
denomination. But the twenty-four-year-old novice, after strenuous prayer and self-examination, and after recovering from a serious and extended illness—miraculously, it seemed to him—had

now resolved his doubts. He would follow what he considered his
God-given mission.

During the first few months at Hanover—when Samuel would
hardly venture outside the pulpit for fear of disgracing the cause
of religion in some way—he little suspected the magnitude of his
success in fulfilling this mission. By any standard of measurement,
Samuel Davies was a major leader of the Great Awakening in the
American colonies and perhaps was unsurpassed as a pulpit orator
either in Great Britain or in America. But despite the international
fame this young Virginian enjoyed during a life span of only
thirty-seven years, and despite his lasting influence, he has largely
been ignored in the twentieth-century appraisals of eighteenth-
century America. Writers of recent decades have been prone to
regard the towering New England preacher and thinker, Jonathan
Edwards, as the embodiment of the Great Awakening in America
while neglecting the more varied and, in some respects, equally
significant contributions of his Virginia contemporary. As the first
permanent New Light, or "New Side," preacher in the Old
Dominion, Davies assumed and executed successfully the task of
gaining religious toleration for his followers in an Anglican society.
He gave the religious revival there a spirit of moderation that it
failed to attain in any of the other colonies. His recruiting for the
French and Indian Wars in the 1750's, in addition to serving the
colonial crown, won from the government a new acceptance of the
dissenting movement in Virginia. His oratorical zeal stirred the
emotions of his contemporaries with a fire that lingered long after
his death.

Much of Davies' success and subsequent reputation rests upon
his versatility. In addition to his internationally acclaimed pulpit
oratory, he wrote and published sermons that were commendable
as literary works and were studied by several generations of preachers. The hymnal verse that he composed distinguished him as
America's first important writer of original hymns. From early
youth, the young preacher had dabbled in poetry-writing, and
eventually he published verse that was read the full length of the

Eastern seaboard. As a minister who saw his duties in a much larger perspective than merely preaching, Davies took an active interest in education for his congregation, being among the first colonial leaders to attempt the education of Negro slaves and of the Indians of the colony. As an active and successful participant in the development of colonial education generally, he was selected to represent his church in Great Britain in 1753 in soliciting contributions for the struggling young Presbyterian College of New Jersey. The success of his mission enabled the school not only to expand operations, but also to erect the first permanent buildings of what is now Princeton University. Davies' career culminated in his selection as president of the college in 1759, an office that he held until his untimely death in 1761.

Fortunately for a present-day appreciation of the man, Davies' literary output was as varied as his accomplishments, and his letters and journals speak to us across the centuries with the voice of a warm and living human being. We witness him on his return voyage from England—a voyage that lasted all of three winter months—desperately seasick and high-mindedly philosophical by turns. We smile with him when, beset with doubts in a foreign land, he records in his diary: "My Spirits are generally low, Tho' I feel a kind of stupid Serenity of Mind." Davies did possess serenity of mind, but it was not at all dull. When slaves to whom he had distributed hymnals congregated in his kitchen for an all-night session of singing and woke him in the early morning hours with what must have seemed at that time a strange distortion of familiar hymn tunes and words, he serenely describes the sounds as "A torrent of sacred harmony [that] poured into my chamber, and carried my mind away to Heaven." On the earthly plane, the serious young minister was not without a leavening of human curiosity, as we learn from the journal he kept on his visit to England. On one occasion he was tempted to attend a comedy with the worldly title *The Careless Husband*. This seems to have been the only occasion on which Davies succumbed to temptation. He comments in his journal: "As I apprehended I should not be known and consequently could give no Offence, I went to gratifie my Curiosity," and concludes wryly, "But the entertainment was short of my Expectations."

It is not the purpose of this book to explore the higher metaphysical question of the relationship between man and his God, but rather to show the efforts of a single individual in the attempt to follow his "path of duty." In pursuing this task, the author has had the generous assistance of institutions and individuals too numerous to mention. However, of the more than two dozen libraries kind enough to make available published and unpublished materials, a special note of gratitude must be extended to the libraries of Princeton University and the Union Theological Seminary of Virginia, to the Presbyterian Historical Society, the Virginia Historical Society, and the Historical Society of Pennsylvania, which have made available many rare, and often valuable, items.

Among those individuals who gave generously of their time and energy, I am particularly indebted to the late Professor Raymond P. Stearns, of the University of Illinois, who read the manuscript in its entirety, providing criticisms and suggestions when needed and advice when sought. I have also benefited much from illuminating discussions with Professors John Frantz of Pennsylvania State University, Charles Nilon of the University of Colorado, Wilbur Jacobs of the University of California at Santa Barbara, David A. Williams of the University of Virginia, Bertram Wyatt-Brown of Case Western Reserve University, and William L. O'Neill of the University of Wisconsin. Homer Kemp of the University of Tennessee deserves special thanks for his careful examination of the text and the removal of more errors than I care to remember. The boards of editors of *The Historian, The Virginia Magazine of History and Biography,* and *The Historical Magazine of the Protestant Episcopal Church* have kindly given me permission to use materials first published under their auspices. Finally, it should be noted that the preparation of this study has been aided by the generosity of the Research Foundation of Oklahoma State University, Colonial Williamsburg Incorporated, and the Council on Research and Creative Work of the University of Colorado.

Since I first began preparation of this study, two important works relating to Samuel Davies have become readily available for scholarly use. Although I used the original manuscript of Davies' diary and the first imprints of his various poems, the reader may wish to refer to the more accessible volumes, my edition of *The Reverend Samuel Davies Abroad: The Diary of a Journey to England and Scotland, 1753–55,* and Richard Beale Davis' *Collected Poems of Samuel Davies, 1723–1761*. In quoting from documentary sources I have made such changes as seemed necessary to make the material more readable and to facilitate the transcription of eighteenth-century manuscript peculiarities into twentieth-century typescript; thus y^e has been changed to the, &c. to etc., & to and, and certain abbreviations expanded. Davies' spelling and capitalization have been allowed to remain unchanged.

G. W. P.

Contents

SAMUEL DAVIES

Apostle of Dissent in Colonial Virginia

I

A Pious Youth

SAMUEL DAVIES' GRANDFATHER, Morgan David, had crossed
the Atlantic in 1684 from the Welsh town of Lantwidvoryde,
in Glamorganshire, to seek a new life in the American domains of
William Penn. Morgan and his small family were on board the
Vine in the early autumn of that year when the vessel sailed into
Delaware Bay with another of the many shiploads of settlers then
pouring into the New World.[1] Most of the weary passengers, like
Morgan, were Welsh, and they were Baptists, a sect that was little
known at that time and little loved. Hoping to find the religious
and the economic liberties that this new land promised, they soon
settled among friends and earlier immigrants in Haverford, Radnor, and Merion townships on the lands of the Penn family.

Morgan and his wife Catherine and their two young sons,
Shionn and David,[2] settled in Merion on the present site of Haverford College, where they had received a grant of one hundred
acres.[3] There they lived and worked much as they had in their

---

[1] Harry Alexander Davis, *The Davis Family in Wales and America* (*Davies and David*), *Genealogy of Morgan David of Pennsylvania* (Washington, D. C., 1927), p. 1.
[2] William Heth Whitsitt, *Genealogy of Jefferson Davis and Samuel Davies* (New York and Washington, D. C., 1910), p. 67.
[3] Davis, *Davis Family*, p. 1.

homeland, the two boys helping their father work the land as they grew toward manhood.[4] When Morgan David died eleven years later, the two sons inherited the family farm as joint tenants and continued to till the Pennsylvania soil.[5] In 1699, four years after Morgan's death, the elder son Shionn married Ann Thomas of Haverford; [6] David did not marry until some seventeen years later, and his bride, Sarah Dickinson, died soon after the wedding.

Within a few months following Sarah's untimely death, the two brothers apparently heard of better opportunities to the south, for they sold their Pennsylvania farm and moved, with Shionn's wife and sons, to a new Welsh settlement in New Castle County, Delaware. Known as the Welsh Tract in Pencader Hundred, this area of thirty thousand acres had originally been granted by William Penn to the leaders of the settlement, David Evans and William Davis of Radnor township.[7] The sons of Morgan David jointly purchased four hundred acres from the Radnor leaders in early 1717,[8] but not before David had engaged in one of those rapid courtships so common to the period and married his second wife, Martha Thomas of the Welsh Tract.[9] It was here that the brothers began to use the name Davis or Davies.[10]

During the next several years, David farmed his land alongside his brother and "built a substantial home of brick," where he may well have joined his wife in her prayers for a son—prayers that eventually were answered on November 3, 1723,[11] with the birth

---

[4] Whitsitt, *Genealogy*, p. 67.

[5] To eliminate possible confusion, the present names of Pennsylvania and Delaware are used.

[6] Davis, *Davis Family*, p. 6. Shionn had a son Evan, who had a son Samuel, whose son was Jefferson Davis (Whitsitt, *Genealogy*, p. 67).

[7] *Records of the Welsh Tract Baptist Meeting, Pencader Hundred, New Castle County, Delaware, 1701 to 1828, Papers of the Historical Society of Delaware*, vol. V, no. xlii, pt. 1 (Wilmington, 1904), p. 3. Hereafter cited as *Welsh Records*.

[8] Davis, *Davis Family*, p. 4. *Welsh Records*, p. 13.

[9] They were married before February 4, 1717, when they both were enrolled in the Pencader Baptist Meeting under the name "Dafis," *ibid.*, p. 20. Martha Thomas had previously been baptized into the church in 1711, *ibid.*, p. 16.

[10] There were numerous variations of the extremely popular Welsh name David. As the Welsh apparently made no systematic use of surnames until well into the nineteenth century, the lack of one in common does not necessarily indicate an absence of relationship.

[11] An Old Testament in the Virginia Historical Society contains the following entry in Davies' hand: "Born in New-Castle County Pennsilvania Nov. 3, 1723."

of Samuel. When he was grown, Samuel commented on his nam-
ing: "I am a son of prayer, like my name-sake *Samuel* the
prophet; and my mother called me *Samuel* because, she said, I
have asked him of the LORD. . . . This early dedication to GOD
has always been a strong inducement to me to devote myself to
Him by my own personal act; and the most important blessings of
my life I have looked upon as immediate answers to the prayers of
a pious mother." [12]

There is no evidence to suggest that young Samuel was one of
those religiously and intellectually precocious children that the
American colonies were wont to produce from time to time. Furthermore, his father is mentioned "as a man of slow mentality, and
of ordinary talents . . . [who] cleared his land . . . and cultivated his farm," [13] "who lived with great plainness and simplicity,
and supported the character of an honest and pious man to his
death." [14] Although the records indicate that David and Martha
Davis could not write even their names, [15] Samuel's mother has
been described as being "possessed of superior natural abilities." [16]
It is likely that she undertook her son's early training before putting him under the tuition of the Reverend Abel Morgan, minister
to the local Baptist meeting. [17] Samuel's association with the school
conducted by the local minister could not have lasted much past
his ninth or tenth birthday, for about that time his mother came
into conflict with the church. Accused of rebelling against the Bap-

---

[12] Davies to Thomas Gibbons, n.d., *Sermons on the Most Useful and Important Subjects, Adapted to the Family and Closet. By the Rev. Samuel Davies, A.M. Late President of the College at Princeton in New Jersey. To Which are Prefixed, a Sermon on
the Death of Mr. Davies, by Samuel Finley, D.D. And Another Discourse on the Same
Occasion, Together with an Elegiac Poem to the Memory of Mr. Davies, by Thomas
Gibbons, D.D.*, ed. Thomas Gibbons (5 vols., London, 1766–1771), I, lxi. This edition
also contains "An Appendix" written anonymously by David Bostwick. Hereafter cited as
Sermons (1766).

[13] Davis, *Davis Family*, p. 12.

[14] [David Bostwick], "Appendix," *Sermons* (1766), I, li.

[15] When selling their land in 1748 in order to accompany their son to Virginia, they
both initialed the deed rather than signed it (Davis, *Davis Family*, p. 13).

[16] William Henry Foote, *Sketches of Virginia: Historical and Biographical*, series one
(Philadelphia, 1850), p. 157. Hereafter cited as Foote, I.

[17] Davis, *Davis Family*, p. 34. Foote, I, 158. Robert Sutherland Alley, "The Reverend
Mr. Samuel Davies: A Study in Religion and Politics, 1747–1759" (Diss., Princeton
University, 1962), pp. 9–10, has a different version of Davies' early education.

tist doctrine, she was cast out of the congregation. According to the record of this action, "The Case of Martha David" was resolved on March 4, 1732, in the following manner:

> The rebellion of Martha David against the Church appeared.
>
> (1) In opposing the truth which she once professed to the church according to the commandment of Christ and the practice of the Apostles under the ministry of the New testament.
>
> (2) In refusing instruction, and despising advice tho' offered many a time by the brethren in particular, and by the church, in general.
>
> (3) In breaking covenant with the church by carrying unconnected pieces of what was talked in the church to the Presbyterians to have their opinion upon them, tho' the church charged her before hand not to do so.
>
> (4) In being so false and unfaithful in carrying her tales so that she has curtailed the truth and increased her falsehoods; and thereby hath wronged the church by her change of opinion, and putting a false gloss on what was said to her—and putting it in the power of the enemies to blaspheme—also to renew the varience between us and the Presbyterians, for which causes she was put out of the church Mar. 4, 1732.[18]

In short, the mother of Samuel Davies, despite the charge of being a gossip, probably found a greater degree of spiritual satisfaction in the Presbyterian view of things religious than in the Baptist. Upon her exclusion from the Baptist meeting, Martha Davis immediately united with her friends in the Presbyterian church at St. Georges, Delaware.[19] This congregation was then under the spiritual care of the Reverend William Robinson, a noted itinerant preacher who later achieved great popularity in Hanover County, Virginia,[20] among the dissenting elements of the Anglican church. Like many of the ministers of that day, Robinson also conducted a rudimentary classical school, where Samuel, probably unwilling and unable to continue with the Baptist school, continued his education [21] for the next several years before eventually uniting with the Presbyterian church [22] as his mother had done.

[18] *Welsh Records*, p. 26.

[19] Davis, *Davis Family*, p. 34.

[20] [John Holt Rice], "Memoir of the Rev. Samuel Davies," *The Virginia Evangelical and Literary Magazine*, I (1819), 116.

[21] Archibald Alexander, *Biographical Sketches of the Founder and Principal Alumni of the Log College. Together With an Account of the Revivals of Religion Under Their Ministry* (Philadelphia, 1851), p. 216.

[22] Davis, *Davis Family*, p. 34. Foote, I, 158.

Throughout the first fifteen years of his life, young Samuel was apparently not unduly concerned with things of a religious nature. He was a normal, sprightly boy, growing up and learning from the example of his parents and the lessons of his tutors. His stay at Robinson's school seems to have been less edifying spiritually than had been hoped, for he is said to have grown "somewhat more careless of the things of religion" while making "great progress in his learning." [23] Nevertheless, according to a friend, toward the close of his period of study at St. Georges something awakened Samuel "to solemn thoughtfulness, and anxious concern about his eternal state . . . and the direful effects of divine displeasure against sin." [24] Another contemporary, the Reverend David Bostwick, reported that the young man began to make a practice of "secret prayer" in the evening, for "he feared lest he should perhaps die before morning." He usually concluded his prayers with the supplication that he should be suitably prepared to enter into the "gospel-Ministry" to which his mother had dedicated him. [25]

By the time Samuel had reached his fifteenth birthday, in 1738, he probably had progressed as far in his studies as Robinson's school could take him, and it was decided that he should continue his education at a classical academy. The Presbyterians considered a formal classical and religious education for their ministers both necessary and desirable. But their insistence upon this training placed them at a serious disadvantage in the competition for souls in America. [26] The American colleges at Cambridge, New Haven, and Williamsburg were too distant to be of much use to the Middle

---

[23] [Bostwick], "Appendix," *Sermons* (1766), I, li.

[24] Samuel Finley, "The Dis-interested and Devoted Christian: A Sermon Preached at Nassau-Hall, Princeton, May 28, 1761. Occasioned by the Death of the Rev. Samuel Davies, A.M. Late President of the College of New Jersey," *ibid.*, I, xxxv.

[25] [Bostwick], "Appendix," *ibid.*, I, li.

[26] "The Presbyterian ministers from the very beginning brought with them to the New World the tradition of a liberal education. Despite the early lack of a sufficient number of preachers, the denomination never entertained a thought of introducing men into the ministry who had not received adequate training in an institution of higher learning, save perhaps in the case of a few exceptionally useful men. Even during the Great Awakening when, due to the revivals, there was a rapid expansion in membership and a consequent shortage of ministers, the Presbyterians never relaxed in their standards of a trained ministry." Wesley Marsh Gewehr, *The Great Awakening in Virginia: 1740–1790* (Durham, 1930), p. 219.

Colonies, and none was altogether suitable for a prospective Presbyterian clergyman. To resolve this dilemma, William Tennent had begun a classical academy on Neshaminy Creek in Bucks County, Pennsylvania, and several of the men trained at this school later founded academies of their own in conjunction with their pastorates. One of the more influential of these so-called "log colleges" founded by Tennent's students was the one Samuel Blair established in 1739 at Fagg's Manor in Chester County, Pennsylvania.[27] The momentous decision to send Samuel to the school that was to have so profound a formative influence on him was made chiefly no doubt by Robinson, who, like Blair, had been a student at the original log college on Neshaminy Creek.[28] The young scholar, therefore, although extremely short of funds, went off to Pennsylvania to prepare himself for the ministry.

At about the same time that Samuel Davies set out for Fagg's Manor, the "New Light" Presbytery of New Brunswick, a body that had broken away from the established Presbyterian Synod of Philadelphia and was leading a revival of personal piety and spiritual experience in religion, ordered William Robinson to undertake a preaching tour in Campbell, Charlotte, and Prince Edward counties in Virginia. Having visited many of the embryonic Presbyterian congregations in those places, Robinson was making his way back to Delaware when he was asked to preach a series of sermons to the dissenters in Hanover County. His message and style impressed the Hanover people greatly, and when he prepared to depart they presented him with a large sum of money, which

[27] Guy Souillard Klett, *Presbyterians in Colonial Pennsylvania* (Philadelphia, 1937), p. 204. Fagg's Manor was "the first Presbyterian theological school in America" (Jacob Harris Patton, *A Popular History of the Presbyterian Church in the United States of America* [New York, 1900], p. 111). "Men intended for secular business were not entirely excluded; but the chief design of the institution was, to prepare youth for the gospel ministry" (Ashbel Green, *Discourses Delivered in the College of New Jersey; Addressed Chiefly to Candidates for the First Degree in the Arts; With Notes and Illustrations, Including a Historical Sketch of the College, From its Origin to the Accession of President Witherspoon* [Philadelphia, New York, and Trenton, 1822], p. 342).

[28] Alexander, *Biographical Sketches*, p. 216. Thomas Clinton Pears and Guy Souillard Klett erroneously state that Davies studied at Tennent's school (eds., *Documentary History of William Tennent and the Log College* [Philadelphia, 1940], p. 174).

Robinson refused to accept. The money was then secreted in one of his saddlebags, but he discovered it and, still unyielding, returned it. Nevertheless, the people continued to press their gratitude upon him until finally he reportedly offered this solution: "I will tell you what must be done with the money—There is a very promising young man, now studying divinity to the North; whose parents are very hard scuffed, and find great difficulty in supporting him at his studies. I will take this money, and it shall be given him to help him through—and when he is licenced, he shall come and be your preacher." [29] The young man, of course, was Samuel Davies, and the money solved his financial problems, making it possible for him to devote himself fully to his studies.

The school at Fagg's Manor was well equipped to meet the young scholar's needs, for Samuel Blair, the master, was himself a noted preacher of the New Light revival [30] and a widely recognized Latin scholar.[31] A native of Ireland, Blair was one of the first pupils to finish his classical and theological studies at the original log college and in turn was responsible for the education of such noted New Light preachers as John Rodgers and Samuel Finley, as well as Samuel Davies.[32] There are no surviving records of Blair's academy. Although any reconstruction of student life or the curriculum is highly theoretical, the academy probably countenanced considerably less frivolity than did most other colleges of the period and must have resembled closely the classical academies founded by two of Blair's students, just as Blair's school was patterned after that of William Tennent.[33] A description of one of these later academies, opened by Robert Smith in connection with his pastorate at Pequea, Pennsylvania, was given by one of the students:

[29] [Rice], "Memoir," p. 116. An "old lady" reportedly told Rice "that is the reason that Mr. Davies came to Hanover; for he often used to say that he was inclined to settle in another place, but that he felt under obligation to the people of Hanover."

[30] Alexander, *Biographical Sketches,* p. 172.

[31] Klett, *Presbyterians,* p. 207.

[32] Alexander, *Biographical Sketches,* pp. 171–172.

[33] Since the purpose of these schools was much the same, their curricula were also probably much the same (Klett, *Presbyterians,* p. 207).

It was the custom of the school to require the pupils not merely to dip into the Latin and Greek classics, or pass in rapid transition from one to the other, by which means a very superficial knowledge of any is obtained, but when once they had commenced an author, to read carefully and attentively the entire work. Besides this laudable and beneficial custom, the scholars of this academy were stimulated to exertion by being brought into frequent competition and by having conferred upon the successful candidates for distinction such honors as were calculated to awake their boyish emulation and to quicken their diligence and attention. Latin was the habitual language of the school and after the pupils had passed through a few of the elementary works, as the colloquies of Corderius and the fables of Aesop, any error which they committed in grammatical propriety either in addressing the teacher or in speaking with one another was punishable as a fault. One literary exercise in the school was contested with more than ordinary emulation. When any class had advanced in its course beyond the Metamorphoses of Ovid and Bucolics of Virgil, the members of it were permitted to enter into voluntary competitions for preeminence. On alternate Saturdays, eight or ten of the better scholars from different classes were allowed to try their skill in the languages in the presence of the principal teacher. Each competitor was suffered to select a sentence within a certain compass of one or two hundred lines, consisting of not more than six or seven hexameter verses. On this selected position, he was the sole examiner, and was permitted to inquire about everything with which he could make himself acquainted by the most diligent previous investigation; such as the grammatical construction of the sentences, the derivation of the words, their composition, relations and quantity, the history or mythology referred to in the passage, the beauty and pertinence of the figures and allusions together with taste and delicacy of the sentiment displayed by the poet. After the whole contest, which usually lasted several hours, was concluded, rewards were bestowed by the master upon those who discovered the greatest address and ingenuity in conducting it.[34]

Samuel Finley, the other Blair student to establish an academy, supervised a school at Nottingham, Maryland, before becoming president of the College of New Jersey at Princeton. At this school, too, students were required to study the standard Latin and Greek authors as well as logic, arithmetic, geography, geometry, ontology, and natural philosophy.[35]

[34] Frederick Beasly quoted in Jacob N. Beam, "Dr. Robert Smith's Academy at Pequea, Pennsylvania," *Journal of the Presbyterian Historical Society,* VIII (1915), 151.
[35] Klett, *Presbyterians,* p. 207.

That Blair's school at Fagg's Manor was successful from an academic point of view there can be no doubt. Among his first group of students, in addition to the two who founded academies of their own, were two future college presidents. Located but an easy ride from Philadelphia, the school was one of the centers of the religious ferment sweeping through the Middle Colonies. The impression made on Davies must have been profound. Blair himself was a powerful preacher. He began a revival of religion in 1740, of which he said: "I think there was scarcely a sermon . . . preached here through that whole summer, but there was manifest evidence of impressions on the hearers, and many times the impressions were very great and general; several would be overcome and fainting." [36] As if to strengthen this work, George Whitefield, who had preached throughout Pennsylvania, Delaware, and New Jersey in 1739, now came to Fagg's Manor and held a public disputation [37] in which "the people were under such deep soul distress, that their cries almost drowned his voice," [38] a distinct possibility since the preacher himself estimated the size of the audience to be in the neighborhood of twelve thousand.[39]

Although Davies never mentioned having heard Whitefield preach, it seems unlikely that one given to silent prayer for his admission into the ministry would have missed a chance to hear this famous man in either 1739 or 1740. That he heard Blair, and heard him often, we can be certain; and we can be even more sure that Blair's preaching had a profound effect upon him, for he referred to him as "the great Mr. Blair" [40] and wrote:

[36] Samuel Blair's narrative of his revival in Foote, I, 111.

[37] Charles Hartshorn Maxson, *The Great Awakening in the Middle Colonies* (Chicago, 1920), p. 60.

[38] Joseph Tracy, *The Great Awakening: A History of the Revival of Religion in the Time of Edwards and Whitefield* (Boston, 1842), pp. 58–59.

[39] John T. Faris, *Old Churches and Meeting Houses in and Around Philadelphia* (Philadelphia and London, 1926), p. 209. "Whitefield was esteemed, in his day, a good judge of numbers. His estimates of his hearers were generally received by his contemporaries. It does not appear that even his enemies ever accused him of exaggeration in this respect" (Tracy, *Great Awakening*, p. 88*n*).

[40] Davies kept a record of his trip to Great Britain in two small notebooks now housed in the libraries of the Union Theological Seminary of Virginia and Princeton University. These have been edited and annotated by the author as *The Reverend Samuel Davies Abroad: The Diary of a Journey to England and Scotland, 1753–55* (Urbana, 1967), September 13, 1753, p. 12. References to this edition will hereafter be cited as *Diary*.

Compar'd with him, the most exalted **Tongue,**
But [strangles] Truth, and does the Subject **Wrong.**
From others heav'nly Truths insipid seem
To them whose Relish was refin'd by him.[41]

Many years later when Davies was asked his opinion of the famous preachers he had heard while visiting in England, he replied that "he had heard no one who in his judgment was superior to his former teacher." [42]

By the spring of 1746, Davies had come to the end of his studies and was prepared to go forth and preach the evangelical doctrines of the New Light. Having acquired a working knowledge of the classics [43] and theology, as well as an acquaintance with the necessary sciences, he was well prepared for his chosen task. Unfortunately he had also weakened his body to such an extent that for the remainder of his brief life he would be susceptible to serious illnesses. At the time his preparatory studies were completed, his slender frame was described as having become "enfeebled" and his health "very delicate." [44]

Shortly after leaving the Blair family, Davies took the first step toward the Presbyterian clergy by appearing before the New Light Presbytery of New Castle, Delaware, which on July 30, 1746, granted him a license to preach for the customary probationary period of six months.[45] Three months later, he was married for the

[41] "On hearing of the Rev. Mr. Samuel Blair's desperate Illness," *Miscellaneous Poems, Chiefly on Divine Subjects. In Two Books. Published for the Religious Entertainment of Christians in General* (Williamsburg, 1752), p. 136. Richard Beale Davis has recently edited and annotated *Collected Poems of Samuel Davies, 1723–1761* (Gainesville, 1968) containing all of Davies' extant poetry. Pagination of his edition conforms to the 1752 edition of the *Miscellaneous Poems*, with additional pages for verses not in the original. Only the original will be cited here for those poems appearing in both volumes. Davis' edition will be cited as *Collected Poems.*

[42] John Rodgers quoted in Alexander, *Biographical Sketches,* p. 193.

[43] He was later able to quote Ovid, Virgil, and Horace in a letter to the Reverend Patrick Henry, Jan. 30, 1753 (*Virginia Gazette,* March 2, 1753, p. 1), as well as Chrysostom and Clement of Alexandria in an open letter to the Anglican clergy, Jan. 9, 1753 ([Rice], "Memoir," p. 208).

[44] Foote, I, 159. One historian has diagnosed this as tuberculosis (Thomas Jefferson Wertenbaker, *Princeton: 1746–1896* [Princeton, 1946], p. 45).

[45] MS Old Testament page, Virginia Historical Society. This Presbytery had been

first time, but all that is known of this first wife comes from two notations Davies made in his Old Testament: "Married to Sarah Kirkpatrick Oct. 23, 1746." And less than a year later: "Separated from her by Death & bereaved of an abortive Son Sep. 15." [46] There is no further mention of this marriage, and during its brief course Davies apparently never indulged his taste for poetry as he was to do during his second marriage.

Having successfully completed his probationary period by filling vacant pulpits in Pennsylvania and Delaware, [47] Davies again appeared before the meeting of the New Castle Presbytery on February 19, 1747, [48] to be ordained. If Davies' ordination followed the Presbytery's customary pattern, one of the ministers of the body appeared at the meetinghouse door immediately before the worship service and asked if anyone had objection to the candidate's ordination. No objection being made to Davies' candidacy, he no doubt was "set apart with fasting, prayer and the laying on of hands of the Presbytery," after which "a minister, before appointed, presided and preached the ordination sermon." [49]

Since the candidate had no congregation of his own, he was officially ordained as an evangelist to all congregations without preachers in Virginia, but especially the one in Hanover County, the center of New Light strength in a colony that had no settled New Light preacher. Hanover was described as "a colony where profaneness and immorality called aloud for his sacred labours" [50] and "where many of the inhabitants, in respect of religion, were but a small remove from the darkness and ignorance of uncultivated

---

organized in 1741 when Samuel Blair and several others had withdrawn from the "Old Light" Presbytery of New Castle. The early records of both have been lost, but since Davies' friends and teacher were members of the new Presbytery and since Davies attended the New Light Synod of New York, this must have been his Presbytery (James Laird Vallandigham and Samuel A. Gayley, *History of the Presbytery of New Castle From its Organization, March 13, 1717, to 1888* [Philadelphia (1889)], p. 10).

[46] MS Old Testament page.

[47] Foote, I, 159.

[48] MS Old Testament page.

[49] Vallandigham and Gayley claim that this was the custom at all ordinations by this body (*Presbytery of New Castle*, p. 7).

[50] [Bostwick], "Appendix," *Sermons* (1766), I, lix.

heathenism." [51] The vocal and energetic dissenters of this area, challenging as they did the authority of the Church of England, were continually plagued by civil and criminal suits against their practices,[52] as well as by the hostility of the attorney general, Peyton Randolph, whom Davies was later to term "my old Adversary." [53] Davies was somewhat reluctant to undertake the mission for fear that he would bring discredit to the dissenting cause by his inexperience in church and political matters.[54] Despite this misgiving and the precarious state of his health, however, he went to Hanover, after being licensed by the General Court, and preached for about a month [55] to those who had financed his studies.

On this first trip to Hanover, Davies found the condition of the dissenters neither especially favorable nor unfavorable. It is true that a significant amount of vocal opposition to the dissenters was present; the government issued proclamations forbidding itinerant preachers from holding public services. Davies, however, so impressed the governor with his knowledge and sincerity that, upon his arrival at Hanover, he could rip one of that official's proclamations from the door of the meetinghouse and preach unchallenged.[56] Young Davies probably owed much of his success with the authorities and his acceptance by Anglicans in general to his scrupulous refusal to attack the established church. When one of his own relatives referred to him as a disruptive force, Davies retorted, "I have

[51] Thomas Gibbons, "Divine Conduct Vindicated, or the Operations of *God* Shown to be the Operations of Wisdom: In the Substance of Two Discourses, Preached at Haberdashers-Hall, London, March 29, 1761; Occasioned by the Decease of the Rev. Samuel Davies, A.M. and President of the College of Nassau-Hall in New Jersey," *Sermons* (1766), I, lxii.

[52] See ch. IV.

[53] *Diary*, March 4, 1754, p. 79.

[54] "The Apostolic Valediction Considered and Applied," *Sermons on Important Subjects, By the Reverend Samuel Davies, A.M., President of the College of New Jersey. With an Essay on the Life and Times of the Author by Albert Barnes. Stereotype Edition, Containing all the Author's Sermons Ever Published,* ed. Albert Barnes (3 vols., New York and Pittsburgh, 1845), III, 479. Henceforth cited as *Sermons* (1845). There are more than two dozen editions of Davies' sermons. Wherever possible I have used the 1845 edition kindly made available by the Library of Congress.

[55] William Dawson to the Bishop of London (Edmund Gibson), April 21, 1747, Dawson MSS, Library of Congress.

[56] Davies to Joseph Bellamy, June 28, 1751, Alexander, *Biographical Sketches,* p. 225.

not spent an Hour since I first opened my Mouth to preach the Gospel, in exposing the Peculiarities of the established Church: and in Conversation with my own People, though I am free to declare my own private Judgments, yet I use my Influence rather to enlarge their Charity, than enflame a bigotted zeal against these Things." [57]

The young preacher did observe what he considered to be widespread inattention to religion. He was appalled by "the general neglect, and stupid unconcernedness about religion, the habitual omissions of its duties, and the vicious practices that glare upon me around, and which are utterly inconsistent with true religion in any denomination." [58] Nevertheless, the preaching of Davies so impressed his listeners that the one month he spent in Hanover was described by a later reporter as "one of those times in which the current of human events, running on with increasing bitterness, takes an unexpected turn . . . and the night of clouds and thick darkness has its morning of brightness and joy." [59] When Davies felt compelled to return home because of his health, he took with him a message from the people in Hanover to the Presbytery asking for his permanent services. [60]

At home in New Castle his worsening health and the death of his wife led Davies to spend "a year under melancholy and consumptive languishments, expecting death." [61] He rejected all offers to settle in Hanover until he might improve, an event that he seriously doubted. Some years later he noted that "divine Providence . . . has generally disposed of me in a Manner different from, and Sometimes contrary to My Expectations, My Purpose and Desires. Such an unexpected and undesired Event was my Separation from my Brethren and Settlement in Virginia." [62]

Although poor health prevented Davies from settling in one

[57] Davies to John Holt, Feb. 27, 1753, Benjamin Rush MSS, Library Company of Philadelphia—Historical Society of Pennsylvania.
[58] Davies to Virginia Anglican Clergy, Jan. 9, 1753, Foote, I, 218.
[59] *Ibid.*, p. 157.
[60] [Rice], "Memoir," p. 117.
[61] Davies to Bellamy, June 28, 1751, Alexander, *Biographical Sketches*, p. 226.
[62] *Diary*, July 2, 1753, p. 1.

charge, he traveled tirelessly, preaching throughout Pennsylvania, New Jersey, and Maryland. However, the bulk of his preaching at this time apparently was done in Maryland where his friend and tutor William Robinson had started a revival in 1745. Davies spent two months there "when the work was at its height . . . though in the extremity of a cold winter." [63] Even at this early stage in his career he seems to have been recognized as a stimulating preacher. This talent coupled with the general shortage of ministers throughout the Middle Colonies resulted in numerous calls asking him to accept a permanent charge; [64] but Davies was still unwilling, because of his precarious health, to accept any of the invitations. Others were, of course, painfully aware of his illness as he continued to ride horseback from congregation to congregation:

> When he was about entering the ministry or had not long entered upon it . . . he was judged to be in a deep and irrecoverable consumption. Finding himself upon the borders of the grave, and without any hopes of recovery, he determined to spend the little remains of an almost exhausted life . . . in the good of souls. . . . He laboured in season and out of season; and . . . preached in the day, and had his hectic fever by night, and that to such a degree as to be sometimes delirious. . . . [65]

In the spring of 1748, about two years following the granting of his license to preach, his health started to improve noticeably. [66] Davies now began to consider seriously the many applications coming his way. [67] One application in particular of those that reached him at St. Georges [68] was signed by more than a hundred heads of

[63] Davies to Bellamy, June 28, 1751, Alexander, *Biographical Sketches*, p. 231. Since Davies mentioned in this letter that "it began, I think, in 1745, by the ministry of Mr. Robinson," Gibbons seems to think that Davies was there during that winter ("Divine Conduct," *Sermons* [1766], I, civ*n*). But if, by his own admission, he was licensed in 1746, he was more likely there in the winter of 1746–1747 (MS Old Testament page).

[64] Davies to the Bishop of London (Thomas Sherlock), Jan. 10, 1752, Foote, I, 167. All letters so addressed are to Bishop Sherlock unless otherwise noted.

[65] Gibbons, "Divine Conduct," *Sermons* (1766), I, lxii.

[66] Davies' illnesses seem to have been most severe when he led an inactive life such as at Fagg's Manor or Princeton. His health seems to have improved noticeably when he engaged in the physical activity of a traveling preacher.

[67] Davies, "Apostolic Valediction," *Sermons* (1845), III, 479.

[68] Gibbons claims that prior to this Davies had "removed from the place where he was to another about an hundred miles distance, that was then in want of a minister" ("Divine Conduct," *Sermons* [1766], I, lxii). These places were probably New Castle and St. Georges, respectively.

16

families in Hanover County and was delivered personally by a representative of this group.[69] Although Davies had fulfilled the commitment made on his behalf by William Robinson [70] during his earlier trip, he still felt a certain obligation to serve the congregation at Hanover: "I had no more thought of it as my pastoral charge, than of the remotest corner of the world; but was preparing to settle in ease near my native place, till the more urgent necessity and importunity of the people here, constrained me to alter my resolution." [71] He had decided to accept the call.

In later years, Davies and the other New Lights were to be charged by their opponents with insincerity and a desire for money. The fact that he answered the appeal of a frontier congregation scattered over several counties at a time when he "was preparing to settle in ease" near his "native place" would seem to be ample refutation of this charge. So it seemed to Davies several years later, when he wrote:

> It was not the secret thirst of filthy lucre, nor the prospect of any other personal advantage, that induced me to settle here in Virginia. For sundry congregations in Pennsylvania, my native country, and in other northern colonies, most earnestly importuned me to settle among them; where I should have had, at least an equal temporal maintenance, incomparably more ease, leisure, and peace, and the happiness of the frequent society of my brethren. . . . But all these strong inducements were overweighed by a sense of the necessity of the Dissenters, as they lay two or three hundred miles distant from the nearest ministers of their own denomination, and laboured under peculiar embarrassments for the want of a settled ministry.[72]

Now approaching his twenty-fifth birthday, Samuel Davies set out for a permanent settlement in Virginia. He was accompanied by his parents, who feared for his health,[73] and by a close friend and fellow student, John Rodgers. Davies had insisted that Rodgers be

[69] Foote, I, 163.
[70] [Rice], "Memoir," p. 116.
[71] Davies, "Apostolic Valediction," *Sermons* (1845), III, 479. A footnote explains that "near my native place" refers to "St. George's, in the territories of Pennsylvania" (now Delaware), where Robinson's old church was located.
[72] Davies to the Bishop of London, Jan. 10, 1752, Foote, I, 167.
[73] Whitsitt, *Genealogy*, p. 37.

his assistant.[74] The two young preachers stopped only momentarily in Hanover before proceeding directly to Williamsburg to be licensed into specific meetinghouses.[75] Lieutenant-Governor Sir William Gooch of Virginia remembered Davies from his previous visit and apparently had been impressed by his moderation.[76] On the assumption that Davies would go to Hanover with or without a permit, he believed that compliance with his request would be the easiest way to avoid trouble; he issued Davies a license.[77] Because Rodgers had preached at Hanover during their brief stop, without benefit of a license and thus illegally, his request to be licensed into specific pulpits was refused, and he was merely permitted to assist Davies temporarily.[78] Nevertheless, Davies had been treated with kindness and respect by the governor and remembered him as having "a ready disposition to allow us all claimable privileges." [79]

When he entered into his duties with his new congregation in 1748, Davies expected to "live and die" among his "dear congregation" in Hanover, even though he had grave doubts, which recurred with every major decision he was forced to make, concerning his qualifications for the undertaking: "It is known to no mortal but myself with what reluctance, fear, and trembling, I accepted your call. The rawness and inexperience of my youth, and the formidable opposition then made both by church and state, when a dissenter was stared at with horror, as a shocking and portentous phenomenon, were no small discouragements in my way." He later commented that for several years he hardly dared venture outside the pulpit "lest, by a promiscuous conversation with the world at large, I should injure the cause of religion." He was convinced, as

---

[74] Samuel Miller, *Memoirs of the Rev. John Rodgers, D.D. Late Pastor of the Wall-Street and Brick Churches in the City of New York* (New York, 1813), p. 24.

[75] Davies to Bellamy, June 28, 1751, Alexander, *Biographical Sketches,* p. 226.

[76] During the colonial period, the official governor of the colony rarely left the Court in England. For instance, the absentee governor of Virginia when Gooch came to the colony in 1727 was George Hamilton, Earl of Orkney—a man to whom Gooch complained of having to send half his salary as resident lieutenant-governor.

[77] Foote, I, 159–60.

[78] John E. Latta to Samuel Miller, July 10, 1811, Miller, *Memoirs,* p. 87. Foote, I, 166.

[79] Davies to Bellamy, June 28, 1751, Alexander, *Biographical Sketches,* p. 226.

he said, that he had embarked on a great exploit equipped with "a sincere desire . . . but little ability." [80] But the simple notation in his Old Testament reflects none of this inner perturbation. It reads: "Settled in Hanover Virginia May 1748." [81]

[80] Davies, "Apostolic Valediction," *Sermons* (1845), III, 479.
[81] MS Old Testament page.

II

The Great Awakening

FROM THE BEGINNINGS of organized religion, there have been those who, doubting the effectiveness of contemporary practices and beliefs, have sought to restore the lost effectiveness through reform. Usually such persons have been shunned and ignored and have exerted little or no influence on that which they tried to change. Occasionally, however, their ideas have caught fire, attracted adherents, and entered into the mainstream of religious thought. The latter occurred during the first half of the eighteenth century when a small group of extremely effective preachers initiated the Great Awakening, a movement that spread throughout the English-speaking world and affected virtually all Protestant denominations.

The chief impetus for this movement came from the German pietist sects of the seventeenth century, which evolved from the private devotional groups organized by Philip Jacob Spener of Frankfurt am Main in the 1670's. Spener established small assemblies of people who met in private homes to pray, sing psalms, and read the Bible. The University of Halle became the theological center of this religious ferment and attracted young men from all over Europe. There, in an atmosphere of intense personal piety, they attained a classical education before going forth to preach.

Joined by other young preachers, they traveled into all parts of the Protestant world calling for a unity of belief and practice based on a religion of the heart that would manifest itself in all aspects of everyday life.

In America the doctrine spread by such men was called the New Light,[1] and it broke out in widely separated places under the influence of several different preachers. Probably the first of these brilliant American evangelists was a young graduate of Halle, Theodorus Frelinghuysen. Frelinghuysen preached his message of moral reform, personal piety, and mystical union with God throughout the Dutch Reformed congregations settled along New Jersey's Raritan Valley during the early 1720's.[2] By 1725 his message had been absorbed by the Presbyterians of the area and had soon spilled over into the adjacent colony of Pennsylvania.

Although the Moravians, Mennonites, and other pietist German groups had long been settled in Pennsylvania, it was a young Presbyterian preacher, Gilbert Tennent, who, inspired by the words of Frelinghuysen, began to spread them among his own denomination in 1727.[3] Tennent had been educated at the famous school of his father, William Tennent, on Neshaminy Creek in Pennsylvania,[4] the academy that also trained Samuel Blair, the teacher of Samuel Davies. The younger Tennent found that he had a captive audience in those Presbyterians who had become dissatisfied with the customarily staid, formal religious observances of their church, especially the lack of fervor in the sermons. Like many men throughout the colonies, he felt that "religion had become a matter of dead formality."[5] It was not long before he was joined by others who had

---

[1] "The doctrine of the 'new Birth,' preached with power and earnestness by the reformers of the eighteenth century, was so novel to those who had been slumbering beneath the establishments of Congregationalism and Episcopacy, that its advocates were called 'New Lights.' This title was not applied to any particular sect, but to all, of every denomination, who followed the disciples of Whitefield." Robert R. Howison, *A History of Virginia, From its Discovery and Settlement by Europeans to the Present Time* (2 vols., Philadelphia, 1846), II, 163.

[2] Maxson, *Great Awakening*, ch. iii.

[3] Alexander, *Biographical Sketches*, pp. 24–37.

[4] *Ibid.*, pp. 25–26.

[5] Gewehr, *Great Awakening*, p. 4.

studied with his father, and a formidable array of preaching talent soon blanketed the Middle Colonies.[6]

The Connecticut River Valley of western Massachusetts next came under the influence of the New Light movement. There, in 1734, Jonathan Edwards of Northampton began a revival that soon spread throughout New England.[7] At the end of the same decade, Samuel Blair undertook a revival of religion at Fagg's Manor in Chester County, Pennsylvania, and his pulpit became the focal point for the spread of the movement southward into Delaware, Maryland, and Virginia.[8]

In many ways, however, these American preachers merely prepared the way for the greatest and most successful of the eighteenth-century revivalists, the Englishman George Whitefield. Beginning with his first preaching tour in 1739, when he "shot across the land like a meteor, flashing light, and creating astonishment and admiration," [9] Whitefield made no fewer than seven hazardous crossings of the Atlantic to preach the New Light in America.[10] He has been termed "the greatest single factor in the Awakening of 1740" because his influence alone "touched every section of the country and every denomination." [11]

During the course of his first preaching tour in 1739 and 1740, Whitefield lifted many thousands to new heights of enthusiasm as he passed from place to place. Whether he spoke through an open church window, from courthouse steps, from the tailgate of a wagon, or from a pulpit, he was an impressive sight with his arms lifted Heavenward,[12] his round face red with exertion, and his booming voice denouncing human indifference and religious in-

---

[6] Brief sketches of all these men can be found in Alexander, *Biographical Sketches, passim.*

[7] There are two major biographies of Edwards: Ola Elizabeth Winslow, *Jonathan Edwards, 1703–1758* (New York: 1940 and 1961), which won the Pulitzer Prize, and Perry Miller, *Jonathan Edwards* (New York, 1949).

[8] Alexander, *Biographical Sketches,* pp. 164–196.

[9] Tracy, *Great Awakening,* p. 213.

[10] The best recent account of Whitefield's preaching in America can be found in William Howland Kenney, 3d., "George Whitefield, Dissenter Priest of the Great Awakening, 1739–1741," *William and Mary Quarterly,* third series, XXVI (1969), 75–93.

[11] Gewehr, *Great Awakening,* pp. 8–9.

[12] *Ibid.,* frontispiece.

sincerity. So effective was he that the crowds frequently interrupted him by "shrieking, crying, weeping and wailing." [13] Often during this first tour, he was followed by Gilbert Tennent, whose language, though similar, was perhaps even more arresting. Tennent's "terrible and searching" words warned rebellious and impenitent sinners of the awful danger they faced of "being struck down to hell, and being damned for ever." [14]

One of the great ironies of early American religious history is that the Great Awakening brought to American Presbyterians internal disunion and eventual disruption as well as new vigor and vitality.[15] This denomination, though it provided such early New Light leaders as the Tennents, Blair, and then Samuel Davies, was inherently weak in organization, a weakness that could be traced back to the late 1600's in the Middle Colonies when two groups of widely different organizational and doctrinal beliefs had formed a tenuous union as the new Presbyterian Synod of Philadelphia. Congregationalists from New England and the Presbyterian settlers lately arrived from Old England were the two unlikely elements of this union, and they were to remain together only briefly. The peculiar problems of the Great Awakening would later expose their fundamental differences and drive the two groups apart.

The Congregationalists, having moved into hostile surroundings, no longer protected by friendly local governments, had been forced to seek strength, and they had sought it in the unity of Presbyterian organization. Even so, they still retained their basic belief in the autonomy of individual congregations, a belief that later contributed to the breaking up of the Synod of Philadelphia and the formation of the New Light Synod of New York. In matters of doctrine, the Congregational elements were considered to be generally "more ardent in their piety" than were the strict Presbyterians. According to a contemporary, they zealously urged that "great care

---

[13] Tracy, *Great Awakening*, p. 108.

[14] *Ibid.*, p. 116.

[15] The major study of this denomination in early America is Leonard J. Trinterud, *The Forming of an American Tradition: a Re-examination of Colonial Presbyterianism* (Philadelphia, 1949). For a study of this group in Pennsylvania, see Klett, *Presbyterians.*

should be taken representing the *personal piety*" of those seeking to enter the ministry and that a "close examination on experimental religion" should precede ordination. Provided they were satisfied on the score of personal piety, they "did not set so high a value on human learning, or require so much of it as indispensable, in candidates for the ministry." [16]

On the other hand, the newer settlers, Presbyterians whose background was of Great Britain rather than New England, insisted upon much more rigorous religious practices and polity. They felt that the only source of ecclesiastical authority was the highest body of the church, the General Assembly—or, in the colonies, the Synod. The newer settlers, as opposed to the Congregational elements, were "zealous for the *Westminster* Confession of Faith, Catechisms, Directory, Presbyterial order, and Academical learning, in the preaching of the gospel." [17]

Within the Synod, the New Light preachers had attracted a large following, which included a number of the former Congregationalists, but it was by no means a majority. Most members of the Synod sympathized with the more conservative views of the Old Light leaders and refused to accept either the New Light doctrines or its practices. The evangelical New Lights had no desire to disrupt or harm the church to which they had devoted their lives, but their unwillingness to confine their activities to their own pulpits could not help but cause trouble. Their readiness to preach wherever they felt a need for their message could only agitate and embitter their opponents. If the minister of the local congregation opposed their preaching and refused them the use of his pulpit, or if he barred the door to the church, then a barn, orchard, graveyard, or any vacant space would be pressed into service. There the revivalist would preach his message, demanding a personal religious experience with complete disregard for the lingering ill feelings of the resident minister, who was often accused of the most damning sin —religious formalism.[18]

[16] Miller, *Memoirs*, pp. 24, 74–75.

[17] *Ibid.*, p. 73.

[18] Thomas Jefferson Wertenbaker, *The Founding of American Civilization: The Middle Colonies* (New York, 1938), pp. 174–175.

If the ill-treated occupant of the local pulpit should happen to protest too vigorously, the more radical New Lights would leave him with no doubt as to his status in their eyes.[19] Should he defend himself against their charges, he would become identified as an opponent of the revival. Often entire congregations were divided into rival groups.[20] Eventually, these disputes found their way into the meetings of the Philadelphia Synod where the two opposing wings of the church brought charges and countercharges and struggled for control.

Control would ultimately lie with those who could muster the most votes. Although the Old Lights were in the majority, they were fast being overtaken by the younger ministers emerging from the log colleges, such as the one Samuel Davies attended at Fagg's Manor. As schools founded primarily to educate men for the Presbyterian ministry, and especially the New Light ministry, these colleges did not minimize the importance of classical education, but they nevertheless stressed the primacy of personal piety and religious experience, attributes they felt the established schools no longer recognized. To the New Lights, it was somehow unjust to deprive a frontier congregation of the service of a pious youth merely because his Greek or his Hebrew was a little weak.[21] As was to be expected, candidates from these schools began to appear before the Presbyteries in much greater numbers than those from the New England colleges or the Old World universities.

The Old Lights of the Synod viewed these young ministers with a mixture of contempt and dread—contempt because they doubted the adequacy of their education and dread because they could see the day when this younger element would control the Synod.[22] For a while the opposition was mainly verbal, and the New Lights continued to thrive, especially in the 1730's with the increased revival activity.

In 1738, however, the Old Lights finally used their majority

---

[19] The best example of these charges is Gilbert Tennent, *The Danger of an Unconverted Ministry. Consider'd in a Sermon on Mark VI. 34. Preached at Nottingham, in Pennsylvania, March 8, Anno 1739–1740* (Philadelphia, 1740).

[20] Alexander, *Biographical Sketches*, p. 51.

[21] Miller, *Memoirs*, p. 75.

[22] Alexander, *Biographical Sketches*, pp. 41–50.

control to take preventive action. At the meeting of the Synod in
that year, the numerically superior Old Lights were able to put
through a resolution requiring all future ministerial candidates who
had not studied at a regular European university or American college to prove their knowledge before a committee appointed by the
Synod,[23] thus assuring continued control of the body by Old Light
leaders. It was in direct violation of this requirement that the Presbytery of New Brunswick at its first meeting in August 1738 licensed John Rowland, a former student of the Tennent school,
authorizing him to begin his probationary period.[24] Members of the
Presbytery, under the leadership of Gilbert Tennent, William Tennent, Jr., and Samuel Blair, formally stated that "in point of conscience," they were not restrained "from using the liberty and
power which Presbyteries all along have hitherto enjoyed," and
that they had "many weighty and sufficient reasons" for admitting
Rowland.[25] A little more than one month later, on September 7, he
was formally admitted to the Presbytery.[26]

The battle was now joined. The Synod of Philadelphia, under the
control of the Old Lights, expelled the entire Presbytery of New
Brunswick [27] in a lengthy charge accusing its leaders of "unwearied,
unscriptural, antipresbyterial, uncharitable, divisive practices." [28]
But the New Lights were not alone, for the issue directly involved
the questions of congregational autonomy and the source of authority within the church as well as the amount of learning necessary for

[23] "Minutes of the Synod of Philadelphia," June 1738, *Records of the Presbyterian Church in the United States of America: Embracing the Minutes of the Presbytery of Philadelphia, From A.D. 1706 to 1716: Minutes of the Synod of Philadelphia, From A.D. 1717 to 1758: Minutes of the Synod of New York, From A.D. 1745 to 1758: Minutes of the Synod of Philadelphia and New York, From A.D. 1758 to 1788* (Philadelphia, 1841), p. 139. Henceforth cited as *Records*. By 1738 there were six Presbyteries in the Synod: New York (organized in 1738 through a merger of the Long Island and East Jersey Presby-teries), New Castle (1717), Philadelphia (1717), Donegal (1732), Lewes (1735), and New Brunswick (1738) (Trinterud, *American Tradition*, pp. 312–313).
[24] Alexander, *Biographical Sketches*, pp. 234–246.
[25] "Minutes of the Presbytery of New Brunswick," 1738, *ibid.*, p. 235.
[26] John Rowland to Thomas Prince, n.d., *ibid.*, p. 237.
[27] There were twenty-six ministers and eighteen elders present at this meeting ("Min-utes of the Synod of Philadelphia," June 1, 1741, *Records*, pp. 155, 158).
[28] *Ibid.*, p. 155n.

ministers. They were supported by remnants of the Congregational element led by Ebenezer Pemberton and Jonathan Dickinson.[29]

Concurrent with the divisions and reforms in New England and the Middle Colonies, Presbyterianism in Virginia was developing from two differing sources—originating with the Scottish and Scotch-Irish Presbyterians in the Great Valley and developing spontaneously among Anglican dissenters in the Hanover neighborhood. A group of Scotch-Irish families grew rapidly in the Cub Creek region of the Little Roanoke River under the leadership of John Caldwell, grandfather of the statesman John Caldwell Calhoun; subsequently, in April 1738, Caldwell petitioned the Synod of Philadelphia to plead the cause of his people before the General Court in Williamsburg.[30] Governor Gooch, who heard the case, once again demonstrated the administrative wisdom and capacity for tolerance which were making his administration one of the most harmonious and successful of the colonial period.[31] He readily gave the Presbyterians permission to worship in their own way without interference. This community thus joined the ranks of the Old Lights.

The development in Hanover County, on the other hand, began with a group of dissenters from the Anglican Church sometime in the late 1730's. Within a short time, this movement, led by Samuel Morris, was to fall under the influence of New Light preachers from the Middle Colonies. Morris, a local bricklayer, and his followers became dissatisfied with the Church of England, not "from any scruples about her ceremonial peculiarities, the usual cause of non-conformity—much less about her excellent Articles of Faith, but

[29] Wertenbaker, *Princeton*, pp. 9–10.

[30] Richard Lee Morton, *Colonial Virginia* (2 vols., Chapel Hill, 1960), II, 583–584. Most of these Scotch-Irish Presbyterians later migrated into Kentucky and the Carolinas, leaving the subsequent Presbyterian movement largely to Anglican dissenters.

[31] *Ibid.*, pp. 500–572. In his first address to the General Assembly in Feb. 1728, the new lieutenant-governor cited his loyalty to the Church of England but added that it would be "consistent with the genius of the Christian religion" and never "inconsistent with the interest of the Church of England" to show tolerance to any dissenters "with consciences truly scrupulous" (*Journal of the House of Burgesses*, 1727–1740, p. 4). Morton's chapter is one of the best treatments available on Gooch. The present author also owes a debt to Edward M. Riley, Director of Research at Colonial Williamsburg, for a personal letter concerning Gooch.

from a dislike of the doctrines generally delivered from the pulpit." [32] They disagreed sharply with the practices of their rector, the Reverend Patrick Henry, uncle of Patrick Henry the Revolutionary orator.[33] For these new dissenters, Henry's sermons were "not savouring of experimental piety, nor suitably intermingled with the glorious peculiarities of the religion of Jesus." [34] Further, it seemed to them that religion was weak and morals were extremely low in the county.[35] Morris soon began to absent himself from the Sunday morning services and to gather some friends at his home.[36] Here they studied the religious books that had been acquired by a few individuals of the group and developed among themselves a new religious zeal.[37] One of the books studied was Martin Luther's commentary on Galatians, a fact that caused Morris' adherents to refer to themselves as "Lutherans," although they had never heard the name used in connection with a denomination.[38]

At this critical point in the group's development, it was exposed to a new and forceful source of inspiration. In 1740 George Whitefield came to Virginia at the invitation of James Blair, the Anglican Commissary of the colony. Although none of the Hanover dissenters journeyed the sixty miles to the capital [39] to hear him preach, they did obtain printed copies of some of Whitefield's sermons in 1743, which they read and discussed in their meetings.[40] Meanwhile the number of dissenters was increasing rapidly, a growth that prompted Governor Gooch to summon the leaders of the group to appear before him and his Council to explain their unorthodox behavior.[41] By

[32] Davies to the Bishop of London, Jan. 10, 1752, Foote, I, 190.

[33] Morton, *Colonial Virginia*, II, 585.

[34] Davies to the Bishop of London, Jan. 10, 1752, Foote, I, 190.

[35] Miller, *Memoirs*, p. 31.

[36] Davies to Philip Doddridge, Oct. 2, 1750, in William Stevens Perry (comp.), *Historical Collections Relating to the American Colonial Church* (4 vols., Hartford, 1870), I, 368.

[37] Miller, *Memoirs*, p. 31.

[38] ———— to John Holt Rice, May 6, 1819 [John Holt Rice], "The Origin of Presbyterianism in Virginia," *The Virginia Evangelical and Literary Magazine*, II (1819), 351. The writer of this letter is referred to as the son of one of the original Hanover dissenters.

[39] *Ibid.*, p. 347*n*.

[40] Davies to Bellamy, June 28, 1751, Alexander, *Biographical Sketches*, p. 22.

[41] Foote, I, 123.

this time, the dissenters had heard of other "Lutherans" whose beliefs they rejected; consequently, they were at a loss as to how to justify the name they had chosen for themselves. As fortune would have it, before they arrived at the inquiry they were caught in a storm and forced to take shelter in a home along the way. During the evening, they explained their beliefs and their predicament to the master of the house. He gave them an old book that they all agreed expressed their views on the doctrines of religion. When they appeared before the governor, they presented this old volume as their creed. Fortunately for Morris and his followers, Governor Gooch not only was of Scottish Presbyterian origin and education, but he also saw the wisdom in making concessions to peaceful dissenters who would pledge allegiance to the civil government. After perusing the book for some time, he pronounced the men Presbyterians and said that the book was "the Confession of Faith of the Presbyterian Church of Scotland; and that they were not only tolerated but acknowledged as part of the established church of the realm." [42]

Morris and his friends returned to Hanover as "Presbyterians." Knowing little of the implications of Presbyterianism, they petitioned the Presbyteries of New Brunswick and New Castle to send them a minister. The two New Light Presbyteries, which were then in the process of uniting as the Synod of New York, had just sent out one of their more prominent preachers, William Robinson, Davies' old friend and teacher, to visit the vacant pulpits in Virginia. The Hanover dissenters persuaded him "to officiate for some time among them." [43] Although he remained in Hanover for less than a week—during which time he was given the money for Davies' education [44]—people came from all over the county to hear him speak in the open air. As a result of this trip, the Hanover church was put in regular order. More important for those who would follow him,

---

[42] —— to Rice, May 6, 1819 [Rice], "Origin," p. 351. This opinion had previously emerged as the result of Synod of Philadelphia to William Gooch, May 30, 1738, and Gooch to Synod [May 1739], Foote, I, 103–104.

[43] Davies to the Bishop of London, Jan. 10, 1752, Foote, I, 190.

[44] [Rice], "Origin," p. 352.

as Davies would later comment, Robinson left "a General Concern about Religion . . . through the neighborhood, and some hundreds . . . were brought anxiously to enquire what shall we do to be saved?" [45]

The "General Concern" that Robinson aroused caused more and more people to drift away from the Church of England, and it became necessary to abandon Morris' home as a gathering place and erect a permanent place of worship. So numerous had the dissenters become and so dispersed were they that no less than five meeting-houses, or readinghouses as they were first called, were constructed.[46] This rapid growth encouraged the young Presbyterian congregation to ask the Synod of New York to send them a permanent leader. But as in the case of Robinson, the Synod found it necessary to send only temporary pastors for the next five years.

The first to arrive was the brother of Samuel Blair, the Reverend John Blair, soon to gain recognition as a noted scholar.[47] Although he, like Robinson, stayed but a short time, his audience was said to be often agitated and emotional to the point of tears and shouting. Morris himself pointed out that one night in particular, under the influence of Blair's voice, "a whole house full of people was quite overcome with the power of the word . . . and they could hardly sit or stand, or keep their passions under proper restraint." [48] In spite of the highly emotional behavior of Blair's audience, however, a later historian noted that his "amiable deportment, genteel manners, and classical language, united with gravity of manners forbid the idea of attaching either vulgarity or disorder to the religion he professed and taught." [49]

During the winter of 1744–45, John Roan visited Hanover and preached in such an intemperate manner that the usually even-tempered and tolerant Gooch was driven to take action. Roan openly attacked the parish ministers, criticizing their low morals and public

[45] Davies to Doddridge, Oct. 2, 1750, Perry, *Historical Collections*, I, 368–369.

[46] Davies to the Bishop of London, Jan. 10, 1752, Foote, I, 183.

[47] John Blair later became professor of theology and vice president of the College of New Jersey (Alexander, *Biographical Sketches*, p. 198).

[48] Morris quoted in *ibid.*, p. 223.

[49] Foote, I, 133.

acts, and incited his hearers to ridicule these government-appointed religious leaders.[50] As a result, Roan was indicted for attacking the Church of England, and two others, including Samuel Morris' son Joshua, were indicted for permitting him to use their homes.[51] But Roan had already left the colony, and the charge against him was later dismissed, as were the charges against Joshua and the other man.[52]

Roan's case spurred Governor Gooch to deliver one of his most devastating charges to a grand jury in the April 1745 session of the General Court. He requested an investigation of "certain false teachers that are lately crept into this government" who, according to the governor, were uneducated and unlicensed and led innocent and ignorant people astray. He said, furthermore, that allowing these persons to continue their attacks on the Anglican clergy would be "unjust to God, to our king, to our country, to our posterity." [53] Gooch, betraying his ignorance of the conditions prevailing within the Presbyterian church, sent a printed copy of the charge against Roan to the Synod of Philadelphia. The Synod immediately replied that it also deplored Roan's activities and did not wish the actions of the New Lights to bring the older Synod into disfavor.[54] After receiving this letter, the governor stated that preachers of any kind would be officially welcomed in the colony and protected by law, but only if they conducted themselves properly and obtained licenses for preaching in specified meetinghouses.[55]

Governor Gooch's indictments against Roan and his two supporters represented a general practice of harassment, both official and

---

[50] *Ibid.*, p. 134.

[51] Gewehr, *Great Awakening*, p. 56.

[52] Foote, I, 142. Alexander, *Biographical Sketches*, p. 224.

[53] Gooch's charge to the grand jury can be found in the *Virginia Gazette*, April 25, 1745.

[54] Robert Cathcart (for the Synod of Philadelphia) to Gooch, May 28, 1745, Foote, I, 138–139.

[55] Gooch to Synod of Philadelphia, June 20, 1745, Foote, I, 139–140. This exchange contained the first public denial by the Philadelphia Synod that the New Lights were Presbyterians: "[They] never belonged to our body, but are missionaries sent out by some who . . . erected themselves into a separate society, and . . . who . . . wee judge ill qualified" (Cathcart to Gooch, May 28, 1745, *ibid.*, p. 139). Both letters were printed in *Pennsylvania Gazette*, Sept. 26, 1745.

unofficial, that was adopted by the government after a series of intemperate attacks on the Anglican clergy by Roan and various itinerant Moravian preachers.[56] Unofficial but nonetheless severe criticism of the dissenters was expressed in "reproaches, sneers, ridicule,
and threats." [57] The Reverend Patrick Henry, no doubt highly incensed by the rejection of his congregation and the attacks by Roan,
raised his voice in protest: "Both Preachers and people are great
boasters of their assurance of salvation. They are so full of it here,
that the greatest number of those who have lately left the Church,
and followed those Enthusiastick Preachers, do confidently assert
that they are as sure of going to Heaven at last, as if they were there
already." [58] He also noted that the enthusiastic preachers "were
very industrious in casting all the reflections they could, upon the
established church and its ministers." [59]

But the Anglican parson Patrick Henry was not the only one
who was personally incensed at the activities of the Hanover dissenters in general and John Roan in particular, and the New Light
preachers were not the only ones to appear in the area. In 1739 the
Reverend John Thompson had been sent to Virginia by the Synod
of Philadelphia [60] and in the course of his journey stopped in Hanover. When he tried to preach from the Presbyterian pulpit, he
found the doors of the church barred against him by the followers
of Morris. According to Henry, who apparently befriended him as
a fellow sufferer of the New Light wrath, the Presbyterians "shut
the doors against him," alleging that he opposed their New Light
leaders. Henry accused the dissenters of locking Thompson out because he was a member of the Philadelphia Synod and thus, in their
eyes, "an enemy to Christ and true religion." [61] Rankled by this in-

---

[56] Morris quoted in Alexander, *Biographical Sketches*, p. 224. See also Morton, II, 592,
for a discussion of the actions of the Moravians and the reaction to them.

[57] Foote, I, 134.

[58] Henry to William Dawson, Feb. 13, 1745, Dawson MSS, Library of Congress.

[59] Henry to William Dawson, Nov. 21, 1747, *ibid.*

[60] Richard Webster, *A History of the Presbyterian Church in America, From its Origin
Until the Year 1760, with Biographical Sketches of its Early Ministers* (Philadelphia,
1857), p. 356.

[61] Henry to William Dawson, Feb. 13, 1745, Dawson MSS.

sult, Thompson returned home to write pamphlets attacking the New Light cause.[62]

Neither the official harassment by the government nor the voluble protests of the Anglican clergy and Old Light Presbyterians could stop the influx of the "Enthusiastick Preachers" of the New Light, for the intemperate Roan was followed by the equally intemperate Gilbert Tennent, accompanied by the milder and more scholarly Samuel Finley. These two preached for a week during the summer of 1745 with no interference from the government, although the harassment resumed after their departure.[63] There now ensued a period of about two years during which no visitors came from the Synod of New York, and Samuel Morris appeared regularly before the county court to be fined for not attending church.[64] By April of 1747, however, the evangelists apparently had resumed their visits, for the governor and Council issued a proclamation stating that those "Itinerant Preachers" who had "crept into this Colony" could not hold any kind of religious services or public or private meetings.[65] The proclamation was duly posted by the sheriff

[62] John Thompson, *The Government of the Church of Christ, and the Authority of Church Judicatories Established on a Scriptural Foundation, and the Spirit of Rash Judging Arraigned and Condemned; or the Matter of Difference Between the Synod of Philadelphia and the Protesting Brethren Justly and Fairly Stated. Being an Examination of Two Papers Brought in by Two of the Protesting Brethren, and Read Publickly in Open Synod in May 1740: And Also an Apology Brought in, Subscribed by the Protesting Brethren, and Read Also in Open Synod in May 1739* (Philadelphia, 1741), and also *The Doctrine of Conviction Set in a Clear Light, or an Examination and Confutation of Several Errors Relating to Conversion. Being the Substance of a Sermon Preached by the Author to His own and a Neighbouring Congregation, With Some Enlargements* (Philadelphia, 1741). Thompson and Davies later became close friends; Webster, *History of the Presbyterian Church,* p. 35.

[63] Alexander, *Biographical Sketches,* p. 224.

[64] *Ibid.,* p. 225.

[65] *Executive Journals of the Council of Colonial Virginia* (April 3, 1747), eds. Henry Read McIlwaine, Wilmer L. Hall, and Benjamin Hillman (6 vols., Richmond, 1925–1966), V, 227–228. "This Board having under their Consideration the Number of Itinerant Preachers lately crept into this Colony and the mischievous Consequences of suffering those Corrupters of our Faith and True Religion to propagate their shocking Doctrines it is Ordered That a Proclamation forthwith issue requiring all Magistrates to discourage and prohibite as far as legally they can all Itinerant Preachers whether New Light men Moravians or Methodists from Teaching Preaching or holding any Meeting in this Colony and that all People can be injoined to be aiding and assisting to that Purpose." The order was executed, *ibid.,* p. 490.

of Hanover County on the door of the Presbyterian meetinghouse.[66]

Largely through the effectiveness of the visiting preachers, the ardor aroused by Robinson in 1743 had now become self-sustaining, enabling the Hanover dissenters to endure opposition and the lack of regular ministerial leadership. Davies later was able to reflect that "the transient labours of my Brethren were extensively blessed and . . . in their absence the people associated to read and pray." [67] To alleviate the problems caused by the lack of a permanent minister, the Synod of New York had determined in September 1745 to move Robinson to Hanover from St. Georges, Delaware; however, Robinson died before assuming his new post. With the exception of a brief visit by Whitefield,[68] the only New Light pulpit in Virginia remained vacant until Samuel Davies arrived for a visit in the spring of 1747.[69]

Such were the difficult conditions facing the newly ordained Davies on his first ministerial assignment. Fortunately for Davies, however, he was aware of Gooch's acceptance of dissenters who expressed deference to his authority.[70] Unlike his less successful predecessors who had gone directly to Hanover, Davies therefore went first to Williamsburg to obtain a license. Here the young preacher, described by the governor as "tall, slim, well-formed . . . pale and wasted by disease, dignified and courteous in manner," was licensed to preach in the four meetinghouses erected by the Morris group.[71] It was an event repeated the following year for the fifth meetinghouse.[72]

---

[66] Foote, I, 160.
[67] Davies to Doddridge, Oct. 2, 1750, Perry, *Historical Collections*, I, 369.
[68] Morris quoted in Alexander, *Biographical Sketches*, p. 225.
[69] Foote, I, 141.
[70] Gooch to Synod of Philadelphia, June 20, 1745, *ibid.*, pp. 139–140.
[71] *Ibid.*, p. 158.
[72] *Ibid.*, pp. 159–160.

III

All the Necessaries of Life

WHEN THE YOUNG New Light preacher first settled in Hanover County, he had but recently lost his wife. He no doubt appeared to many members of his congregation as a possible suitor for their daughters, for the ministry was even then one of the few occupations considered totally respectable in a class-conscious society. Davies, however, selected as his second wife a girl from Williamsburg. He wasted little time in courtship. On October 4, 1748, shortly after permanently settling in Hanover, he married Jane Holt, member of a family well known in the colonial capital.

Jane's father, William Holt, had once served as mayor, and her brother John was learning the printing business from William Hunter, the public printer of the colony and publisher of the *Virginia Gazette.* John later was to become prominent throughout the colonies as the partner of James Parker—who published both the *Connecticut Gazette* and the *New York Gazette*—and as sole publisher of a series of newspapers in New York State and Norfolk, Virginia. He would also become one of Benjamin Franklin's deputy post masters.[1]

---

[1] There are several varying accounts of John Holt: "Narrative of George Fisher," *William and Mary Quarterly,* series one, XVII (1908), 154*n*; "The Holt Family," *Tyler's Quarterly Magazine of History and Genealogy,* VII (1926), 284–285; Victor H. Paltsits in *Dictionary of American Biography,* s.v. "John Holt." Only the last seems accurate.

There is nothing surprising about the marriage of Davies so soon after his permanent location in the colony. Such marriages were common during the entire colonial period, especially on the frontier. In fact, single young men were looked upon with suspicion. What is of interest about this marriage is that Jane was a member of a well-known Church of England family in no way connected, apparently, with the Hanover dissenters. It is quite probable that some of Davies' success in the colony may have been the result of this union. Certainly, his marriage to Jane Holt did give him a certain measure of acceptance that he otherwise might not have had.

Even so, Davies brought to the marriage a variety of qualifications that far outweighed the prestige of a prominent family name. Leaders of the New Light movement would have been hard pressed to find a better-qualified representative of their cause than this accomplished young minister. In a colonial Virginia society at the height of its brilliance, highly urbane and literate, here was a New Light spokesman who was well educated, articulate, and diplomatic. He was an attractive man, tall and erect although showing the signs of his recurring illnesses, a poet and eloquent orator who brought to the pulpit a strong classical education and who tempered a forceful spiritual drive with moderation and toleration. As a consequence, Samuel Davies slipped easily into the spiritual life of Hanover. Any loneliness he felt as the only New Light preacher in Virginia must surely have been allayed by the activities of a strenuous schedule and his warm acceptance in the community.

When Davies arrived at his new home he could not have foreseen that this was to be the one and only pastorate of his career, spanning a mere twelve years, from 1748 to 1759, nor that his life would extend only two years beyond that. Yet the few years in Hanover, made even briefer by a fourteen-month interlude in Great Britain, were to be full and deeply satisfying to the young preacher, a fact that he would acknowledge more than once. Despite his uncertain health, Davies was to pursue an active career in the pulpit, as rewarding as it was varied. He was already writing poetry when he accepted the New Light pastorate, and he would gain increasing pleasure from this activity as well as from his other writings and their publication. In his personal life, he was happily married and the father of a growing family. His income was barely sufficient, but it seemed to give him little concern. Most important to the sensitive young man, he had found a good friend shortly after settling in Hanover, one who would listen to him, criticize and stimulate his thoughts, exchange pleasantries, and provide direct assistance during the remainder of his life.

It was to this friend, John Holt, the brother of his wife, that Davies spoke of being a "contented Mortal." Davies had just completed the third year of his pastorate, and he was contrasting his country life with that of Holt in the polite society of Williamsburg:

> Amid the Hurries of a busy Life, and the refined Nonsense of the polite Vulgar, of which you have copious Entainments, I believe at Times it may give you the Pleasure of Variety to hear from a happy Preacher, whose life differs as much from yours as a Mole's or an Oyster's from the Aerial Eagle's or a polite Lap-Dog's. I can tell you I am as happy as perhaps the Creation can make me: I enjoy all the Necessaries and most of the Conveniences of Life; I have a peaceful Study, as a Refuge from the Hurries and Noise of the World around me; the venerable Dead are waiting in my Library to entertain me, and relieve me from the Nonsense of surviving Mortals; I am peculiarly happy in my Relations, and Providence does not afflict me by afflicting them. In short, I have all a moderate Heart can wish; and I very much question if there be a more calm, placid and contented Mortal in Virginia.[2]

They engaged in a lively correspondence about a multitude of common interests.[3] Although John seems to have been firm in his Anglican beliefs, the two men of differing tastes and religious backgrounds developed a genuine and lasting friendship as well as a close family relationship. They aided and assisted each other to the end of Davies' life. The minister once spoke of having read some of his writings to Holt's senior associate, the public printer William Hunter, who may have first known Davies through Holt.[4] At

[2] Davies to Holt, Aug. 13, 1751, Rush MSS.
[3] Apparently all that remains of this correspondence are the seventeen letters from Davies to Holt in the Rush MSS. Regrettably Davies seems to have preserved little, and those of Holt are no longer extant.
[4] Davies to Holt, July 7, 1749, *ibid.* This is actually a postscript to that of July 4, 1749.

another time, Davies' friendship for his brother-in-law prompted him to poetry when he heard that Holt was going to England:

> Say, shall a Brother, Sir, nay more, a Friend
> To you these rude Effects of Friendship send? [5]

And a few years later, when Holt's business in Williamsburg was failing, Davies went out of his way to speak to an acquaintance in New York, "a noted Mercht, and my peculiar Friend," in an attempt to find a place for Holt in the trade of "Iron, Shoes, Paddles, Biscuits, etc." [6] Family ties apparently were close, too, for the mother of John and Jane Holt made frequent visits to the household in Hanover, visits that were returned by the Davies family. [7]

In addition to Holt's role as supplier of books and information, Davies came to depend upon the printer as his sole adviser on writing and publishing. Throughout his residence in Hanover, Davies regularly published sermons, poems, and essays, most of which appeared either in the *Virginia Gazette* or as separate publications. Davies trusted Holt's judgment completely, allowing him to edit and publish his efforts wherever and however he liked. It was up to Holt to determine whether they should appear in the *Gazette* or separately as pamphlets. It was Holt who decided whether an article should be printed in whole, in part, or at all. In March 1751, Davies wrote to Holt complimenting the printer on his introduction to one of Davies' poems and included with his letter a collection of poetry—an important enclosure that was later to become *Miscellaneous Poems*. This volume of fifty poems—the only collection of Davies' poetry to be published during his lifetime—appeared over the Hunter imprint in early 1752, hardly four years after he settled in Hanover. It is safe to assume that in publishing the collection Holt complied with Davies' request to "correct and dispose of as you please" and to "pick and cull such as you think worthy of public View." [8] A decade later, just before his death, Davies penned his

[5] Davies to Holt, Nov. 25, 1749; *ibid.*; *Collected Poems*, p. 141.
[6] Davies to Holt, Aug. 13, 1751, Rush MSS.
[7] Davies to Holt, Feb. 10, 1749, Nov. 25, 1749, Aug. 23, 1760, Jan. 21, 1761, *ibid.*
[8] Davies to Holt, March 2, 1751, *ibid.*

last letter to his faithful friend, observing that "I always intend for you the first Offer of all my little Business as an Author." [9]

It is certain that Davies received very little income from his writing, and he himself noted that the purpose of his verse, like his prose, was primarily to encourage people to seek salvation.[10] His life in Hanover continued to have a small economic base—at one time his yearly income was about £100—but he observed that he could "make a shift to live upon it." [11] Davies made a few trips to Williamsburg, purchased books frequently, and even considered the purchase of a slave with his £100 a year,[12] but he did feel the economic pinch now and again. When it came time, later during his residence at Hanover, for him to visit England on a fund-raising trip for the College of New Jersey, he had to insist that his sponsors buy his clothes for the trip.[13]

Home life in Hanover centered around Davies' beloved "Chara" (his favorite term of endearment for his wife) and their family. His wife bore him six children, whom the minister liked to call "the little Pledges of our mutual Love." One, a daughter, died at birth, but five—three sons and two daughters—survived to complete the home Davies enjoyed so thoroughly. The three boys arrived first— William in 1749, Samuel in 1750, and John Rodgers in 1752— before their father's trip to England. The two girls were born after his return to Hanover—Martha in 1755 and Margaret in 1757.

The love Davies felt for his Chara was apparently so great that he experienced agonizing moments in which he feared it might replace love for his God. He paid a moving tribute to her in his poem "Conjugal Love and Happiness," which contained this stanza:

[9] Davies to Holt, Jan. 21, 1761, *ibid.*

[10] Davies, *Miscellaneous Poems*, p. vii.

[11] Davies to Bellamy in William Henry Foote, *Sketches of Virginia: Historical and Biographical*, series two (Philadelphia, 1856), p. 42. Hereafter cited as Foote, II.

[12] In February of 1749, Davies wrote to Holt: "I understand, by your information, that the Governour has a Negro Wench to sell. . . . If you think her fit for me, and that her Price is reasonable, please to request his Honour to keep her for me—I want One very much; therefore would be willing to give a good Price for a good one." It is not known whether the purchase was made.

[13] *Diary*, Sept. 20, 1753, p. 14.

> *Chara,* beneath thy Influence I felt
> The charming Flame; my Soul was taught to melt
> In Ecstasies unknown, and soon began
> To put the Stoic off, and soften into Man.
> The Veil of Modesty, in vain confin'd
> Th' alluring Beauties of thy lovely Mind:
> The shining Charms beam'd thro' the fair Disguise;
> Blush'd in thy Aspect, dazzled in thy Eyes;
> In every Word, in all thy Conduct known,
> And in thy artless Face, well-copy'd, shone—
> So thro' refulgent Clouds breaks the bright Morning Sun.
> I saw, I lov'd, I sought to gain,
> The blooming Fair; nor sought in vain.
> Thy yielding Bosom soon began to glow
> With the same Flame thy Charms taught me to know.
> Thy Soul, unskill'd in those inhumane Arts,
> Thy Sex affect to torture captive Hearts,
> A constant Lover did disdain to vex,
> Or with unkind Delays and treach'rous Wiles perplex.
> Thy Soul, that knew not what dissembling meant,
> With modest soft Reluctance, blush'd Consent.
> In Transport lost the joyful News I heard;
> And vow'd my Life the Favour to reward.
> A solemn Rite the willing Contract seal'd,
> To stand, 'til Death divide us, unrepeal'd.

Yet at the height of his reverie, Davies in the same poem was seized by fear that this love was supplanting his love for God:

> But here, ah! here a guilty Scene appears!——
> Oh! break my senseless Heart, and flow my Tears!
> How manifold and strange my Frailties be!
> *Chara,* I find Temptations ev'n in thee!
> When fondly in thy loving Arms I rest,
> And thy resistless Charms enflame my Breast,
> The pleasing Tempter seizes all my Heart,
> Or leaves my GOD but the inferior Part.
> Almighty Grace! th' Extravagance controul
> Of this unruly Pow'r that captivates my Soul.[14]

Expressions of love and concern for Chara were also assigned regularly by Davies to the privacy of his journal, especially during

---

[14] *Miscellaneous Poems,* pp. 59–61.

the months he spent in England. He almost canceled the foreign trip because Chara was ill; and, even amid an enthusiastic reception in Great Britain, he painfully missed his wife and his home. At one point he made the entry, "At night finished a Letter to my Dearest, with such tender affections as I could hardly bear." Again, "my dear Chara has often recurred to my Thoughts, and frequently I imagine myself talking to her." [15] Just prior to reaching England, when he was in sight of land, Davies' "heart spontaneously dictated" a poem to Chara, which he also set down in the journal:

> While Objects various, strange and new,
> In numerous Prospects rush to View,
> The Tho'ts of Friends, the Tho'ts of Home
> Engross my Heart and still find Room.
> Chara, with what strange, magic Art,
> Dost thou, so distant, charm my Heart? [16]

The youthful minister's attitude toward his children was characterized by a tension between joy in them and apprehension about the state of their souls. At the birth of his third son, the namesake of his friend and schoolmate John Rodgers, Davies again turned to his favorite medium for expressing his innermost thoughts. He composed a poem debating the problem of predestination in which he agonized over the possible fate awaiting his son:

> Thou little wond'rous miniature of man,
> Form'd by unerring Wisdom's perfect plan;
> Thou little stranger, from eternal night
> Emerging into life's immortal light.

The poem reached a climax with the line, "Thou embryo-angel, or thou infant fiend," and concluded with a prayer for the son's soul:

> Maker of souls! avert so dire a doom,
> Or snatch her back to native nothing's gloom! [17]

Such an overriding concern for the state of the soul meant that the discipline of religious instruction and the encouragement of holi-

---

[15] *Diary,* Jan. 9, 1755, p. 139.

[16] *Ibid.,* Dec. 22, 1753, p. 40; *Collected Poems,* p. 160.

[17] "On the Birth of John Rodgers Davies, the Author's Third Son," *Sermons* (1845), III, 495; *Collected Poems,* pp. 199–200.

ness in life tended to come first in Davies' family relations. Consequently, he often assumed the character of teacher. A message to his friend in London, Thomas Gibbons, suggests that such periods of instruction on occasion found the children naturally reluctant to learn:

> We have now three sons and two daughters; whose young minds as they are open I am endeavouring to cultivate with my own hand, unwilling to trust them to a stranger; and I find the business of education much more difficult than I expected. My dear little creatures sob and drop a tear now and then under my instructions, but I am not so happy as to see them under deep and lasting impressions of religion; and this is the greatest grief they afford me. Grace cannot be communicated by natural descent; and if it could, they would receive but little from me.[18]

Indeed, the religious emphasis found in the Davies household may have produced one of the major disappointments of his life—the unfavorable reaction of his children. Only one of the daughters expressed serious concern in matters of religion. The others seem to have been either skeptical about their father's beliefs or openly hostile. One of the sons went so far as to express a preference for "the Romanists," while another refused throughout his adult life to attend church. Despite his love for and enjoyment in his children, Davies fell prey to the tragedy of so many dedicated preachers: his children did not come to share his views.[19]

It seems inconceivable that Davies could have suppressed his views on religion even if he had known their ultimate effect on the children. His dedication to his own idea of religion and his deep commitment to teaching it to others pervaded all forms of his expression. Davies felt that the minister's sole office was to be instrumental in "the Salvation of Souls," and he faithfully pursued this mission, with friends such as Holt and with his family. Davies the man was Davies the preacher. He insisted that the purpose of all literary composition, in whatever form, was to lure men from sin.[20]

---

[18] Davies to Gibbons, n.d., *Sermons* (1766), I, lxvi.

[19] "A Recovered Tract of President Davies: Now First Published," *The Biblical Repertory and Princeton Review*, IX (1837), 360–362.

[20] *Miscellaneous Poems*, p. vii.

Thus, poetry quite naturally became a religious medium for him. He used it to preach and to teach, as well as to express himself. On occasion he even directed his poetic talents toward serving members of his congregation in need of appropriate epitaphs. He apparently was able to dash off these inscriptions with little or no preparation; when he was once asked to write a short verse for an epitaph, he noted, "Tho' I had neither Leisure, nor Composure, I wrote 3." [21]

Although Davies excused himself from the select company of those poets able to please the most discriminating critics—"None but an Homer or Virgil, a Milton or Pope, can furnish them with proper Entertainment"—he suggested that his verse might be acceptable nonetheless in service to "the Interests of Religion and Virtue." [22] He quoted George Herbert's line to make the point: "a verse may hit him whom the Sermon flies." [23] It was this same orientation, toward serving his God through poetry, that led Davies early in his career to turn to hymn writing: it added another dimension to his preaching efforts. The latter action was more significant on another count, however, for it broke with tradition and established him as a pioneer in American hymnology.

Despite his modest disclaimer that it was not in his province to write poetry suitable for "Persons of a refined and judicious Taste," Davies' verses clearly found a mark. They were read not only by his congregations and fellow dissenters, but also by a large audience of stanch Anglicans, as evidenced by the account books of the *Virginia Gazette* and the extant records of private library holdings of Anglican planters. The poems were copied in newspapers and early magazines from South Carolina to New Hampshire. Several poems were printed in British magazines. They obviously attracted attention to the minister and his work, for the verse was attacked and de-

---

[21] *Diary*, Nov. 13, 1753, pp. 26–27. One of these was:
> Ye that in Beauty, or in Youth confide,
> Come view this Monument, to burst your Pride;
> The Charms of Beauty, Youth in Flowery Bloom,
> Wither'd at Morn, lie Mouldering in this Tomb,
> And you may meet the Same surprizing Doom.

[22] *Miscellaneous Poems*, p. vi.

[23] *Ibid.*, p. vii.

fended heatedly in the *Virginia Gazette* for a period of about two years. The hymns, those that were published, were widely distributed also. Many of them were even appended to British printings of his individual sermons.[24]

Inwardly, though, Davies was less confident than his success as preacher and writer would indicate. Periodic spells of illness and frequent periods of doubt concerning his capabilities heightened an introspective, meditative bent in the young preacher. Since poetry was such an easy and intimate medium for him, it was here that he most often revealed his inner nature. Virtually all of these meditations focused in the Godhead and the joys of salvation, but seldom were they unaccompanied by nagging doubts about his relationship to God. Would the ultimate goal of the Christian escape his personal grasp? He wrestled constantly with the problem. He read and imitated such religious meditations as Young's *Night Thoughts* and Thomson's *Seasons*, and he also knew Baxter's *The Saints' Everlasting Rest*, which was familiar to all educated Calvinists. Baxter's treatise called for the unceasing self-examination that Davies practiced so thoroughly. Much of Davies' verse followed closely the Baxter formula, which was to go to the scripture for material, call on memory to create a setting for it, use judgment to reason it out, and then express it in a soliloquy, thus arousing the heart to apprehend the material.[25] Davies' opening poem in his published collection was such a soliloquy, observing the Baxter guidelines. The fourteen stanzas were based on John 21:17 and entitled "Lord Thou knowest all Things, Thou knowest that I love Thee." In the particular lines following, he was expressing the struggle that always seemed to arise from his meditations:

> My God! the Wretch that does not love Thy Name
> To Life and Being forfeits all his Claim,
> And may he sink to nothing whence he came.
> . . . .

[24] See especially Davis' "Introduction" to *Collected Poems*, pp. xi–xxv, from which this information is drawn.

[25] Louis L. Martz, "Foreword" to *The Poetry of Edward Taylor*, ed. Donald E. Stanford (New Haven, 1960), p. xxvii.

Oh! if my Heart does not to Thee aspire,
If ought with equal Fervour I desire,
I'm self-condemn'd, and doom myself to Fire.
. . . .

Yet ah! in some dark Hours I hardly know
Whether I love my gracious GOD or no.
. . . .

And yet methinks in some bright Moments too,
I feel the heav'nly Flame divinely glow.
. . . .

Oh! if I love Thee not, as Fears suggest,
Why am I, in Thine Absence, thus distrest?
. . . .

Whence this immense Ambition in my Mind,
That scorns all Joys but those of heavenly Kind?
Why should a Worm, an animated Clod;
Disdain all Bliss beneath a boundless GOD?
. . . .

I love my GOD, or else I nothing love;
And the pure Flame e'er long shall burn above,
And from its native El'ment ne'er remove.[26]

Working in the Hanover study he enjoyed so much, Davies would also utilize verse as a means of meditating upon and sharpening the content of his sermons. He described this creative process in the prefatory remarks to the fifty poems collected and published during his lifetime. The complete title of the volume was *Miscellaneous Poems, Chiefly on Divine Subjects. In Two Books. Published for the Religious Entertainment of Christians in general.* Most of the selections were grouped in Books I and II, but they were followed by an Appendix of "Devout Ejaculations and Soliloquies" containing other, usually shorter, pieces. In Book II, he collected those poems that had been composed "to improve a vacant Hour on Saturday Evening after study; and to give me a more lively Impression of the Subject of Discourse for the ensuing Day." [27] In further explanation, he observed, "It has been my usual Method for some

[26] *Miscellaneous Poems*, pp. 1–5.
[27] *Ibid.*, p. iii.

Time, after studying a Sermon, to cast a few Thoughts into a poetical Form, either containing the Substance of the Sermon, or expressive of my Disposition in composing it." [28] One of many such poems composed during the Saturday evening hours was "annext to a Sermon adapted for Self-Examination, on I John iii. 7, 8." He titled the poem "The Doubting Christian" and, as was typical of much of his verse, eventually turned to examining his own spiritual state:

> HAPPY the Man whose peaceful Breast
> A smiling Conscience charms to rest;
> Whose pious Heart and Life express
> The living Characters of Grace!
>
> He humbly claims the Promises,
> And calls their richest Blessing his:
> In Peace he lives, and dies in Peace,
> And peaceful soars to heav'nly Bliss.
>
> Thrice happy he! But ah! I feel
> The Twinges of Suspicions still;
> Dark boding Fears and wild Surmise,
> And Jealousies perpetual rise.
>
> Perplext with various Characters,
> My Mind is tost 'twixt Hopes and Fears:
> Here some kind Tokens rise, but there
> The dismal Counter-Tokens glare.
>
> I humbly hope, in some bright Hour,
> My State is safe, my Heav'n secure:
> But soon the shining Moment flies,
> And soon tremendous Glooms arise.
>
> Thus in a dubious Twilight lost,
> With various Waves, alternate, tost,
> O'er Life's tempestuous Sea I roam,
> Uncertain where shall be my Home:
>
> Uncertain where my Soul must go,
> To Fields of Joy, or Lakes of Woe:
> Before me the vast Prospect lies,
> But cover'd with Uncertainties.
>
> . . . .

[28] *Ibid.*, p. 87.

Thou seest my Passions to Thy Name
Kindle, tho' with a feeble Flame
And shall a Spark of heav'nly Love
From its own native Regions move?

O! shall the meanest of Thy Friends,
Forever dwell with hateful Fiends?
No! let me claim the humblest Place
In the bright Mansions of Thy Grace.[29]

Even as a doubter, however, Davies' faith in ultimate salvation and his joy of anticipation usually overcame the fears, as in these lines:

Since of Thy Love I tasted first,
All other Pleasures I disgust:
Since first Thy Beauties charm'd my Sight,
Created Charms yield no Delight.

O! if I'm doom'd Thy Frowns to feel,
Why didst Thou e'er Thy Smiles reveal?
Why with Thy Glories charm my Eye,
O! why torment me with the Views
Of Bliss I must for ever lose?

. . . .

But hence each dire Surmise! away!
My gracious God would not display
His Glories to enflame my Heart,
If I were destin'd to depart.
He would not cruelly deride
My Soul with Bliss to be deny'd;
Nor kindle Love to pant in vain,
And rack me with augmented Pain.
No! His own Self will satisfy
The Wishes He has rais'd so high.[30]

In all, Davies must have written well over one hundred poems, a few of them quite long, for some ninety-odd have survived to this day.[31] Most of it was the poetry of meditation so popular among the

[29] *Ibid.*, pp. 103–104.
[30] *Ibid.*, pp. 117–118.
[31] The total poetic effort of Samuel Davies is substantial enough and important enough to warrant a full-scale study, but it obviously cannot be undertaken here. Until a more thorough examination becomes available, readers interested in this inspirational verse of

religious writers of the seventeenth century and later. In form, it resembled the hymns of Isaac Watts and Philip Doddridge, and it could be traced also to the work of such poets as Milton and to the Bible and the classics. If Davies had been classifying it, using the terminology of his day, he probably would have called it the form of the "Pindaric Ode."

But it was the poetry's quality of sublimity that best expressed and revealed the inner nature of the Hanover pastor and that made it so effective. In his poetry as in his life, Davies was a moderate, hewing a middle line somewhere between the extremes of the cold, learned rationalism of the Virginia Anglicans and the emotionalism of George Whitefield, an emotionalism that was even characteristic of some of the dissenting preachers in the colonies. Always first with Davies was the need to reach the human heart, and this could not be accomplished by reason alone. Sinners must be made to see the magnificence, the awesomeness—the sublimity—of God and the Christian concept. In this respect, the leader of the Great Awakening in America expressed well "the relationship between evangelical dissent and 'pre-Romanticism.' " [32] Although Burke and other forerunners of the Romantics developed the eighteenth-century concept of the divine, Davies and other Calvinist clergymen, notably Jonathan Edwards, gave it a special emphasis. These men believed with Burke that the truly sublime consisted of such elements as power, vastness, infinity, magnificence, and fear-admiration, "a kind of tranquility tinged with terror, which might reach the souls of men." [33] Thus, virtually all of Davies' writing, both poetry and prose, shared this predominant quality: it was sublime, in aim, imagery, and theme.

Davies continually depicted the awesomeness of God in opposition to the weakness of man:

the Great Awakening may turn to the previously mentioned collection by Richard Beale Davis, especially his excellent introduction wherein the poetry is briefly described and placed in its literary and religious milieu. This section draws heavily upon Davis' edition.

[32] Alan Heimert, *Religion and the American Mind from the Great Awakening to the Revolution* (Cambridge, Mass., 1966), p. 173.

[33] Davis, "Introduction" to *Collected Poems,* pp. xviii–xix.

> THOU only Good! Eternal ALL!
> What am I when compar'd with THEE?
> A Piece of animated Clay;
> An Atom sporting in thy Ray—— [34]

God was seen at one point as

> So bright a Glory shall He dart around,
> The dazzling Deluge shall the Sun confound,[35]

and again:

> —O! the dire Terrors of the THUND'RER's Wrath!
> O! the immense Severity
> Of the dread Law! the dire Reward
> Of Sin! the Vengeance of the flaming Sword
> Of Justice! O! dire Fruits of the forbidden Tree! [36]

During a time of uncertainty over his salvation, the pastor observed:

> I view the Ocean vast and wide,
> Where Time unites its ebbing Tide;
> Now, hoping, would th' Adventure make,
> Now trembling, shudd'ring startle back.[37] . . . . .

In a footnote to the poem "The Conflagration" (based on II Peter 3:2), he said, "There is no Theme, perhaps, in the Compass of Nature, that so far exceeds human Language and Imagination, as the Conflagration." [38] Passages from the poem itself bore out this assertion:

> Horrendous Sight! A World in Flames!
> Thunders loud rumbling thro' the Air!
> Dire Lightnings flashing fiery Streams,
> And glaring red and vengeful there!
>
> . . . .
>
> There overwhelm'd, the rebel Worms
> Lie ever, ever, ever lost!

[34] *Miscellaneous Poems*, p. 22.
[35] *Ibid.*, p. 73.
[36] *Ibid.*, p. 83.
[37] *Ibid.*, p. 104.
[38] *Ibid.*, p. 113n.

Beaten with everlasting Storms,
On fiery Eddies whirl'd and tost.

But ye dear Saints, ye pious Few,
JESUS shall screen your feeble Souls:
Safe from on high your Eyes shall view
The burning Earth and melting Poles.[39]

Davies was fascinated with a storm; it represented for him the power of God, as well as God's mercy in sparing the weak human being from its fury. A vivid description of a storm at sea was set down during his trip to England. To Davies, the sea itself held many qualities of the sublime, and a storm at sea was doubly sublime:

When the Storm thickens, and the Ocean rolls,
When Nature trembles to the frightful Poles,
The pious mind nor Doubts nor fears assail,
Tempests are Zephyrs, or a gentler Gale.

. . . .

The Lightening flashes a malignant Glare
Thro' the thick Gloom, and helps but to descry
The Horrors of the Dark, and Danger's Frown

. . . .

The mountain break, in a tumultuous Roar;

. . . .

Sure 'tis the War of Elements; the shock
Of Nature in Convulsions; 'tis the Wreck
Of Worlds! What horrid Images can shew
The dreadful Scene! What loud tremendous Sounds,
What wild, tumultuous Verse can represent
The blended Roar of Thunder, Winds and Waves
In Tumult—Now how naturally Distress
Casts up to Heaven the wild imploring Eye,
And eager cries for Help—Now, now we sink!

. . . .

Now we shall rise no more. Strange! we emerge
Toss'd like a Cork, we float from Wave to Wave,
From the huge, watry Precipice we plunge

. . . .

—O thou Ruler of the Seas,
Send forth thy mighty Mandate, "Peace, be still,"

[39] *Ibid.*, pp. 111–112.

And calm their Rage—But can even Mercy hear
Such daring Rebels, who in one vile Breath
Blend Prayers and Curses? But alas! my Heart
Look home; thou art not innocent; my Guilt
May hurl these furious Hurricanes in Air,
And Arm each Billow of the Sea against me.[40]

From the point of view of American literary history, however, it was Davies as hymn writer who was most significant as poet. Music and harmony affected him deeply; he always carefully indicated a familiar tune for his early hymns, and his later "Odes" were set to music by a Princeton graduate. Davies, like Edward Taylor in his *Preparatory Meditations*, composed his hymns to go with sermons on the same subjects, in many cases preparing his congregation for the Lord's Supper. Even a century and a half after his death, many of his hymns were popular among churchgoers, and several denominations were still using his "Communion Hymns." [41] He seems to have been the first resident of the American colonies to write hymns as a regular and serious endeavor and the first to have had them published. Louis F. Benson has noted that "If the distinction be observed . . . between metrical renderings of the Psalms and other passages of Scripture . . . on the one hand, and 'hymns of mere human composure,' on the other; then, with that understanding, Davies is entitled to the still greater renown of being the first hymn writer of any moment in America."

Traditionally this distinction has been accorded to a Connecticut Indian named Samson Occum,[42] but this claim cannot be sustained in light of the fact that his authorship is open to question. Furthermore, the first hymns attributed to him were not published until

[40] *Collected Poems*, pp. 160, 161–162. For the original version with Davies' corrections, see *Diary*, Nov. 18, 1753, p. 28; Jan. 26, 1755, pp. 140–142.

[41] The best study of Davies the hymn writer is still Louis Fitzgerald Benson, "President Davies as a Hymn Writer," *Journal of the Presbyterian Historical Society*, II (1903), 277–286. See also his "The Hymns of President Davies," *ibid.*, pp. 343–373.

[42] See W. DeLoss Love, *Samson Occum and the Christian Indians of New England* (Boston, 1899), pp. 176–187. The standard study of American hymnody is Henry Wilder Foote, *Three Centuries of American Hymnody* (Cambridge, Mass., 1940). The hymn in the English-speaking world is discussed in Louis F. Benson, *The English Hymn: Its Development and Use in Worship* (Richmond, 1962).

1774, whereas those of Davies first appeared appended to sermons as early as 1756.[43] In 1769, his friend and correspondent Thomas Gibbons published his own *Hymns Adapted to Divine Worship* [44] and included sixteen of Davies' in an appendix. In effect this was the fulfillment of a promise Gibbons had made in the first edition of Davies' sermons, wherein he commented on the author's habit of annexing "Hymns of his own composition" to his pulpit orations: "Had this been uniformly the case they might have accompanied his Discourses to the press, but as it is not, I have omitted them; but, if death or incapacity prevent not my design, I intend hereafter to collect what Hymns of his have fallen into my hands, and publish them together with some of my own." [45] Again, in 1787, the Baptist John Rippon printed seven of Davies' hymns in *A Selection of Hymns*.

The significance of Davies' efforts as a writer of hymns is not a mere matter of dates, albeit he does have priority here; it depends as well on a recognition of the prejudices with which he had to contend. According to Benson, the New Light preacher and those who immediately followed him were the founders of a revolt against the exclusive practice of psalm singing in the American churches. The pioneer work of Isaac Watts had appeared shortly before Davies' birth, but it was not until 1787 that his own church permitted the singing of Watts' hymns.[46] Benson asserts that "these facts throw a color of originality, perhaps even of venturesomeness, around Davies' work as a writer of hymns, and invest it with a historical significance quite apart from any actual merit in the hymns themselves." [47] But they hold more than historical interest. Many were successful in finding their way into collections, thus attaining a wide degree of circulation and, presumably, extensive use in worship; they were therefore important for their content as well as for

[43] Benson, "President Davies," pp. 280–281.
[44] Thomas Gibbons, *Hymns Adapted to Divine Worship* (London, 1769).
[45] *Sermons* (1766), I, x–xii.
[46] "The Synod . . . do hereby allow, that Dr. Watts' imitations of David's Psalms . . . be sung in the churches and families under their care." "Minutes of the Synod of Philadelphia and New York," May 24, 1787, *Records*, p. 535.
[47] Benson, "President Davies," pp. 281–282.

their early composition. Their value is further enhanced by the fact that American Presbyterianism, throughout its history, has produced few writers of hymns whose influence can compare with that of Davies.

Although the poetry was primarily a poetry of meditation, meant for private edification or religious instruction, it has assured him a place of permanent importance in American literary history. In his own day, his verse received far more attention than that of his Anglican contemporaries, and it still stands as an important medium for understanding one of the leaders of the Great Awakening. His hymns, moreover, show Davies to have been an innovator of both historical import and artistic merit. Perhaps Richard Beale Davis has best summarized the importance of Davies as a poet:

> One may never call his verse great poetry and by no means all of it good poetry. But it was the rhymed representation of a significant American movement, the Great Awakening. And with all due allowance for the *Bay Psalm Book* and Michael Wigglesworth and a number of New England fugitive religious poets it was Samuel Davies . . . who brought Polyhymnia, the muse of sacred poetry, before the American public.[48]

[48] Davis, "Introduction" to *Collected Poems*, p. xxiv.

IV

The Fires of Eloquence

U NLIKE most eighteenth-century American revivals, the one occurring in Virginia was singularly free of the emotional excesses that brought disrepute to the Great Awakening.[1] Much of the moderation of the Virginia revival resulted from the nature of the members of the local congregations. They were outside the mainstream of Presbyterian development, and, if they were less susceptible to "wild reveries of enthusiasms," it must have been due in part to their Church of England background. Their former mode of worship had no doubt left them with a certain sense of dignity and decorum, which they refused to abandon even after their withdrawal from the established church. Samuel Davies answered the needs of the Virginia dissenters perfectly, for he fitted well his own description of the proper preacher for the area, which he set forth in a letter to Jonathan Edwards. Davies asserted that such a preacher must not be a "fiery, superficial" pulpit orator, but "a popular preacher, of ready utterance, good delivery, solid judgment, free from enthusiastic freaks, and of ardent zeal." [2] Davies'

[1] James R. Graham, *The Planting of the Presbyterian Church in Northern Virginia* (Winchester, 1904), p. 25.
[2] Quoted by Davies in a letter to Bellamy, July 4, 1751, *The Presbyterian Magazine*, IV (1854), 513.

54

striking combination of these qualities, plus his dignity and solemnity, readiness to answer the needs of a frontier people, and exemplary personal life, led increasingly large numbers of Anglicans to turn away from the cold, rationalistic sermons and uninspired lives of their Church of England clergy.

As the champion of moderation and religious toleration in Virginia, Davies did not actively proselyte nor did he enter into a round of name-calling with either his Anglican or his Presbyterian opponents. This is not to say that he did not enjoy entering into a good argument when such was presented. In fact, he occasionally went out of his way to engage in these mental exercises, but he was not impetuous and never abused his opponent with vitriolic language. He attacked arguments rather than individuals, taking great delight in demolishing a chain of reasoning while maintaining a friendly relationship with his adversary, regardless of the difference in their religious beliefs. In the journal of his trip to England, he recorded that he "spent an Evening with Dr. Benson, and had a friendly Dispute with him about subscribing Articles of Faith" [3] and that he "went to Mr. Denham, a Presbyterian minister and had a long and difficult Dispute with him. . . . It was my Happiness to have my Tho'ts ready, and I . . . silenced him." [4] Another time he wrote that he "spent the Evening with Mr. Thomson Junior, an ingenious young Baptist Minister, who tho' educated a strict Calvinist, has embibed the modern Latitudinarian Principles. I had an amicable Dispute with him about the Lawfullness and Expediency of Subscribing Tests of orthodoxy, besides the Scriptures." [5] In none of these instances did he speak disparagingly of his opponents for holding doctrines unlike his own. So evident was this trait of tolerance that his intimate friend John Rodgers noted, "I never saw him angry during several years of unbounded intimacy, though I have repeatedly known him to have been ungenerously treated." [6]

[3] *Diary,* April 14, 1754, p. 86.
[4] *Ibid.,* Feb. 11, 1754, pp. 71–72.
[5] *Ibid.,* Feb. 14, 1754, p. 73.
[6] Rodgers to Samuel Finley (c. 1764), Finley, "The Dis-interested and Devoted Christian," *Sermons* (1766), I, xxxix.

This willingness to exchange views with those of unlike minds was to characterize Davies throughout his brief career. His journal reveals numerous instances of his placing himself in positions that most would have tried to avoid. He "preached for one Mr. Dews . . . in a Baptist Congregation" [7] and "visited Mr. Winter, a Congregational Minister," although he did find the latter disagreeable because of "his dry orthodoxy, and severe Reflections upon those that deviated from rigid Calvinism." [8] Davies was known to speak favorably of Lutherans, as when he described "his Majesty's Chaplain" as "a good old Lutheran Minister." [9] After visiting a group of Pennsylvania Lutheran ministers, he commented, "How pleasing it is to see the Religion of Jesus appear undisguised in Foreigners! I am so charmed with it, that I forget all national and religious Differences; and my very Heart is intimately united to them." [10]

Davies' catholicity made it impossible for him to be a Presbyterian exclusivist and deny the validity of all systems of worship other than his own. His inherent generosity would not even permit him to judge the personal worth of his brother-in-law, John Holt, with whom he had no need to disguise his true feelings. He declared in a letter to Holt, "I care but little whether Men go to Heaven from The Church of England, or Presbyterian; if they do but go there. . . . O! that I could see the established Clergy inflamed with Zeal." [11] Much the same attitude was expressed to a correspondent in England when he observed: "If I am acquainted with the temper of my own mind I do not rejoice in the increase of our members as captures from the Established Church . . . if Men are walking the Heavenly Road, it affords me but little uneasiness that they are not of my mind about every circumstance." [12]

Davies must have been making a true expression of his beliefs when he constantly decried the tendency to lump men together into

[7] *Diary*, Dec. 30, 1753, p. 45.
[8] *Ibid.*, Jan. 7, 1754, p. 51.
[9] *Ibid.*, Jan. 9, 1754, p. 52.
[10] *Ibid.*, Sept. 17, 1753, p. 13.
[11] Davies to Holt, Aug. 13, 1751, Rush MSS.
[12] Davies to Doddridge, Oct. 2, 1750, Perry, *Historical Collections*, I, 369–370.

artificial factions or denominations. In addition to expressing these beliefs to his relatives, he even wrote the Bishop of London that

> I confess, my lord, with pleasure, that there are sundry of the laity in the sphere of my acquaintance in the Church of England, who are persons of good morals and have a veneration for the religion; and some of them, I doubt not, are sincere Christians, whom I cordially love: and . . . with more ardent affection than those of my own denomination, who appear destitute of real religion. . . . The pious conformists can witness, that I have not been officious in endeavouring to proselyte them to my party; and that, when conversant with them, I rather choose to dwell on those infinitely more important and delightful peculiarities in which we differ. I also cheerfully own . . . that sundry of the established clergy [are] gentlemen of learning, parts and morality.[13]

But if Davies was blessed with a strain of generosity, there were those among his adversaries who were not so fortunate. Attacks on the New Lights continued, and Davies sought opportunities to state his position publicly. In an open letter to the Virginia Anglican clergy, he denied that he was preaching "the rigid peculiarities of Presbyterianism" or "the raw innovations of 'New Lights.'" He claimed to be advocating "the generous truths of catholic Christianity . . . the good old doctrines of the Church of England, of the Reformation, and to say all in a word, of the Bible." And if the Anglican clergy wished to know what "strange charme . . . enchanted people . . . to leave the stated communion of the established church, and to profess themselves dissenters," they could ask his "hearers of every denomination" and be told that it was not his condemnation of the Church of England "but the plain, peaceable preaching of such doctrines . . . in weakness, and in fear, and in much trembling. And . . . it was an eager thirst after these doctrines, rather than a dissatisfaction with the peculiar modes of worship in that church, which first induced them to dissent."[14]

The sentiments expressed in this message were reinforced by those in a letter written to the Anglican Commissary of the colony a year earlier in which Davies denied at great length the charges

---

[13] Davies to the Bishop of London, Jan. 10, 1752, Foote, I, 202.

[14] Davies to the Anglican Clergy of Virginia, Jan. 9, 1753, *ibid.*, pp. 216–217.

that he and his associates were trying to fragment the religious organization of Virginia:

> I am not fond, sir, of disseminating sedition and schism; I have no am-
> bition to Presbyterianize the colony. But . . . I have a sincere zeal
> . . . to propagate the catholic religion of Jesus. . . . I pretend to no
> superior sanctity above the established clergy, who are piously aiming at
> the great end of their office. . . . I pretend to no Apostolic powers and
> privileges, immediate revelations and impulses, but renounce the claim
> as presumptuous and enthusiastical. . . . [But] I cannot stand an un-
> concerned inactive spectator of the ruin of my fellow sinners. . . . I
> would exert myself to the utmost, in my little sphere, for their recovery;
> and since I am disabled by some conscientious scruples, to attempt it in
> the communion of the established church, I humbly conceive, I am war-
> ranted to attempt it in a separate communion.[15]

Davies' best statement of principle, however, and his most forceful
denial of the charges of proselyting levied against him was made
in a sermon, "The Sacred Import of the Christian Name," in which
he delivered a long and scathing denunciation of the tendency
evinced by all denominations, including his own, to seek to win
converts from others:

> Let us consider the Christian name as a catholic name intended to bury
> all party-denominations.
>
> . . . .
>
> What party names have been adopted by the Protestant churches,
> whose religion is substantially the same common Christianity, and who
> agree in much more important articles than those in which they differ;
> and who therefore might peaceably unite under the common name of
> Christians? We have Lutherans, Calvinists, Arminians, Zwinglians,
> Churchmen, Presbyterians, Independents, Baptists, and a long list of
> names which I cannot now enumerate. To be a Christian is not enough
> now-a-days, but a man must also be *something* more and better, that is
> he must be a strenuous bigot to this or that particular church. But where
> is the reason or propriety of this?
>
> . . . .
>
> For me to glory in the denomination of any particular church, as my
> highest character; to lay more stress upon the name of a presbyterian or
> a churchman than upon the sacred name of Christian; to make a punc-

---

[15] Davies to William Dawson, 1752, *ibid.*, pp. 217–218.

tilious agreement with my sentiments in the little peculiarities of a party the test of all religion; to make it the object of my zeal to gain proselytes to some other than the Christian name. . . . These are the things which deserve universal condemnation from God and man; these proceed from a spirit of bigotry . . . [which] hinders the progress of serious practical religion, by turning the attention of men from the great concerns of eternity, and the essentials of Christianity, to vain jangling and contests about circumstantials and trifles. Thus the Christian is swallowed up in the partisan, and fundaments lost in extra-essentials.

. . . .

My brethren, I would warn you against this wretched mischievous spirit of party. . . . You may, if you please, call yourselves *presbyterians* and *dissenters*. . . . But . . . I can appeal to yourselves . . . whether it has not been the great object of my zeal to inculcate upon you the grand essentials of our holy Religion, and to make you sincere practical Christians. Alas! . . . unless I succeed in this, I labour to very little purpose, though I should presbyterianize the whole colony.[16]

The extreme emotionalism that accompanied many of the revivals was an even greater source of concern than was the charge of proselyting, for the entire New Light movement was under attack. Although some, like Davies, considered this to be a "trifle," there were others among his friends and opponents who considered this emotionalism an integral part of the Great Awakening. Throughout most of the colonies, bodily responses were an important part of the revival; [17] yet they were never manifested to any great extent in Virginia, where Davies was the leader. Davies himself did not encourage such displays,[18] but he did believe it possible that physical manifestations were valid evidence of salvation.

Even though he was best known for the "solemnity of his manner"—which to one hearer "produced a greater effect on his mind than any sermon he had ever heard"—Davies was criticized for inspiring "a copious flow of tears" as well as "faintings and trem-

---

[16] "The Sacred Import of the Christian Name," *Sermons* (1845), I, 215–218.

[17] The worst instances of the emotionalism that occurred under the preaching of John Davenport are described in Tracy, *Great Awakening*, pp. 252–254.

[18] Gewehr, *Great Awakening*, pp. 87–88. Gewehr states that "whatever may be said of the New Lights as a group, Davies never indulged in any wild reveries of enthusiasm of which so many of them were accused."

bling." [19] Such criticism was rare and often failed to evoke a response; however, Davies was quick to challenge a pseudonymous pamphlet signed "Artemas," which sarcastically referred to Davies as "the Geneva doctor" and described the bodily effects of his preaching in ludicrous language. He reportedly answered the charges in a scathing rebuttal titled "A Pill for Artemas," which denied the necessity of extreme emotionalism but claimed at the same time that it might be desirable. [20]

The charges against Davies in this pamphlet were much the same as those he had found being circulated on his arrival in Hanover. John Caldwell, an Old Light Presbyterian in New Hampshire, had published a pamphlet in 1742 accusing the New Light preachers in New England of trying to bring about "a sudden and terrible fear of divine wrath, or the miseries of hell" and of deliberately causing "in some a Sensation of Cold, in Most a very extraordinary Warmth all over the Body, causing People to cry as if distracted, to shed Tears in great Plenty, throwing many into Convulsions, and a few for some Time into Despair." The Caldwell tract, which had been reprinted by the Virginia public printer, concluded with the statement:

> Alas! why should so great Stress be laid upon shedding Tears, and convulsive Motions? Are these true Evidences of good Dispositions? Do they not spring from mechanical Causes? Are they not the Effect of a sudden Motion of the Blood and Animal Spirits in Persons of Abounding Fluids and weak Nerves? The aptness of Children and Women to weep more easily and in greater Abundance than grown Persons and Men is a plain proof of this; Anatomy convincing us that their Fluids are more numerous in Proportion to their Solids, and their Nerves weak. [21]

[19] "A Recovered Tract of President Davies," p. 363.

[20] *Ibid.*, pp. 363–364. Apparently neither of these two pamphlets is extant. This is the only reference to them.

[21] *An Impartial Trial of the Spirit Operating in this Part of the World; by Comparing the Nature, Effects and Evidences, of the Present Supposed Conversion With the Word of God. A Sermon Preached at New Londonderry, October 14th, 1741* (Boston, 1742), pp. 26–27. When William Parks, the public printer, reprinted this tract on Nov. 11, 1747, he wrote a preface that was openly partisan and hostile to leaders of the Great Awakening. At one point he even referred to the evangelists who were touring Virginia as incendiaries,

Because the Caldwell pamphlet had been circulated in Virginia after his visit in 1747, Davies felt compelled to answer it when he assumed his duties at Hanover in early 1748. Davies titled his answer *The Impartial Trial Impartially Tried and Convicted of Partiality*. He denied the allegations of Caldwell and referred to the emotional outbursts as evidences of "uncommon religious concern," adding:

That it was the substance of a work of this matter, and not the circumstances of it, or the supposed or real disorders that attended it; which we [the New Lights] vindicated and promoted, may be seen from what has been written for its vindication and promotion.

There were some circumstances and appendages attending this work which we conceived were no esstential parts of it. . . . Such were . . . the effects of their inward concern on the animal passions, and thereby on the bodies of some; the suddenness of their first impressions, and comfortable deliverance; the degree of their joys and sorrows. In a word all the things Mr. Thornton [22] relates as the evidences of it (making allowances for his misrepresentations) we accounted either insignificant circumstances, which would neither prove nor disprove it to be divine, or probable indications of intense exercise of mind. And why should we view them in a worse light? Must we conclude a sinner's conviction of his sin and danger irrational because it is so affecting to his soul that it affects his body too? Must we pronounce his sense of condemnation under the penalty of the violated law delusive or diabolical because it is attended with such commotions as would not be thought strange in one that sees himself condemned to death at a human bar, as weeping, crying, swooning?

Finally we readily concede, there were sundry irregularities and instances of misconduct that attended this work; and which some good men were but too zealous in promoting, or too lax in suppressing, before they were thoroughly acquainted with them and their consequences. . . . I would not hereby intimate that the work in general was of this nature, or the subjects and promoters of it generally attended with these frailities. I have the comfort to know it was otherwise.[23]

"Enemies not only to the established Church, but also common Disturbers of the Peace and Order of religious Societies where ever they came" (Preface, p. xiii).

[22] See *The Impartial Trial, Impartially Tried and Convicted of Partiality* (Williamsburg, 1748), p. 34, where he exposes Caldwell as an Irish thief named Thornton, who had fled to America and changed his name.

[23] *Ibid.*, pp. 40–41. In a sermon entitled *The Nature and Extent of Christ's Redemption*, delivered and published in 1753, the Reverend William Stith refuted parts of

Davies apparently had considered the relationship of a mental state to a physical state. He was aware of the extent to which religious revivals had been accompanied by bodily disturbances and observed that in America such outbreaks had generally been confined to New England. Indeed this had been the occasion for the original publication of Caldwell's pamphlet. Davies indicated, however, that such manifestations were almost universally deplored, and he noted that although there were in New England "many great and good men, perhaps superior to any in America, yet it is certain, and they themselves have bewailed it, that sundry irregularities have attended the Word of God there." [24]

In a sermon Davies gave before his Presbytery in 1752, he urged his fellow preachers to strike a balance between "the wild reveries of *enthusiasm*," which characterized the more impetuous New Lights, and "the droaning Heaviness and serene Stupidity" of the Old Light Presbyterians and Anglicans. According to Davies, a sermon should be delivered "with a *grave* and *affectionate Solemnity*." Preachers indeed should be passionate and warm, he said, but should beware of appearing too emotional and fanatical, for such behavior exposed their beliefs to public contempt and could encourage irrational behavior by their listeners. Such a state, he suggested, was usually only transitory and would "soon stagnate into *Stupidity*, or hurry them into enthusiastical Extravagancies." On the other hand, Davies advised against appearing unconcerned in the pulpit, declaring that the delivery instead should be "*vigorous and affectionate* and expressive of the deep Impressions the tremendous Things we speak make upon our own Hearts." [25]

Davies' pamphlet. Stith, the third president of the College of William and Mary, reflected the Virginia aristocracy in stoutly defending the rights of colonial Englishmen against absentee government while radically opposing religious dissenters. After his return from England in 1755, Davies wrote a reply to Stith's sermon entitled *Charity and Truth, Or . . . the Way of the Multitude Exposed, In Six Letters, To the Rev. William Stith, A.M., President of William & Mary College.* Inasmuch as Stith died while the reply was being written, Davies never published it. The work was published in 1941, by the Department of History of the Presbyterian Church in the U. S. A., edited by Thomas Clinton Pears, Jr.

[24] *Ibid.*, p. 41.

[25] *A Sermon Preached Before the Reverend Presbytery of New-Castle, October 11, 1752* (Philadelphia, 1753), pp. 17–18.

If Davies did not condemn the Church of England and its priests as instruments of salvation, and if he did not encourage the emotional excesses that put the movement in a bad light, how then was he able to bring about a mass defection from the established church? The lamentations of both the ecclesiastical and governmental authorities in the colony [26]—and ample evidence bears out such complaints [27]—indicate that he must have done something to encourage the rise of dissent in the colony. This he did: he preached and lived a theology that was palpably relevant to the needs of his time and place.

Throughout the eighteenth century, the clergy of the Church of England came more and more to preach rationalistic discourses on matters of abstract morality.[28] Although most prevalent in England where it did much to provoke the Methodist phase of the Great Awakening, this tendency gradually infected the American clergy as well. If this style of preaching brought about protest in Britain, it was bound to arouse even more dissatisfaction in the colonies where it lacked the vitality demanded by the necessities of precarious semi-frontier conditions. Even in the more settled areas of the New World, life seemed to be spent in a continual struggle for survival, a struggle that could be made more violent at any moment by disease, crop failure, Indian attack, or the actions of England's covetous enemies. Thus, the uncertainties of life in America constantly kept the prospect of Heaven and Hell before the people.[29]

Religious appeals, in order to be effective, had to bear some relation to everyday American life. Religion had to help the people in the things that most affected them; it had to help them solve the problems of life on a frontier and prepare them to face death.

---

[26] See, for example, Robert Dinwiddie to the Bishop of London, June 5, 1752, Perry, *Historical Collections*, I, 396, and William Dawson to the Bishop of London, March 11, 1754, *ibid.*, p. 409.

[27] Thomas Dawson to the Bishop of London, Aug. 13, 1755, Dawson MSS.

[28] Charles Smyth, *The Art of Preaching. A Practical Survey of Preaching in the Church of England; 747–1939* (London, 1940), p. 162.

[29] An interesting comment on this aspect of American religious life is Cyclone Covey, *The American Pilgrimage; the Roots of American History, Religion and Culture* (New York, 1961).

The message preached by the New Lights satisfied these requirements more than that of any other group, especially the Anglicans.
By the test of the age, the Church of England was doomed to ultimate failure, for the strength of any colonial religious body was
eventually determined by the degree of its acceptance of the Great
Awakening. The Presbyterians, who accepted the Great Awakening
almost completely, became numerically strong and immensely popular. Those who opposed it, led by the established church in Virginia, entered into a period of decline.[30]

During this time, England supplied the Anglican church in the
colonies with priests as well as Episcopal control. The preachers
were most concerned that their sermons should meet the test of
reason, and their efforts in this direction produced plain edifying
discourses that often degenerated into moral platitudes or abstruse
doctrinal debates devoid of purpose or meaning for the listeners.
In criticizing this tendency, one Episcopal scholar observed that
sermons "of all compositions can never be immortal when the
preacher seems to have no particular message to deliver . . . beyond a general impression that it is more prudent on the whole to
believe the Gospel, in a modified sort of way, than not." This was
the case in the Church of England at midcentury, and the same situation had come to prevail throughout the colonies,[31] especially in
the church in Virginia.[32]

The established clergy in Virginia were no better than average,
"about on a par with their brethren at home before the beginning
of the Wesleyan movement." [33] The lower classes derived little or
no benefit from their ministrations and exercised little or no control
over church affairs. Plagued by extremely large parishes and a
shortage of clergymen, the typical Anglican clergyman in Vir-

[30] Gewehr, *Great Awakening*, p. 86.

[31] Smyth, *Art of Preaching*, p. 162.

[32] For the best discussion of the problems faced by the Church of England in Virginia,
see George MacLaren Brydon, *Virginia's Mother Church and the Political Conditions
Under Which it Grew* (2 vols., Richmond and Philadelphia, 1947 and 1952), I.

[33] H. J. Eckenrode, *Separation of Church and State in Virginia: A Study in the Development of the Revolution*, special report of the Department of Archives and History,
Virginia State Library (Richmond, 1910), p. 33.

ginia delivered a Sunday sermon and lived a properly ordered life devoid of religious enthusiasm. In opposition to this formalistic routine, the evangelical missionaries arrived, preaching a new religion. "Their sermons were not the rationalistic homilies of Anglican divines but the burning, moving appeals of enthusiasts. The people, with all the Englishman's susceptibility to religious feeling, responded powerfully. The awakening of popular emotions in the ordered life of old Virginia was startling in its manifestations because this was the first occasion. The poorer people, hitherto unreached by the establishment, were stirred to the core." [34] Samuel Davies was one of these evangelical missionaries, and he answered well the demands of his listeners, causing one of his acquaintances to observe that:

> Sublimity and energy of thought
> Enliven'd with devotion's fervid vein,
> And inextinguishable zeal to save
> Immortals from immortal misery,
> Characteriz'd, ennobled, and refin'd
> Thine every sermon.[35]

Davies made the uncertainty of life on the frontier one of the chief emphases in his preaching. His message was one of preparation, so that his listeners would be better able to face death, should it suddenly confront them. In both his sermons and his letters, death was one of the most frequently recurring topics. Davies felt that he was preaching to those whose deaths were imminent, and he was constantly urging them to prepare for the event. "I preach as if I ne'er should preach again; And as a dying man to dying men," [36] he once told Gibbons. Another time he noted that his real mission was "to save my country, and, which is of much more consequence, to save souls—from death—from that tremendous kind of death a soul can die." [37]

[34] *Ibid.*

[35] Thomas Gibbons, "An Elegiac Poem to the Memory of the Rev. Samuel Davies, A.M.," *Sermons* (1766), I, cvii.

[36] Davies to Gibbons, n.d., *ibid.* p. lxviii.

[37] Davies to Gibbons, n.d., *ibid.*, p. lxvi. This is apparently a different letter than the one cited in note 36.

The preparation of souls for imminent death was in fact the core of Davies' theology. To better prepare his listeners for the ultimate event, Davies demanded a unity of Christian life—a unity of inward belief and outward action. He concentrated on behavior here on earth and called for Christians to emulate Christ by living a life of virtue and holiness, a life of positive righteousness rather than negative goodness. Such a theology had a certain positiveness that fitted the time and place. Favorite targets of Davies were those whom he considered lacking in religious zeal; consequently, he preached not only to sinners, as most New Lights did, but also to lukewarm church members.

Because Davies insisted that his hearers emulate Christ and strive for a better life in this world, it might be charged that he abandoned certain elemental principles of the Presbyterian church and advocated "good works" as a means of salvation. Nowhere in his extant sermons or letters, however, did he expect anyone to depend upon good works for deliverance. Always, like the moderate Calvinist he was, he saw works as but external evidences of the grace by which one was saved. In an unequivocal reply to a commentary by Thomas Sherlock, the Bishop of London, on the problem of judgment, he noted "that according to the Law, good Works or Holiness, were not only the distinguishing Characteristics of those that Should be acquitted, or the Rule *According* to which they should be judged; but also the meritorious Cause and sole Ground of their Acquittance, or that for which they should be judged righteous: But according to the Gospel, good works have the former Place only, and Christ's Righteousness alone occupies the Place of the latter." [38]

Seldom did Davies state so clearly his position on doctrine, and never did he state it so forcefully to his congregations. He cannot be accused, therefore, of disparaging doctrine, even though his Calvinism fails to emerge from his sermons with anything like the above strength. Usually he believed that matters of doctrine consisted only of irritating trifles that served to divide men into com-

---

[38] "Remarks on the VII ch of Dr. Sherlock's Discourse on Judgements," Rush MSS.

peting religious groups. Righteousness, or holiness, usually was placed above such things. In writing to his Anglican brother-in-law of his respect for good men of all churches, Davies stated, "An Episcopal Christian shall always attract more of my Esteem; than a Pharisee or a Profligate of my own Denomination—If I am conscious of my own Temper, my greatest Concern for myself . . . and for Mankind, is, That our Hearts may be right with God; That we may be quicken'd by Grace, who were dead in Trespasses and Sins; and that Holiness may be implanted in our spirits by Divine Agency." [39]

In light of his seeming emphasis on good works, he left himself open to charges of neglecting doctrine and had to defend himself against such accusations at least once in his career. In an undated letter to an unnamed correspondent, Davies set forth those doctrines whose omission he felt was deplorable, as well as the relationship he perceived between doctrine and works. He denied that salvation could be the result of good works, just as he denied that holiness could be present without grace. He conceived holiness to be a unity of inner attitude and outward action; to deny this was equivalent to making the flagrant assertion that "God can take Pleasure in the Wicked as such, while they are here upon Earth." If God approves the wicked on earth, then "why may he not delight in them in Heaven?" If this were even remotely possible, Davies saw "no Necessity of Regeneration and Holiness as a Prerequisite to future Happiness." The entire concept impressed him as an absurdity that could not be embraced without rejecting Christianity. [40]

Although he expressed his theology and exerted a strong personal influence through poetry, letters, and essays, the greater impact made by his sermons is undeniable. They were obviously effective, in both content and manner of delivery, for they gained wide acceptance among a broad spectrum of the population in Great Britain as well as in the American colonies. The sermons were not only delivered orally, but many were also published, re-

[39] Davies to Holt, July 4, 1749, Rush MSS.
[40] Davies to ———, n.d., MS letter fragment in Princeton University Library. Apparently written from Philadelphia prior to his trip to England in 1753.

published, and kept in print for more than a century after his death. His audiences, moreover, represented many levels of society and a variety of religious beliefs.

It is probable, in fact, that Samuel Davies had no peer among his fellow preachers; at least, there is ample evidence that he stood with such giants of his calling as Jonathan Edwards, George White-field, and John Wesley. Certainly, he aroused universal admiration wherever he preached and won the esteem of his prominent fellow preachers. His reputation, unlike that of some of his contemporaries, did not diminish upon his death but continued to grow.

William Buell Sprague, who studied the efforts of hundreds of American preachers, claimed that Davies spoke with a "glowing zeal, combined with exemplary prudence, and an eloquence more impressive and effective than had then ever graced the American pulpit." [41] Another commentator, an early historian of the log college movement, spoke of Davies as the "first of American preachers." [42] Robert Reid Howison, a Virginia historian, observed that it was "not extravagant to say that Samuel Davies was in many respects the greatest preacher that America has ever known." [43] Anonymous reviewers of one edition of his works asserted that Davies, among all "American preachers of pure doctrine in powerful and persuasive diction must . . . ever hold the first place," [44] that during his life he was probably the most admired preacher in the Presbyterian church, and that his sermons were "the most generally acceptable ever published in this country." [45]

Perhaps these assessments overstate the case for the significance of his sermons because such men had reason to be biased in his favor, but even the prominent modern historian of religion in America, William Warren Sweet, has placed Davies' works among the

[41] William Buell Sprague, *Annals of the American Pulpit or Commemorative Notices of Distinguished American Clergymen of Various Denominations, From the Early Settlement of the Country to the Close of the Year Eighteen Hundred and Fifty-Five. With Historical Introductions* (9 vols., New York, 1859–1869), III, 141.

[42] Alexander, *Biographical Sketches*, p. 169.

[43] Howison, *Virginia*, II, 178.

[44] "Review of Samuel Davies, *Sermons on Important Subjects*. . . , ed. Albert Barnes (New York, 1841)," *The Biblical Repertory and Princeton Review*, IV (1842), 144.

[45] "A Recovered Tract of President Davies," p. 350.

greatest of the eighteenth century.[46] According to Sprague, "he made his way among all classes of people, and was alike acceptable to all, from the most polished gentlemen to the most ignorant African slave." [47] It was this universal acceptability that continued long after his death and made the numerous editions of his sermons so immensely popular among readers of every station in life. His popularity was singularly manifested during the course of his visit to England and Scotland. There he preached more than sixty sermons,[48] many of which were printed and received a wide distribution. At least one of the published sermons was in Welsh.[49] Publication was a concern of Davies, for he wrote to his English friend the Reverend Thomas Gibbons, "I want to live after I am dead, not in name, but in public usefulness: I was therefore about to order in my will that all my notes . . . might be sent to you correct and publish such of them as you might judge conducive to the public good." [50] Whether such a bequest appeared in his will is uncertain; nevertheless, Gibbons brought out a three-volume collection of Davies' sermons in 1766, supplemented in 1771 by an additional two volumes. These were "Printed for the Benefit of the *Author's* Widow." Among the list of 661 subscribers to 847 sets of the first edition are found the names of many of Davies' friends and associates.[51] In all, there were more than twenty different printings of the collected sermons between the time of Davies' death and the last edition in 1867. Countless imprints of individual sermons also appeared. As late as 1846, a Methodist reviewer, referring to Da-

[46] "Among the many prolific eighteenth-century preachers, few if any can be read more profitably today than Samuel Davies" (William Warren Sweet, *Revivalism in America, its Origin, Growth, and Decline* [New York, 1944], p. 70).

[47] Sprague, *Annals*, III, 141.

[48] *Diary, passim.* No doubt he preached the same sermon several times, but how often cannot be determined.

[49] *Pregeth ar yr Adgyfodiad Cyffredinol, yn Saesonaeg, gan y Parch. Samuel Davies, Diweddar Olygwr ar y Colledge Princeton, yn Jersey Newydd, yn America. Wedi ei Chyfieithu i'r Gymraeg gan y Parch. M. Jones* (Nghaerfryddin, 1789). It was reprinted under a slightly different title in 1798.

[50] Davies to Gibbons, Sept. 12, 1757, *Sermons* (1766), I, iv.

[51] *Ibid.*, p. i. Included among the subscribers to one or more sets were John Gillies, Colonel James Gordon, the Reverend Patrick Henry, Devereaux Jarrat, the Marquis of Lothian, the Earl of Lauderdale, the Earl of Leven, Benjamin Rush, and the Lord Provost of Edinburgh University, *ibid.*, pp. cxxvii–cliv.

vies as "a Congregational minister," claimed that he was second only to John Wesley in the circulation of his printed works.[52] Thus Davies continued in "public usefulness," as he had wished, and exerted a lasting effect upon several generations of preachers and orators.

It was primarily the content of these sermons that laid claims to future significance, for it was here that Davies' theology expressed itself. The theology was from first to last orthodox Calvinistic, dealing primarily with eschatology, with Divine Grace and Man's Salvation. As Richard Beale Davis phrases it: "Sinful man and God's Grace, these were the all-absorbing themes. . . ."[53] Davies preached this message many times and at great length, promising his listeners a ready welcome in Heaven if they would but repent. The sinner was made conscious of his own inability to save himself and was encouraged to place himself in the hands of a merciful God. "However vile and abandoned a sinner has been," he said at one point, "yet upon his repentence he becomes GOD's dear son, his favourite child. He will from that moment regard him, provide for him, protect him, and bring him to his heavenly inheritance, as his son and heir."[54]

The grim possibility of death was, of course, a frequent reference, emphasizing the immediate need for repentance and salvation. Many sermons bore such titles as "The Nature and Universality of Spiritual Death," "The Doom of the Incorrigible Sinner," "The Certainty of Death," and "The Guilt and Doom of Impenitent Hearers." Even the precarious state of his own health was utilized by Davies in making his point. Referring to a recent illness in one of his sermons, he told his listeners, "I have this day been solicitously thinking in what way my life, redeemed from the grave, may be of

[52] R. W. A., "Review of Samuel Davies, *Sermons on Important Subjects* . . . , ed. Albert Barnes (New York, 1842)," *The Methodist Quarterly Review*, XXVIII (1846), 138, 144. The reviewer also admonished his readers: "it should be remembered that the author of these sermons was a Calvinist, and that some of the peculiarities of his creed would naturally find a place in them; but notwithstanding all their objectionable features, we must be permitted to pronounce them as among the most eloquent and useful sermons ever issued by the American or English press," *ibid.*, p. 145.

[53] "Introduction" to *Collected Poems*, p. xvii.

[54] "The Divine Mercy to Mourning Penitents," *Sermons* (1766), II, 119.

most service to my dear people." He concluded by observing: "I have this day set life and death before you: I have opened to you the method of salvation through Jesus Christ; the only method in which you can be saved; the only method that could afford a gleam of hope to such a sinner as I in my late approach to the eternal world." [55] His health was a matter of serious concern to the earnest young preacher. Once, after recovering from a severe bout with fever, he said, "I am just beginning to creep back from the valley of the shadow of death, to which I made a very near approach a few days ago." [56] And more often than not, he found a God-given plan in his recovery, as when he expressed the belief that he had been spared during his early sicknesses so that he could serve the Virginia dissenters. [57]

The sermons' constant call to prepare for unexpected physical death was accompanied by a warning to avoid what was worse, the death of the soul. Thus Davies observed: "A creature treading every moment on the slippery brink of the grave, and ready every moment to shoot the gulph of eternity, and launch away to some unknown coast, ought to stand always in the posture of serious expectation." [58] For death could not be avoided. "So extensive have been the havoc and devastation which death has made in the world for near six thousand years," he said, "that this earth is now become one vast graveyard, or burying-place for her sons. . . . The many generations . . . are now in the mansions under ground." [59]

Death, according to Davies, "lurks in ambush for you, ready every moment to spring upon his prey. . . . Methinks it becomes you to prepare for what you cannot avoid." [60] And lurking behind physical death was the even greater danger of eternal damnation. If Davies and the other New Lights could make sinners aware of this universal threat, then the sinners' alarms would lead to a sin-

---

[55] "The Method of Salvation Through Jesus Christ," *ibid.*, I, 31, 50.
[56] Davies to Gibbons, Sept. 12, 1750, *ibid.*, I, lxxi. He concluded, "it seized me in the pulpit, like a soldier wounded in the field."
[57] "Apostolic Valediction," *Sermons* (1845), III, 479.
[58] "Indifference to Life Urged From its Shortness and Vanity," *ibid.*, I, 421.
[59] "Life and Immortality Revealed in the Gospel," *ibid.*, II, 9.
[60] *Ibid.*, p. 21.

cere desire to change their sinful natures. Thus, sinners would be led to realize that their guilt could be erased only through following Christ, as set forth by God.

Davies expressed his own hopes of following this path to salvation when he observed that "as for myself, I am just striving not to live in vain. . . . I have but little, very little, true religion. My advancements in holiness are extremely small . . . [and] to maintain a secret walk with God, to be holy as he is holy, this is the labour, this the work." [61] Although continually lamenting his own shortcomings, he seldom spoke publicly on the components of conversion and the process of conviction. Rather, he talked of specific manifestations of these states, usually under the heading of "experimental religion." By this he meant an inner change so profound as to cause an alteration in the course of one's life. This is what Davies called for when he told his associates of the New Castle Presbytery to stress "the Nature and Necessity of Regeneration, of Faith, Repentence, and other Christian Graces" in their sermons and to adapt them "to the various cases of Saints and Sinners, to instruct, to wound, to comfort and support, according to their respective Exigencies." [62]

In sum, Davies hoped to effect a unity of religious life, beginning with conviction and followed by a sincere change of heart and a complete spiritual cleansing. The change would ultimately be evidenced in right living. His one demand was that religion be shown in everyday life, and he frequently warned his congregations that "a divine revelation must not be calculated merely to amuse us, and gratify our curiosity with sublime and refined notions and speculations" but must be adapted "to direct and regulate our practice, and render us better as well as wiser." [63]

He consequently urged those who desired to demonstrate Christianity in their everyday lives to strive constantly for virtue and holiness. Without such striving one could be a Christian in name

---

[61] Davies to Gibbons, n.d., *Sermons* (1766), I, lxvii.

[62] *A Sermon . . .* , *October 11, 1752*, p. 13.

[63] "The Divine Authority and Sufficiency of the Christian Religion," *Sermons* (1845), I, 7–8.

alone. Christ was the model for the virtue and holiness urged by Davies, and his reference for the desired relationship between inner attitude and outward act. In one of his sermons, "The Sacred Import of the Christian Name," he was especially specific about virtue and vice. Sounding like a nineteenth-century preacher of the Social Gospel, Davies claimed that the "resemblance and imitation of Christ is essential to the very being of a Christian," for this was "the most perfect pattern of living holiness and virtue that ever was exhibited in the world." He challenged his hearers with the question: "If you claim the name of Christians, where is that ardent devotion, that affectionate love to God, that zeal for his glory, that alacrity in his service, that resignation to his will, that generous benevolence to mankind, that zeal to promote their best interests, that meekness and forbearance under ill usage, that unwearied activity in doing good to all, that self-denial and heavenly-mindedness which shone so conspicious in Christ, whose holy name you bear?" Then Davies defined the characteristics of a Christian:

> A Christian is a complication of all the amiable and useful graces and virtues: temperate and sober, just, liberal, compassionate and benevolent, humble, meek, gentle, peaceable, and in all things conscientious. A Christian is a good parent, a good child, a good master, a good servant, a good husband, a good wife, a faithful friend, an obliging neighbour, a dutiful subject, a good ruler, a zealous patriot, and an honest statesman; and as far as he is such, so far, and no farther, he is a Christian. And can there be a more amiable and excellent character exhibited to your view? It is an angelic, a divine character.[64]

In a sermon titled "The Connection Between Present Holiness and Future Felicity," Davies asserted that virtuous living was the ultimate expression of religious belief. He had not come to place an emphasis on works, however, but merely was applying a pragmatic test in judging the sincerity of religion. He held that a true divine revelation could change a person's life and that "the sacred writings give us a complete system of practical religion and morality." [65]

In stressing the unity of inward belief and outward action, Davies

---

[64] "The Sacred Import of the Christian Name," *ibid.*, pp. 223–224.
[65] "Divine Authority," *ibid.*, p. 8.

failed to be specific in defining a good Christian action. Although he constantly spoke of right living, he seldom gave such specific examples as those in "The Sacred Import of the Christian Name." He seems to have expected his hearers to supply such examples themselves. However, he did describe graphically the Christian inner attitude, which, if properly cultivated, would grant its possessor a sense of devotion and joy. Joy, not only in his future but also in his present life, would be the greatest reward for the true Christian. To Davies this was reason enough for one to strive after holiness. "Eternal felicity," of course, was the ultimate attainment of the religious person, but Davies also proclaimed that "without holiness here it is impossible for us to enjoy heavenly happiness in the future world." [66] He further defined holiness as that which consists "in an habitual delight in all the duties of holiness . . . and an earnest desire for communion with God. . . . If we love God for his holiness, we shall delight in that service in which our conformity to him consists; if we love his law we shall delight in that obedience which it enjoins." [67]

If Davies' listeners were aware of the message he was attempting to convey, they must have been shocked out of any self-satisfaction derived merely from not being sinful. This he attacked as "*negative* goodness," which was insufficient either to prepare one for death or to make one a true Christian. What was demanded, he asserted, was that "the temper of . . . minds must be changed by the power of divine grace: and . . . must be turned from the love and practice of all sin, to the love and practice of universal holiness." The Christian "must be enabled to live righteously, soberly, and godly" in a sinful world without falling prey to it.[68]

Basically, Davies was attacking what he considered to be the hypocrisy of those who tried to show in practice that they were Christians but who lacked the proper inner attitudes—those, in other words, who found religious duty bothersome but who, for various reasons, sought to act like Christians. In Davies' mind religious ac-

[66] "The Connection Between Present Holiness and Future Felicity," *ibid.*, pp. 160–161.
[67] *Ibid.*, p. 267.
[68] "The Curse of Cowardice," *ibid.*, III, 97.

tions unaccompanied by a sense of inner piety were a "deadly poison . . . abominable to God" and more harmful than no action at all.[69] He insisted that the true Christian did not practice holiness merely from fear of punishment, nor did the Christian harbor a hidden wish to retain some favorite sins and avoid some unpleasant duties. On the contrary, the Christian found his greatest delight in "universal holiness," for the joys of heaven would be much diminished were he to carry the smallest sin there. He avoided "sinful pleasures" while habituating himself "to so much strictness in religion." [70]

As a result, many of Davies' sermons, such as "The Danger of Lukewarmness in Religion," were directed toward those lacking religious zeal—halfhearted, insincere persons who lived righteously while deeply resenting it. Such persons, in Davies' opinion, were hypocrites who lacked the inner attitude proper to Christians and needed regeneration as much as did the worst of unsaved sinners. In his evangelical messages, Davies often emphasized the rigors of hell in order to "alarm the secure Conscience with the Glare of Conviction" and "awaken hardy Impenitents by the Terrors of the Lord," but he also spoke to those who were already saved and admonished them to enjoy "the pleasure of a justified state" while pursuing "the increase of holiness," humbly relying on God and embracing the promise of joy in heaven as their due.[71]

Like most revivalists of any age, Davies seemed to place too much emphasis on his demands for what he termed "universal holiness." Yet the demands are understandable in view of his fear for the spiritual state of those around him who overemphasized temporal things. It was a fear that no doubt increased when he occasionally noted the same tendency in himself. Above all else, therefore, one had to enjoy being a Christian, for the main difference between true Christians and the various classes of sinners was this: "God, Christ, holiness, and the concerns of eternity are habitually uppermost in the hearts of the former; but to the latter they are

[69] "The Danger of Lukewarmness in Religion," *ibid.*, I, 280–281.
[70] "The Connection," *ibid.*, p. 166.
[71] *Ibid.*, p. 169.

generally but things by the by, and the world engrosses the vigour of their lives." [72] The strongest bent of a Christian was "God-ward," and religion was not forced and unnatural in such a person. If a Christian occasionally felt reluctant to pursue the right course, he was merely reflecting human nature, a natural opposition of the flesh to the spirit.[73]

It was possible for Davies to become entrapped in his other-worldliness when he was not cautious. But he was too practical a person to exclude from his attention all material considerations. For him God was present in everyday affairs, and, as in his statements on the presence of joy,[74] he often failed to differentiate between heaven and earth for the Christian.[75]

If Davies' preaching on death and zealous Christian living was relevant to his frontier congregations, then certainly his fiery sermons on the theme of defense during the French and Indian War were pertinent and probably accounted for much of his ultimate success in Virginia. Like such prominent contemporary Calvinists as Jonathan Edwards, Davies saw God's hand in all natural occurrences, whether they be the Lisbon earthquake, the death of General Braddock, or the barbarities of the French and Indians. He believed that the war was divine punishment for sins; however, in true Calvinist tradition, he saw such punishment primarily as a challenge to God's people to repent of their sins and increase their endeavors on behalf of God's earthly Kingdom. With such sermons as *Religion and Patriotism: The Constituents of a Good Soldier* (1755), *Virginia's Danger and Remedy* (1756), and *The Curse of Cowardice* (1758), Davies equated patriotism with Christianity and became, through his pulpit, the colony's best recruiting officer.

In Davies' opinion, the causes of the sufferings were both personal and collective. Wars, to Davies, were brought about by an unChristian lust for power—a desire to dominate others. "What in-

[72] "The One Thing Needful," *ibid.*, p. 391.
[73] "The Devine Life in the Souls of Men Considered," *ibid.*, II, 392–393.
[74] "The Connection," *ibid.*, I, 160–161.
[75] For an example, see "Saints Saved With Difficulty, and the Certain Perdition of Sinners," *ibid.*, p. 408.

76

fernal cause is it," he once asked his hearers, "that sets the world in arms? . . . Whence is it that swords and guns, and other instruments of death, are become necessary utensils in life, and a piece of furniture for kingdoms?" They came, he answered, like all conflicts of whatever nature, from the ungovernable lusts warring within the human soul, for "the lust of dominion, the lust of riches, the lust of vain glory and applause, have set the world in arms from age to age." [76] As if to presage coming events, he noted that "one man has no right to superiority over others, except it was originally derived from their consent." "What," he then asked, "could prompt a man to risk his own life, to embroil nations, to lay countries waste, and to destroy the lives of thousands of his fellowmen?" Only "the lawless lust of power." [77]

In addition to these terrible sins of commission by individuals, the colony as a whole was accused of a grave sin of omission: Virginia had made no serious efforts to prevent the war. "These calamities," he charged his hearers, "have not come upon us without warning. We were long ago apprised of the ambitious schemes of our enemies, and their motions to carry them into execution: and had we taken timely measures, they might have been crushed before they could have arrived at such a formidable height. But . . . our country has been sunk in a deep sleep: a stupid security has unmanned the inhabitants . . . and hence little or nothing has been done for the defense of our country." [78] The only way to prevent such wars and to end the one at hand was to take strong action and carry the horrors of battle to the enemy:

And will these violences cease without a vigorous and timely resistance from us? Can Indian revenge and thirst for blood be glutted? or can French ambition and avarice be satisfied? No, we have no method left but to repel force with force, and to give them blood to drink in their turn, who have drank ours. If we sit still and do nothing or content ourselves, as, alas! we have hitherto, with feeble, dilatory efforts, we may expect these barbarities will not only continue, but that the Indians, headed by the French, will carry their inroads still farther into the

[76] "Serious Reflections on War," *ibid.*, III, 199–200.
[77] *Ibid.*, p. 200.
[78] "Religion and Patriotism," *ibid.*, p. 421.

country, and reach even unto us. By the desertion of our remote settlements, the frontiers are approaching every day nearer and nearer to us: and if we cannot stand our ground now, when we have above a hundred miles of a thick-settled country between us and the enemy, much less shall we be able, when our strength is weakened by so vast a loss of men, arms, and riches, and we lie exposed to their immediate incursions. Some cry, "Let the enemy come down to us, and then we will fight them." But this is the trifling excuse of cowardice or security, and not the language of prudence and fortitude. Those who make this plea, if the enemy should take them at their word, and make them so near a visit, would be as forward in flight as they are now backward to take up arms.[79]

Despite such militant words and his many other calls to arms, Davies was essentially a man of peace, preaching the words of a Prince of Peace. As such, he was faced with the universal dilemma of the good man in a sinful and violent world. He did not choose withdrawal, but instead sought to change the world according to his own concepts of right action. No doubt he expressed his personal desires when he said that "nothing can be more agreeable to the God of Peace, than to see universal harmony and benevolence prevail among his creatures, and he has laid them under the strongest obligations to cultivate a pacific temper towards one another, both as individuals and nations. *Follow peace with all men,* is one of the principal precepts of our holy religion. And the great Prince of Peace has solemnly pronounced, *Blessed are the peacemakers.*" [80]

In general, Davies' sermons were artful combinations of hortatory messages calling for religious or secular action and discussions of theological or philosophical abstractions. The abstractions, however, were never allowed to intrude upon the central theme of repentance and salvation. If anything did obscure the import of his sermons, it was his reluctance to come to the point. Davies' practice of using overly long introductions must have dulled his listeners. The purpose of the introductory discourse was to put his hearers in a receptive frame of mind for the call to action, which occurred near the middle of the sermon. "There is not one of us in this assembly," he might begin, "but what has heard of Christ and salva-

[79] "Curse of Cowardice," *ibid.,* p. 88.
[80] *Ibid.,* p. 84.

tion: there is not one of us but has had the rich blessings of the gospel freely and repeatedly offered to us." [81] Perhaps more characteristic of what he was attempting was his request: "O sirs, let us all keep our souls in a praying posture, throughout this discourse." [82]

After the introduction the sermon moved fairly rapidly through the call to action into a brief and pointed conclusion. The closing portion of the sermon was usually devoted to those who had remained unaffected by the other parts and was apparently intended to remind them of the consequences awaiting them on the day of judgment:

> I cannot but fear, after all, that some of you, as usual, will continue careless and impenitent. Well, when you are suffering the punishment of this sin in hell, remember that you were warned, and acquit me from being accessory to your ruin. And when we all appear before the supreme Judge, and I am called to give an account of my ministry: when I am asked, "Did you warn these creatures of their danger? Did you lay before them their guilt in making light of these things," you will allow me to answer, "Yes, Lord, I warned them in the best manner I could, but they would not believe me; they would not regard what I said, though enforced by the authority of thy awful name, and confirmed by thine own word." O Sirs, must I give in this accusation against any of you? No, rather have mercy upon yourselves, and have mercy upon me, that I may give an account of you with joy and not with grief! [83]

Davies projected his messages—whether he was preaching on death or virtuous living—in a manner equaled by few pulpit orators of his time. Physically, he presented an impressive figure in the pulpit, appearing to one observer "like the embassador of some great king." [84]

A later writer described him as:

> tall, well proportioned, erect, and comely; his carriage easy, graceful, and dignified; his dress neat and tasteful, and his manners polished. . . . He was endowed with a voice strong, clear, and musical, . . . a

---

[81] "The Nature and Danger of Making Light of Christ and Salvation," *ibid.*, I, 129.
[82] "The Nature and Process of Spiritual Life," *ibid.*, p. 96.
[83] "Nature and Danger," *ibid.*, p. 142.
[84] Quoted by William Wirt Henry, *Patrick Henry, Life, Correspondence and Speeches* (3 vols., New York, 1891), I, 13.

perfect command of strong, ornate, and perspicuous diction, and an animation in delivery which lighted up his features, pervaded every look, gesture, and movement, and seemed to blend the simplicity of nature with the highest culture of art.[85]

One of those who went to hear him preach is reputed to have said that the "sight of the man . . . made a deeper impression on him than all the sermons he had ever heard before." [86] Davies apparently never lost his dignity in the heat of delivery, as did some of his contemporaries. "He never seemed to make a gesture; he only uttered his sentiments with becoming motions of his body, and tones and modulations of his voice." [87] One of the few physical descriptions left by one who knew Davies personally comes from his associate in the Synod of Philadelphia and New York, the Reverend David Bostwick of Jamaica, Long Island, who spoke of him in these terms:

> His talent at composition, especially for the pulpit, was equalled by few, and perhaps exceeded by none. His taste was judicious, elegant, and polite, and yet his discourses were plain and pungent, peculiarly adapted to pierce the conscience and affect the heart. His diction was surprisingly beautiful and comprehensive, tending to make the most stupid hearer, sensibly feel, as well as clearly understand. Sublimity and elegance, plainness and perspicuity, and all the force and energy that the language of mortals could convey, were the ingredients of almost every composition. His manner of delivery, as to pronunciation, gesture, and modulation of voice, seemed to be a perfect model of the most moving and striking oratory.[88]

When Davies entered the pulpit, he carried with him small booklets in which he had stitched carefully transcribed copies of his sermons. Once in the pulpit, however, he read the sermons only when his duties had been too time-consuming to allow his usual practice of memorization. A nineteenth-century writer claimed that he "often read them, and often preached without reading, or omitted some of his preparations, or added to them, as circumstances and his

---

[85] *Ibid.*
[86] Alexander, *Biographical Sketches*, p. 170.
[87] Foote, I, 303.
[88] [Bostwick], "Appendix," *Sermons* (1766), I, li.

own feelings prompted." [89] Although Davies was not bound by any rigid text or habit of delivery, the sermons were available for ready reference, for repeated delivery on various preaching tours, or for publication.

Even as he adapted the content of his sermons to the needs of his congregations, Davies suited his style of delivery to the nature of his audience. He could include himself among his hearers and share their problems or he could assume the posture of God's spokesman and authoritatively declare God's will in such terms as "I can assure you as certainly as if you heard it proclaimed with an immediate voice from heaven what the will of God is in this case." [90] He also could vary his style of expression from one of flowery beauty to one of thunderous force, depending upon whether he was preaching a God of love or a God of justice. His emphasis on love was usually more dominant than his emphasis on justice, as might be gathered from his sermon, "God is Love":

> Love is a gentle, pleasing theme, the noblest passion of the human breast, and the fairest ornament of the rational nature. Love is the cement of society, and the source of social happiness; and without it the great community of the rational universe would dissolve, and men and angels would turn savages, and roam apart in barbarous solitude. Love is the spring of every pleasure; for who could take pleasure in the possession of what he does not love! Love is the foundation of religion and morality, for what is more monstrous than religion without love to that God who is the object of it? . . . Love is the softener and polisher of human minds, and transforms barbarians into men; its pleasures are refined and delicate, and even its pains and anxieties have something in them soothing and pleasing. In a word, love is the brightest beam of divinity that has ever irradiated the creation; the nearest resemblance to the ever-blessed God; for "God is Love." [91]

But Davies occasionally warned of God's justice, more often than not associating it with the condemnation of insincerity: "Surely such [insincere] prayer must bring down a curse upon you instead

[89] Foote, I, 302.
[90] "A Time of Unusual Sickness and Mortality Improved," *Sermons* (1845), III, 151–152.
[91] "God is Love," *ibid.*, I, 315–316.

of a blessing: such sacrifices must be *an abomination to the Lord*, . . . and it is astonishing that he has not mingled your blood with your sacrifices and sent you from your knees to hell; from thoughtless, unmeaning prayer to real blasphemy and torture." [92] Davies was willing to play upon all the motives for human behavior (a subject which he studied carefully) [93] as a means of encouraging a prescribed course of action in either an unsaved person or an insincere Christian.

As an orator, Davies served as a model for many of his contemporaries, both religious and secular—"the means of kindling the hidden fire of eloquence in other bosoms," according to one historian.[94] He undoubtedly was influenced by evangelists such as Wesley and Whitefield, who initiated a new style of pulpit oratory in the eighteenth century, relying heavily on the arts of public speaking to appeal to the emotions, as well as to the intellects, of their hearers. Most of the young New Light preachers adopted this method after Whitefield's successful preaching tour of America in 1739. Davies himself acquired his pulpit practices at the feet of his New Light mentor Samuel Blair at Fagg's Manor, employing some but not all of the methods of Whitefield. Davies always insisted that he was not an enthusiast in feeling or method. His effect was somewhere between that of his rationalistic Anglican associates and the highly emotional impact of his Baptist contemporaries. Many young preachers patterned their pulpit oratory after Davies, and the Reverend James Waddell, especially, "caught from Davies the inspiration which afterwards made him almost his equal in sacred pathos." [95] Henry Jones Ford, writing early in the twentieth century, even credited Davies with founding "a school of oratory that profoundly affected forensic method in America, whether in the

---

[92] "Lukewarmness in Religion," *ibid.*, p. 277.
[93] The Rush MSS contain an undated paper titled "A Synoptical View of the humane Passions containing 9 Tables—Set down in Regular Order by the Revd. Sam Davies." Davies had originally given it the title "Synoptical Tables of the humane Passions." This is a careful schematic diagram of the causes of human action, indicating that Davies had made some study of the matter.
[94] Howison, *Virginia*, II, 180.
[95] *Ibid.*

forum, in the pulpit or at the bar." According to Ford, it was the peculiar work of Davies and his successors

> to systematize the new method, imparting to it dignity and character, and establishing its artistic canons. In so doing a distinctively American school of oratory was founded, whose best examples vie with the finest passages of literature the world can furnish. . . . The fact that the style has degenerated until it is now insufferable does not detract from the merit of the masters who unconsciously originated it, in adapting pulpit method to the needs of the times. With them that style was unaffected, natural and sincere. The literary emancipation in which they were leaders remains as a permanent gain since to it modern prose owes its ease and freedom.[96]

In colonial America, the sermon was probably the most significant form of communication. In addition to receiving religious instruction, congregations were accustomed to hearing the latest news of all types from the pulpit. This remained the case until the emergence of the political orator at the time of the Revolution, and it is highly probable that these later speakers deliberately patterned their style after the prominent preachers of the day. It has been suggested that Davies influenced this later oratory through his impact on Patrick Henry, one of the best-known orators of the Revolution. Henry reportedly claimed he was "first taught what an orator should be" by listening to Davies preach.[97] Alan Heimert, observing that Davies was noted for the warmth of his voice and the use of a variety of sounds in his sermon delivery, states that he may have influenced a distinctive Southern style of oratory through the agency of Henry.[98]

The young Patrick Henry was a member of his uncle's Anglican parish in Hanover when Davies was at the height of his popularity as a preacher, and it was Henry's habit to take his mother, who was a Presbyterian, to hear the sermons of the dissenting preacher. When he had grown to manhood, he continued, along with his sisters, as a regular attendant at the Presbyterian meetinghouse.[99]

[96] Henry Jones Ford, *The Scotch-Irish in America* (Princeton, 1915), pp. 390, 399–400.
[97] Howison, *Virginia*, II, 180.
[98] Heimert, *Religion and the American Mind*, p. 231.
[99] William E. Dodd in *Dictionary of American Biography*, s.v. "Patrick Henry."

The effect this master of pulpit oratory had upon his youthful listener must have been something akin to that which Samuel Blair had had on Davies. Regardless of the direct influence Davies may have had on Henry, Henry said in later years that as an orator his own success was owed to the example set by this man. Davies' struggles for religious toleration and his tremendously patriotic sermons surely struck a sympathetic chord in the freedom-loving nature of his hearer. Years later, when Henry rose in the Hanover courthouse to speak against the royal veto of a Virginia law, he may have remembered the great leader of the nonconformists who had so often argued for religious rights against the same men he now faced. Again, in St. John's Parish Church at Richmond, when Henry made his "Liberty or Death" speech, urging Virginians to join together in resisting their enemies, he may have remembered Davies' similar plea of almost two decades before: "Let us then in the name of the Lord of Hosts, the God of the armies of Israel, let us collect our whole strength, and give one decisive blow." [100] Patrick Henry expressed the similar thought that "an appeal to arms and to the God of Hosts is all that is left us! . . . Sir, we are not weak if we make a proper use of those means which the God of nature hath placed in our power." [101]

There are many parallels between the war sermons of the great preacher and the famous speech of the great patriot, although this affinity could be attributed to their similarity of outlook and a likeness of conditions. Both men spoke of the common tendency to ignore danger and stressed that a society must be prepared for war whether desiring it or not. Both men felt the dangers of their situations to be real, convinced that a form of slavery was the only possible alternative to an active defense. Both men denied the concept of

[100] "Curse of Cowardice," *Sermons* (1845), III, 93.

[101] There is no accurate record of Patrick Henry's "Liberty or Death" speech, but it was pieced together from contemporary reports by William Wirt in his *Sketches of the Life and Character of Patrick Henry*, first published in 1817 in Philadelphia. A later, more eulogistic biographer, William Wirt Henry, published it in his *Patrick Henry, Life, Correspondence and Speeches*, I, 265–266. The similarity between Davies and Henry is noted by William Wirt Henry and by Patrick Henry's latest biographer, Robert Douthat Meade, *Patrick Henry*, pp. 70–74.

peace at any price. An interesting comparison of style may be seen in Henry's speech and Davies' sermon on the death of General Braddock.

As a preacher, then, Davies may have been unsurpassed by any of his contemporaries, either in America or Great Britain. Whether writing sermons for publication or delivering them from the pulpit, he excelled at meeting the needs of his audience, propounding a practical theology that was particularly appropriate to the exigencies of frontier life. He exercised a moderation in the pulpit that appealed to the Anglican-trained dissenters, and his tolerance for differing views eroded the ingrained resistance of the Anglican clergy and civil authorities. When the French and Indian War threatened Virginia's welfare, Davies placed patriotism on the side of Christianity and became one of the colony's finest recruiters. Fiery in delivery and a master of the art of oratory, he undoubtedly exerted at least some influence on the future Revolutionary orator Patrick Henry, even though the underlying purpose of all of Davies' oratory was to bring sinners to repentance. As will be seen later, the conversion of sinners was after all his one basic mission in fulfilling the role of a diligent pastor to a burgeoning congregation.

V

The Duties of a Good Pastor

A FREQUENT VISITOR to Hanover observed that "when I go amongst Mr. Davies people, religion seems to flourish; it is like the suburbs of Heaven."[1] Such testimony leaves little doubt that Davies was highly successful in his role as local pastor, even as he achieved international fame as a champion of the New Light movement. His pastoral work was "local" only in the frontier sense of the term, however, for at one time he served as many as seven congregations in five counties. Much of this burden was assumed by a succession of young ministers attracted to Davies by his accomplishments and personal qualities. During most of his tenure in Hanover, in fact, he was training one or more of these assistants.

Within a remarkably short time after settling in Hanover, Davies had become one of the most sought after preachers in the Presbyterian church and, in fact, one of the most prominent and popular speakers in the Old Dominion. Virginians traveled many miles to hear the New Light pastor speak in Hanover, and leaders of congregations throughout Virginia "became desirous to obtain some portion of his service in their immediate neighborhood."[2] John

[1] ——— to John Gillies, Sept. 5, 1755, "Old Documents," *The Virginia Evangelical and Literary Magazine*, IV (1821), 544.
[2] Foote, I, 168.

86

Holt Rice, writing many years after Davies had left Virginia and drawing on his personal acquaintance with some of the surviving members of the Hanover congregation, found "satisfactory evidence that he produced a powerful impression wherever he went" and that "his powers of persuasion seemed sufficient for the accomplishment of any purpose." Many of Rice's stories have an apocryphal ring, but they no doubt reflect the impression Davies made on his contemporaries. According to Rice, "A mother might often be seen," as one progressed through the countryside, "rocking her infant in a cradle, sewing some garment for her husband, and learning her catechism at the same time." A young girl "employed in spinning" might be observed to "place her book of questions at the head of the wheel, and catching a glance at it as she ran up her yarn on the spindle, would thus prepare for public catechism." Even farm boys, "accustomed to follow the plough," were reportedly "often to be seen, while their horses were feeding at midday, reclining under an old oak in the yard, learning the weekly task."[3] Rice was himself a Presbyterian and thus, presumably, had a certain amount of sympathy for Davies and his mission. A century after Davies came to Hanover, however, even a Methodist reporter observed that "in accomplishing the great objects contemplated in the Christian ministry, few men . . . in any age have been more highly honored than Davies."[4]

The appeal of this young minister stemmed largely from the outward manifestations of his character. In contrast to many of the Anglican clergy with whom he was compared, he stood forth as a model of virtue and propriety. Twentieth-century historians have described him as "one of the holiest apostles as well as one of the greatest intellects of his time,"[5] a judgment corroborated by those who came in contact with him throughout his career. Even the Anglican Commissary of the colony, William Dawson, was reportedly

---

[3] [Rice], "Memoir," pp. 201–202. The many possible but improbable stories about Davies should not necessarily be accepted as fact but merely as indicative of the impressions Davies left on his contemporaries and their descendants.

[4] R. W. A., "Review, *Sermons on Important Subjects* (1842)," p. 138.

[5] Philip Alexander Bruce, Lyon G. Tyler, Richard L. Morton, *et al.*, *History of Virginia: Colonial Period, 1607–1763* (3 vols., Chicago and New York, 1924), I, 328.

impressed by Davies' zeal and success and spoke somewhat enviously of him to his superior, the Bishop of London: "The Dissenters were but an inconsiderable number before the late arrival of certain Teachers from the Northern Colonies . . . [and] since Mr. Davies has been allowed to officiate in so many places . . . there has been a great defection from our Religious Assemblies. The generality of his followers, I believe, were born and bred in our Communion." [6]

Dawson's complaint was justified, for under Davies' leadership the Hanover Presbyterians soon became a force to be reckoned with in the political and religious life of the supposedly Anglican colony. Brought together under their own leader, the dissenters possessed a solidarity that made them conscious of their power and led them to assert it; by 1752 they were able to force promises from candidates for public office in return for their support.[7] As early as 1753 the Hanover clergyman noted that his adherents numbered five or six hundred,[8] a sizable voting block for a local election in colonial America. As might be expected, this rapid increase in numbers and political strength of the Presbyterians under Davies' ministrations was viewed by Anglican authorities as a serious threat to the religious and political stability of the colony.

The man himself, however, was never certain of his success as a pastor and was constantly pessimistic regarding his work. But in everything he undertook, he achieved more than he expected. His replacement during his trip to England reported "considerable appearances of success" in several areas where Davies supposedly "was apprehensive he had laboured much in vain." [9]

His practice of ministering to more than one meetinghouse caused some critics to label him an itinerant, an epithet that he found perhaps more distasteful than any other.[10] Popular preacher that he

---

[6] Dawson to the Bishop of London, n.d., Perry, *Historical Collections*, I, 384–385.

[7] Gewehr, p. 89n.

[8] Davies to Holt, Feb. 27, 1753, Rush MSS.

[9] John Wright to Gillies, n.d. (c. 1754), John Gillies, *Historical Collections Relating to Remarkable Periods of the Success of the Gospel and Eminent Instruments Employed in Promoting it* (Kelso, Va., 1845), p. 433n.

[10] Dinwiddie to the Bishop of London, June 5, 1752, Perry, *Historical Collections*, I, 396.

was, he was constantly besieged with requests to preach to the many independent congregations [11] and, as a result , became something of a circuit rider as well as a settled pastor. Foote reports that "Amid all his labours . . . Davies found time and strength and disposition to make frequent missionary excursions to the sections of the country now included in the counties of Cumberland, Powhatan, Prince Edward, Charlotte, Campbell, Nottoway and Amelia." [12] These missionary tours and "the habit of Mr. Davies either to preach at the places where he lodged, or to give a lecture to the family and servants" [13] left him open, of course, to the charge he so scrupulously tried to avoid—that of being an itinerant. The government never used this as an excuse to revoke his license, however, and Davies continued as an occasional wandering preacher until he left the colony.

The conversions resulting from these tours formed the nucleus of at least two future churches.[14] On such trips, which frequently took him as far south as North Carolina, he generally preached in the woods and evidently laid the foundation for much of the later revival movement in this area. Even after his departure from Hanover, when "the Baptists spread over Virginia like a torrent, and their converts proceeded to give a public account of their religious awakening and experience," it was said to be common for a convert to begin his testimony by saying, " 'At such a time and place I heard the Rev. Mr. Davies preach, and had my mind deeply impressed.' " [15]

To assist on these difficult journeys through the wilderness, Davies customarily took with him one of the younger members of his congregation. The young man was expected to serve not only as a companion during their lonely days on the trail, but also as a pioneer or scout. One of his major duties was to ride ahead and find lodging for the night,[16] no easy task in a semi-frontier area where settlement was sparse and the people might be reluctant to invite a controversial

[11] Foote, I, 168.
[12] *Ibid.*, p. 214.
[13] *Ibid.*, p. 215.
[14] "A Recovered Tract of President Davies," p. 364. Foote, I, 215–216.
[15] "A Recovered Tract of President Davies," p. 362.
[16] Foote, I, 215.

ORANGE

SPOTSYLVANIA

KI:
GEO

Port Royal ●

CAROLINE

LOUISA

HANOVER

North Wales ●

ALBEMARLE

GOOCHLAND

James R.

Hanover ● KI:

New Castle

CUMBERLAND

HENRICO

● Richmond

James R.

CHESTERFIELD

CHAR

● Petersburg

AMELIA

PRINCE
GEORGE

SU

LUNENBURG

BRUNSWICK

SOUTH

0   10   20   30
MILES

Map by Larry Hirst based on a sketch by G.W.P.

WEST-
MORELAND

RICHMOND   NORTH-
            UMBERLAND

SEX

G   LANCASTER

AND   Rappahanock R.
ony R.   MIDDLESEX
QUEEN

NT   GLOUCESTER

JAMES   YORK York R.
CITY
Y.   Williamsburg ●
ames R.   WAR-   ELIZABETH
        James   WICK   CITY
        Town ●

ISLE OF   James R.
WIGHT

                      PRINCESS
                        ANNE

          NORFOLK

NANSEMOND

Chesapeake
   Bay

ACCOMACK

NORTHAMPTON

Atlantic Ocean

Counties of
Eastern Virginia
about 1750

preacher into their homes. One of the young men of Hanover who served most in this capacity was a boy named John Morton.

In one of the stories that survived Davies' departure from Virginia, Davies and young Morton reportedly came to the house of the latter's older cousin Joseph Morton. The elder Morton, described as "a rigid Churchman," was reluctant to provide them with shelter, but after conferring with his wife he agreed to take them in for the night. From all accounts, the two Anglicans were impressed by Davies and "the dignity and suavity of his manner," and accompanied him to his next preaching stop in Cumberland County. In the course of their journey, Mrs. Morton apparently expressed a desire to participate in the communion service that was a feature of the minister's visits, and she prepared to do so even though her husband at first remained aloof. But in the intermission after the "action sermon," Morton must have changed his mind, for he called Davies and asked to join in the service. The preacher was evidently pleased with the course of events, and "after a little conversation, gave him a token of admission, and the husband and wife went together to the Lord's Table." [17]

The account of Joseph Morton's experience depicts a prominent facet of Davies' pastoral work, his use of communion tokens. Historically, both pagans and Christians had made use of some kind of identification piece in order to recognize communicants, and Calvin had brought this practice into Protestantism as early as 1560. The basic function of tokens was to limit participation in religious rites to those who had received the requisite instructions and had given proper testimony of their faith. Virginia Presbyterians adhered to this practice closely, identifying it with the process of catechetical instruction. Thus, before the administration of the sacrament, all present were examined on the "chief heads of religion" with tokens being given to those who successfully answered the questions.

---

[17] Narrative of William Morton in James W. Alexander, *The Life of Archibald Alexander, D.D., LL.D., First Professor in the Theological Seminary, at Princeton, New Jersey* (New York, 1856), pp. 180–181. Similar facts are found in Foote, I, 215–216. One of John Morton's daughters was the mother of John Holt Rice, a fact lending credence to many of his stories.

In using tokens, Davies was following the established customs of Scottish Presbyterianism and apparently was trying to make his practice conform to his claim of being a member of the Church of Scotland.[18] But instead of using the Presbyterians' traditional small stamped metal disks, the New Light minister distributed engraved cards that allowed him to present longer inscriptions or passages of his own poetry pertinent to the event, such as:

> Do this says Christ 'till Time shall end.
> In Memory of your dying Friend.
> Meet at my Table and Record
> The Love of your departed Lord.[19]

The cards also were probably less expensive than metal disks, although they were made from steel engravings, which no doubt had to come from England.[20] Davies placed a high value on these cards and exercised painstaking care in their preparation.

The extensive demand for the services of the Hanover clergyman was of course related to his role as the only New Light preacher permanently settled in the colony for many years. With seven pulpits located in five different counties—three in Hanover and one each in Henrico, Goochland, Louisa, and Caroline [21]—Davies found himself ministering to about three hundred families. He often rode eighty or ninety miles from one meetinghouse to another.[22] Even with this number of communicants scattered over such a large area, he still felt it his duty to apply for an eighth preaching place as early as 1750.[23] He constantly noted the neglected condition of

[18] Davies had previously made this claim to Governor Dinwiddie when he had been granted his permanent licenses; Dinwiddie to the Bishop of London, June 5, 1752, Perry, *Historical Collections*, I, 396.

[19] *Journal of the Presbyterian Historical Society*, II (1903), picture facing p. 277.

[20] Mary McWhorter Tenney, *Communion Tokens, Their Origin, History and Use, With a Treatise on the Relation of the Sacrament to the Vitality and Revivals of the Church* (Grand Rapids, 1936), p. 84 and also pp. 11–16, 17, 25. This is the standard work on this subject.

[21] Foote, I, 169.

[22] Davies to the Bishop of London, Jan. 10, 1753, *ibid.*, p. 183.

[23] "Petition of the New Kent Co. Presbyterians to the County Court," "Records of the New Kent, Co. Court," April 12, 1750, *ibid.*, pp. 169–170. William Dawson to the Bishop of London, July 23, 1753, Perry, *Historical Collections*, I, 407.

other frontier congregations, "about fifteen or twenty families in Cumberland . . . and about the same number contiguous in New Kent." [24] The extent of his labors is best indicated by the fact that the formation of Hanover Presbytery, which took place at the end of 1755, involved five ministers, serving an area that Davies had formerly served alone.[25]

Although most of the early work in the colony was accomplished by Davies alone, his constant pleas for assistance were soon answered by visiting ministers sent by the Synod of New York and the New Brunswick Presbytery; [26] and eventually, as the number of Presbyterians increased, still other New Light preachers settled permanently in the colony. The first of his visiting assistants, the Reverend James Davenport, brought with him a controversial background. Davenport had had a stormy career as a revivalist in New England, having been twice declared insane and driven out of Connecticut for his Savonarola-like bonfires. Early in his career he seems to have embodied all the hostility-arousing traits of the typical stereotype of a revival preacher, but he was apparently somewhat calmer when he arrived in Virginia in 1750.[27] After stopping at the Davies' household, slightly more than three hundred miles from his home in Hopewell, New Jersey, he went about "a hundred and twenty miles further, even to Roanoke River, and came within thirty miles of North Carolina." He was absent from his home for more than four months, traveled an estimated 1,590 miles, "and generally preached once every week, and sometimes twice or thrice." [28] Davies was not only happy with the concern shown by the Synod but also impressed with Davenport's work, for he wrote "blest be God, [he] did not labour in vain." [29]

Shortly after Davenport's visit, Davies began his serious attempts,

---

[24] Davies to the Bishop of London, Jan. 10, 1753, Foote, I, 183.

[25] "Early Minutes of Hanover Presbytery," Dec. 3, 1755, ed. William M. E. Rachal, *Virginia Magazine of History and Biography*, LXIII (1955), 54.

[26] "Minutes of the Synod of New York," Oct. 5, 1749, *Records*, p. 240.

[27] Sprague, *Annals*, III, 80–92. Charles A. Dinsmore in *Dictionary of American Biography*, s.v. "James Davenport."

[28] Davenport to ——— Williams, Oct. 16, [1750], Sprague, *Annals*, III, 89.

[29] Davies to Bellamy, June 27, 1751, Gillies, *Historical Collections*, p. 432.

through the good offices of Joseph Bellamy, to bring the Reverend Jonathan Edwards into the colony as his co-worker in the movement, going so far as to raise funds for Edwards' support.[30] The Hanover pastor apparently gave little thought to personal honors when he invited the famous Edwards to join him, for by so doing he was jeopardizing his own position of prestige and leadership in Virginia. Instead, the Virginian's comment on Edwards was that "Of all the men I know in America, he appears to me the most fit for this place, I would cheerfully resign him my place."[31] Edwards had recently been removed from his pulpit at Northampton, Massachusetts, and was admittedly having difficulty finding a new position. "I am now," he lamented, "thrown upon the wide ocean of the world, and know not what will become of me, and my numerous and chargeable family."[32]

Despairing of ever finding a new pulpit in New England, Edwards might have joined Davies in Virginia except that the invitation arrived too late. The matter is duly noted in one of his letters: "I was in the latter part of the last summer, applied to, with much earnestness and importunity, by some of the people of Virginia, to come and settle among them in the work of the ministry; who subscribed handsomely for my encouragement and support, and sent a messenger to me with their request and subscriptions; but I was installed at Stockbridge, before the messenger came."[33] In view of this failure there can only be speculation on the possibly remarkable accomplishments of two such religious leaders working together.

It is possible that Davies had not expected Edwards to make a favorable response to the request for his services, for an invitation was extended to Bellamy in the same letter, seeking the latter's assistance.[34] Bellamy refused to come to Virginia for reasons unknown. It may have been that he was reluctant to substitute for the more famous Edwards or to take second place to Davies himself.

[30] Davies to Bellamy, July 4, 1751, Foote, II, 41–43.
[31] *Ibid.*, p. 41.
[32] Edwards to John Erskine, July 5, 1750, *The Works of President Edwards: With a Memoir of his Life*, ed. Sereno Edwards Dwight (10 vols., Boston, 1830), I, 411.
[33] Edwards to Erskine, July 7, 1752, *ibid.*, p. 498.
[34] Davies to Bellamy, July 4, 1751, Foote, II, 43.

But not all of Davies' efforts to recruit some kind of permanent assistance ended in failure. After much urging, he did obtain the services of a young graduate of the College of New Jersey, the Reverend John Todd, continually telling the Synod of "the great necessities of the people, in the back parts of Virginia, where multitudes were remarkably awakened and reformed . . . [and] have been thirsting after the ordinances of God."[35] Todd had been graduated from the college in 1749 and, immediately after his licensing in 1750 by the Presbytery of New Brunswick, had been sent into Virginia at Davies' request.[36] This 1750 mission must have been for a temporary visit only, however, for as late as November 1752 Edwards noted "the probability of the settlement of a Mr. Todd, a young man of good learning and of a pious disposition, in a part of Virginia."[37] Todd was installed the same month,[38] but seven months later Davies was again asking for help, protesting to Bellamy that those who had put themselves under the care of New Castle Presbytery and had repeatedly asked for assistance were "still destitute of ministers," some congregations having been more than a year without a sermon.[39]

The permanent settlement of John Todd in Virginia was extremely gratifying to Davies, although it undoubtedly caused some concern among those who were deprived of their original pastor. It certainly caused concern among opponents of dissenters generally. In fact, Todd's installation was accepted only reluctantly by the new governor, Robert Dinwiddie, who previously had disapproved of Davies' serving as many as seven pulpits. The sharp-tongued, plainspoken Dinwiddie, who lacked the graciousness and tolerance of his predecessor Gooch, refused Todd a license for an eighth pulpit and permitted him to preach only as an assistant to Davies. The governor himself described the conversation with Davies, brought about by this refusal:

[35] Edwards to [William] M'Culloch, Nov. 24, 1752, Edwards, *Works*, I, 518.
[36] Webster, *History of the Presbyterian Church*, p. 608.
[37] Edwards to M'Culloch, Nov. 24, 1752, Edwards, *Works*, I, 518.
[38] Foote, I, 216.
[39] Davies to Bellamy, June 27, 1751, Gillies, *Historical Collections*, p. 432.

I told him I thought it impossible for him to discharge the duties of a good pastor to so many different congregations dispersed at so great a distance one from the other. I took upon me to tell him what I conceived to be the duty of a Minister . . . and that as he did not discharge these duties, which I conceived he could not do without a close residence with his hearers, I must look upon him as an Itinerant preacher more out of lucrative view than the salvation of the people. After a long silence he desired I would not look upon him as an Itinerant preacher, which character he abhor'd, but agreed with me that in the Meeting houses already Licensed he could not discharge the essential duties of his Ministry and therefore desired me to admit one Mr. Todd for his assistant. I told him I had a due regard for people of tender consciences, and . . . he was admitted to be his assistant.[40]

No doubt Davies was unimpressed by the governor's discourse on the duty of a minister, and he was probably somewhat disappointed in not obtaining a permanent pulpit for Todd. But his greatest disillusionment must have been caused by Dinwiddie's attitude, for he had previously written: "We have a new Governor, who is a candid condescending gentleman. And as he has been educated in the Church of Scotland, he has a respect for the Presbyterians, which I hope is a happy omen."[41] Of course, the charge that Davies was a preacher more interested in money than in the salvation of souls was so false as to cast doubt on the writer's sincerity, and it is possible that this description sent to the Bishop of London was motivated more by political expediency than by personal conviction. In fact, when Davies reached Glasgow on his embassy for the college, he found that Dinwiddie had written letters of commendation to his friends and brother-in-law, asking their support for the school.[42]

Todd, the new assistant, was in the vanguard of a succession of effective preachers who would eventually unite into the Presbytery of Hanover. Many congregations were still in need of resident ministers, a need evinced by Todd's unsuccessful attempt to be licensed

[40] Dinwiddie to the Bishop of London, June 5, 1752, Perry, *Historical Collections*, I, 396.
[41] Davies to Edwards, March 2, 1752, quoted in Edwards to Erskine, July 7, 1752, Edwards, *Works*, I, 498.
[42] *Diary*, July 5, 1754, p. 106.

into three new meetinghouses.[43] With Todd serving four of the seven original pulpits, Davies had more time to expand his work on the southern frontier. It was here in 1755 that Davies assisted in the founding of the historic Briery Church in Prince Edward County, made up of former Tidewater families.[44] The situation evidently proved to be satisfactory to both men, for Davies was relieved of much of his work as well as his fears of inadequacy, and Todd eventually was recognized as a permanent fixture in the Virginia religious community.[45] The two New Light preachers soon became fast friends.

Davies himself officiated at Todd's installation, preaching the sermon and giving over to him part of the original Hanover congregation.[46] The new assistant proved to be an effective preacher and efficient pastoral leader, as well as a friend upon whom Davies could depend for sound advice.[47] When Davies was uncertain whether to undertake the trip to England on behalf of the College of New Jersey, it was Todd to whom he turned for advice and counsel.[48] Todd accompanied Davies to Philadelphia, where Davies embarked for Great Britain, prompting a journal entry that he "parted with my favourite Friend Mr. Todd, not without Tears." [49] And finally, it was Todd who entered the Hanover pulpit as permanent successor when Davies left for his new duties at Princeton in 1759.[50]

Todd later became the recognized leader of the Virginia Presbyterians, encouraging them in their opposition to George III and in their inclination to follow the frontier to the west.[51] His personal reputation was second only to Davies' own. One contemporary praised God for sending Todd to Virginia, noting that "Mr. Todd gave us a most instructive sermon. I never hear a sermon, but one

[43] Foote, II, 45.
[44] Morton, *Colonial Virginia*, II, 595.
[45] Foote, II, 45.
[46] *Ibid.*, p. 46.
[47] *Diary*, July 13, 1753, p. 9.
[48] *Ibid.*, July 2, 1753, p. 6.
[49] *Ibid.*, Oct. 11, 1753, p. 20.
[50] Webster, *History of the Presbyterian Church*, p. 609.
[51] Foote, II, 47.

from Mr. Davies, with more delight. O that the Lord would be pleased to send us a minister with as much piety as Mr. Todd." [52]

Soon after Todd was permanently settled in the colony in 1752, the Synod of New York temporarily appointed the Reverend Nehemiah Greenman and the Reverend Robert Henry to go to Davies' aid.[53] Greenman, a Yale graduate and a resident of New Jersey,[54] had previously failed to carry out a similar synodical commission,[55] and there is no evidence that he complied this time. On the other hand, Robert Henry, a native of Scotland and a recent graduate of the College of New Jersey,[56] went immediately to Virginia where he became permanent minister to two congregations in Charlotte and Prince Edward counties. When Davies returned from England, he served at Henry's installation.[57]

Another of Davies' early associates was the Reverend John Brown, whose ordination sermon Davies preached[58] just prior to leaving for England. Brown was a native of Ireland[59] and, like Henry, a graduate of the college at Princeton. He immediately assumed responsibility for vacant pulpits at New Providence and Fairfield in the Shenandoah Valley.[60] After establishing a grammar school and fathering two future United States senators and a minister to France, Brown eventually moved into Kentucky.[61]

For a brief time, the Reverend Alexander Craighead was also numbered among the permanent New Light preachers in the colony. Craighead had been one of the original seceders from the Synod

---

[52] "Journal of Col. James Gordon, of Lancaster County, Va.," Oct. 22, Nov. 1, 1761, *William and Mary Quarterly*, series one, XI (1903), 225.

[53] "Minutes of the Synod of New York," Sept. 29, 1752, *Records*, p. 248.

[54] Webster, *History of the Presbyterian Church*, pp. 654–655.

[55] "Minutes of the Synod of New York," Sept. 27, 1751, Sept. 28, 1752, *Records*, pp. 246, 247.

[56] Webster, *History of the Presbyterian Church*, pp. 650–651.

[57] Foote, I, 220. Both of these congregations had been independently organized by the aforementioned Joseph Morton and his wife (Webster, *History of the Presbyterian Church*, p. 651).

[58] *Diary*, Oct. 11, 1753, p. 20.

[59] Webster, *History of the Presbyterian Church*, p. 656.

[60] Foote, II, 96.

[61] Webster, *History of the Presbyterian Church*, p. 657.

of Philadelphia.[62] His career within the Presbyterian church had already been long, varied, and stormy when he finally became associated with the New Lights of the Presbytery of New Castle in 1754. Originally he had been a member of the conservative Donegal Presbytery on the Pennsylvania frontier, but about 1739 he was excluded from that body because of his advocacy and practice of itineracy. Although Craighead was also a member of the New Brunswick Presbytery for a while, he left that group when it refused to adopt the Solemn League and Covenant. He then became a member of Reformed Presbyterian Church of Scotland through the Anti-Burger Synod of the Associated Presbyterian Church. About this time, 1749, he went to the Virginia frontier in an attempt to organize an Anti-Burger church. It was not until he formally joined the New Castle Presbytery some five years later that he was considered a member of the New Light group. Craighead remained in Virginia only briefly in his New Light capacity. After Braddock's defeat, he led his entire congregation into an area of North Carolina that was free of the Indian threat.[63]

As a result of this influx of New Light preachers into Virginia, Davies' travels were considerably curtailed. Even though he continued to travel to pastor-less congregations at the behest of his Synod and Presbytery, he was no longer their sole source of pastoral care. Davies gained no extra leisure time, however. He found many other tasks that demanded his attention, all of them in keeping with his concept of the ministerial function.

[62] Charles Augustus Briggs, *American Presbyterianism; its Origin and Early History, Together With an Appendix of Letters and Documents, Many of which have Recently Been Discovered* (New York, 1885), pp. 247, 261–263.

[63] Webster, *History of the Presbyterian Church*, pp. 434–437.

VI

The Great Concerns of Religion

CHIEF AMONG THE DUTIES that Davies undertook in conjunction with his preaching was that of educating the people of his congregations. It was a task that was not confined to the young, for he directed his efforts at persons of all ages, nor was it confined to the white people among his listeners, for he promoted education among many Negroes and Indians as well. In this respect, the New Light pastor was true to the ideals of education that the Presbyterian church demanded of its preachers and encouraged among its communicants. Throughout the colonies it was not uncommon for ministers of Davies' denomination, regardless of their Synod, to fill the role of teacher, often establishing schools in their own homes when they could not obtain a regular schoolhouse.[1] It was universally accepted that they were charged with both the religious and secular instruction of children. Davies and the Virginia Presbyterians met with unqualified success in both tasks and were soon recognized as the best educators in the colony.[2]

Probably because of the vast numbers under his pastoral care, Davies established no school. Instead he distributed books and other

---

[1] For instance, William Tennent, Samuel Blair, William Robinson, and Robert Smith. See above, ch. I.

[2] Gewehr, *Great Awakening*, p. 221.

educational materials to those who attended his sermons. One commentator has noted that "households generally were furnished with a few standard works, of good old times; and were expected to study them carefully." People who had been members of Davies' churches usually had "books or remnants of books, such as Watson's Body of Divinity, Boston's Fourfold State, Luther on the Galatians, Flavel's Works, Baxter's Call to the Unconverted, and Saint's Everlasting Rest, Alleine's Alarm, and others of similar character." The writer's concluding comment that "Davies's churches were schools in which the people were taught better things than the ancient sages ever communicated to their disciples," while no doubt an overstatement of the case, does indicate the lasting impression Davies made on his followers and their descendants.[3]

That such works mentioned in the foregoing account were seriously studied by the members of Davies' congregations seems plausible in view of the importance attached to education by the Presbyterians, the extent to which eighteenth-century literature was dominated by writings of a religious nature, and the general shortage of reading material on the Virginia frontier. Davies knew of many "in such low circumstances, that they cannot spare money to purchase good books," as well as many more "so stupidly ignorant and insensible of their want of instruction, as to excuse themselves from it as a needless expence." In fact, there were "few houses in Virginia well furnished in this important respect."[4]

A voracious reader himself,[5] Davies constantly borrowed all types of reading material from John Holt and at least once asked to borrow old magazines and newspapers.[6] In addition, Davies asked Holt to purchase books for him on Holt's many trips to England. Books for his own education were mentioned in almost all of his letters to

[3] [Rice], "Memoir," p. 202.
[4] Davies to Robert Crutenden, March 1755, "Old Documents," *The Virginia Evangelical and Literary Magazine*, I (1819), 540. This letter also appeared in Foote, I, 284; the Library of Congress copy has the following handwritten notation: "Almost Certainly his friend R[obert] Crutenden, of London."
[5] "How do I long for Retirement in my Study," *Diary*, July 21, 1754, p. 111.
[6] Davies to Holt, March 2, 1751, Rush MSS.

Holt, and he often recommended and loaned books to Holt and others. On one occasion Davies wrote, "I have lent Brother Billy Mr. Brainerd's Life, with a View [that] you also might peruse it. . . . I would have you read Mr. Edwards III Reflection page 295." [7] He constantly asked his relative to supply him with particular works desired at the moment: "Please to bring me the Night Tho'ts, Prior's Solomon, Young on the Conflagration, and on Job, and Gibbon's Juvenilia." [8] After having read the materials, Davies would make known his opinions to his favorite correspondent. Such comments were both favorable and unfavorable, as when he said, "I am wholly disappointed in Prior; . . . the Vol. you sent me is generally a profane or trifling Miscellany," or when he referred to "our favourite" Addison.[9] Of all the books that Davies was able to buy or borrow, one of his abiding favorites (if not the favorite) was Edward Young's *Night Thoughts*, about which he wrote, "of all the poetical Pieces I ever read, the Night thoughts, I think have been most serviceable to me; and I shall keep them as my companion, till I commence an Immortal."

Other activities, however, kept Davies from reading and studying as much as he would have wished. In an effort to husband his time, he began the study of shorthand for use in putting down his sermon notes and other writings. Davies relied on Holt in this matter too, for in a letter written during his early years in Hanover he thanked his friend for a "tachygraphical Piece" received and asked him to send to England "by the first opportunity for Weston's Stenography of Short Hand." [10] Later, he observed that he would be "glad to receive Weston's short Hand, tho' the Price should be 30 or 40 shillings," [11] an expensive item indeed for one with an income of but a hundred pounds. The use of some system of shorthand or abbreviated writing was quite common in this period.

[7] Davies to Holt, Sept. 5, 1751, *ibid.*
[8] Davies to Holt, Sept. 12, 1751, *ibid.*
[9] Davies to Holt, Aug. 7, 1752, *ibid.*
[10] Davies to Holt, Sept. 5, 1751, *ibid.*
[11] Davies to Holt, Sept. 12, 1751, *ibid.*

Davies made limited use of a system that he apparently developed for himself; [12] however, he does not seem to have been as successful in this endeavor as was John Wesley.[13]

The books, the magazines, and the shorthand studies were all part of an attempt to advance his own education, which had as its immediate goal the attainment of a degree from the College of New Jersey. He told Holt of his ambition in a letter dated August 7, 1752, in which he said, "I intend to stand Candidate for the Degree of M.A. at the next Commencement in October at the College of New Jersey. This has obliged me to revise the various branches of Literature and improve myself in them, particularly in Natural Philosophy, when I could redeem a few Hours from the Advocations of my Function, which have been peculiarly numerous this Season." [14] But his progress was delayed, and it was not until September of 1753 that Davies "delivered a Thesis (*Personales Distinctiones in Trinitate sunt æternæ*) and Vindicated it in a public Dispute against 3 Opponents; and afterwards was honoured with the Degree of Master of Arts." [15]

Naturally, the efforts at personal improvement did not cease with the attainment of a degree. Requests for books and magazines continued, and during his remaining years Davies became acquainted with a large number of writings ranging from the Greek and Latin classics to those of his contemporaries. Since Davies was not one to parade knowledge that he did not have, his copious quotations and citations indicate that he had read widely in several fields.[16] His sermons are well illustrated with accurate quotations from more than two dozen ancient writers, among them Augustine, Plato, and

[12] The Princeton University Library has a forty-six page manuscript of biblical comments in Davies' abbreviated writing. It has never been deciphered.

[13] For examples of Wesley's system, see *The Journal of the Rev. John Wesley, A.M. Sometime Fellow of Lincoln College, Oxford, Enlarged From Original MSS., With Notes From Unpublished Diaries, Annotations, Maps, and Illustrations*, ed. Nehemiah Curnock (8 vols., London, n.d.), I, 207–208, 300, 331.

[14] Davies to Holt, Aug. 7, 1752, Rush MSS.

[15] *Diary*, Sept. 26, 1753, p. 16.

[16] For examples of this, see Davies to ——— Donald, April 5, 1757, which contains his commentaries on three volumes of Bolingbroke's works, "A Recovered Tract of President Davies," pp. 349–364.

Tacitus. In almost every case he includes both the original and his translation. Accompanying these quotations from the classics are an equal number of citations from works of his contemporaries, including Addison, Pope, Watts, Whitefield, and Thomas Prince.

Any list of the writings of which Davies revealed such a working knowledge raises the question of how, with all of his many duties as a preacher and pastor, he found time to read so much. That he spent his all too scarce leisure moments reading is evident from the passages in the journal he kept during his voyages to and from England, during which he finished reading several books.[17] Furthermore, like John Wesley, he was able to read while traveling by horseback.[18]

Even though Davies was interested in books for his personal use, he was more concerned with the education of those under his care than with his own improvement. He made frequent appeals for books to his friends and acquaintances in England and Scotland, and during his English trip he met members of the Society in London for Promoting Religious Knowledge among the Poor, one of the many education-oriented religious organizations flourishing during that period. This body had, as one of its purposes, the furtherance of education among nonconformists in the colonies. Davies was able to obtain from this group several large shipments of books, which he distributed among those he deemed best able to put them to use. His letters to England are filled with reports on the distribution of specific titles, such as the letter that mentions *The Compassionate Address,* Doddridge's *Rise and Progress,* and Baxter's *Call.*[19] This letter, addressed to the Society, apparently prompted a second shipment of books. Following the latter gift, Davies again replied, this time as a member of the body, that he had announced the arrival of the books at the end of a sermon, inviting all persons (both black and white) who could read and were too poor to buy books to come to his house to receive them. After lamenting "what are 4 or 500 books, among so many thousands," he asked the charit-

---

[17] *Diary,* Jan. and Feb. 1755, pp. 139–146.
[18] *Ibid.,* July 16, 1754, p. 109.
[19] Davies to Crutenden, March 1755, "Old Documents," p. 540.

able group to continue its shipments, especially requesting multiple sets of Watts' *Catechisms*.[20]

In the area of formal education, Davies did not establish a grammar school or classical academy in conjunction with his pastorate, but he did encourage his New Light associates in Virginia to do so, and he occasionally took a young man into his home to prepare him personally for college or the ministry. At one time or another he supervised the tuition of John Wright, John Martin, William Richardson, James Waddell, and James Hunt, all of whom became Presbyterian clergymen. Davies never considered himself capable of carrying their education to completion as was done at the classical academies, however, and he looked to the College of New Jersey as the proper place for the students to complete their studies.[21]

Of his associates in Virginia who conducted schools, John Todd probably had the best, and Davies divided his support between Todd's school and the schools of the Hanover Presbytery, which later developed into Hampden-Sydney and Washington and Lee colleges.[22]

What Davies did to support these fledgling institutions is difficult to determine accurately. On a more or less regular basis he tutored several young men who later became his colleagues, and he guided the studies of at least one student who prepared for Princeton in his spare time while working as a schoolmaster.[23] The latter was the Reverend David Rice, who was recruited into the ministry by Davies and who accompanied Davies to the College of New Jersey to continue his own education.[24]

The Presbyterians were woefully short of ministers, and Davies did his best to alleviate the shortage. Whereas the New Lights had made striking gains during the early part of the Great Awakening because of the ability of their log colleges to supply them with more new clergymen than any other denomination, their continued

[20] Davies to Crutenden, March 2, 1754, Foote, I, 287–292.

[21] *Ibid.*, pp. 220, 221.

[22] Foote, II, 471.

[23] Elizabeth Venable Gaines, *Cub Creek Church and Congregation, 1738–1838* (Richmond and Texarkana, 1931), p. 22.

[24] Sprague, *Annals,* III, 246.

insistence upon an educated ministry caused them to lose more and more ground to the Baptists and Methodists. These groups, having no qualms about the lack of a classical education, were gradually replacing the Presbyterians as the leading elements of the revival movement. As a result, Davies became an active recruiter of students for both the classical schools and the College of New Jersey. Thus it was that David Rice studied, after a fashion, with Davies, and James Waddell was encouraged to study with John Todd, enabling Waddell to enter directly into the ministry without attending any college at all.[25]

In these cases and that of Henry Patillo, it can be seen that Davies was more than a recruiter for the ministry; he tried to guide and prepare the young men as best he could. Patillo was a native of Ireland who had met Davies at Roanoke in 1751 and accompanied him to Hanover, where the young recruit began his theological studies. Like Waddell, Patillo attended neither a classical academy nor a regular college. He received the bulk of his education under Davies and became a member of the Hanover Presbytery in 1757, serving throughout Virginia and North Carolina.[26] Another of Davies' protégés, the Reverend William Richardson, later became closely associated with his mentor in missionary work among the Indian tribes of North Carolina.[27]

But despite Davies' efforts to alleviate the shortage of ministers within the Presbyterian church, most of his activities were directed toward regular communicants and their many Negro slaves. The people of the Old Dominion had not yet developed the abiding fear of the educated Negro group that was to characterize Virginians a century later; neither had psychotic fears of a slave rebellion emerged as yet as a major factor in the Southern mentality. Unlike many of those who would follow him into Virginia, Davies felt that his duty was to teach the principles of Christianity to all who would listen.

His work among the Negroes of Hanover County was a source

[25] Graham, *Presbyterian Church in Northern Virginia*, p. 122.
[26] Webster, *History of the Presbyterian Church*, pp. 676–677.
[27] Rachal, "Early Minutes of Hanover Presbytery," pp. 165–166.

of pride. "Never have I been so struck with the appearance of an assembly," Davies observed, "as when I have glanced my eye to that part of the meetinghouse where they usually sit . . . with so many black countenances eagerly attentive to every word they hear, and frequently bathed in tears." [28] Within two short years after his settlement in Hanover, the new pastor had brought at least a dozen Negroes into the church; [29] in another two years he claimed to have baptized about forty; [30] and by 1755 he was able to say that about three hundred attended his services regularly and that "a considerable number of them (about an hundred) have been baptized, after a proper time for instruction." [31] Much of the time that Davies set aside for religious instruction of the Negroes was devoted to teaching them how to read the numerous books sent over from England.

Apparently Davies was one of the earliest leaders, if not the first, to concern himself actively with the education of Negro slaves in America. As late as 1843, one writer noted that he had "seen persons, born in Africa, who were baptized by Mr. Davies, and by his care had been taught to read: and have seen in their hands, the books given to them by this eminent preacher." [32] Davies believed that many Negroes exhibited the unity that he believed to be an essential part of religion. "A considerable number of them," he said, "have given credible evidences, not only of their acquaintance with the important doctrines of the Christian religion, but also a deep sense of them upon their minds, attested by a life of strict piety and holiness." [33]

In his desire to teach Negroes to read, thus enabling them to read the basic texts of Christianity, Davies found his own funds insufficient to purchase the necessary tools and was forced to rely on gifts of religious books from his friends in England. "I doubt not

[28] Davies to Crutenden, March 1755, "Old Documents," p. 540.

[29] Davies to Doddridge, Oct. 2, 1750, Perry, *Historical Collections*, I, 396.

[30] Davies to Bellamy, June 27, 1751, Gillies, *Historical Collections*, p. 432.

[31] Davies to Crutenden, March 1755, "Old Documents," p. 540.

[32] "Review of Charles C. Jones, *The Religious Instruction of the Negroes in the United States* (n.p., 1842)," *The Biblical Repertory and Princeton Review*, XV (1843), 26–27. A similar claim was made in "Aliquis," "Biographical Sketch of President Davies," *The Presbyterian Magazine*, III (1853), 571.

[33] Davies to Crutenden, March 1755, "Old Documents," p. 540.

. . . but you will continue your zealous efforts in this Apostolic service," he wrote. "I am in hopes, a divine blessing will attend it. Spelling *Books*, and *Watts's* two Sets of Catechisms, are now most wanted among the Negroes." [34]

The letters in which Davies acknowledged the gifts of books greatly impressed members of the Society both singly and as a group. The first letter so pleased its recipient, Robert Crutenden, that he sent it on to some friends, noting that it was "the first of this kind I ever received, and as far as I know the first attempt of the nature that has ever been made with any considerable success." He proposed that Davies and other American Presbyterians send a group of young Negroes to the College of New Jersey where they could be prepared for missionary work in Africa, an idea that persisted in America but was never brought to fruition.[35] The books by Isaac Watts that Davies requested so often were apparently not on the list of those supplied by his benefactors, but a special collection was made to buy them. This "large donation of books," wrote Davies, "gave me the most agreeable surprise that I ever met with in my whole life." [36]

Chief among the English friends and suppliers of books were the Wesleys, John and Charles, whom Davies had met while on his mission for the college. Although he did not entirely agree with the Wesleys, he was in accord with their "Spirit of Religion" and was willing to accept the help of these two English preachers, who were major figures in the efforts to educate the poor. Several of Davies' letters requesting books were sent on to John Wesley, who thought so highly of the man and his mission that he copied the letters in his journal.[37] Picturing the Negroes as *"African Savages"*

---

[34] Davies to J. F., Feb. 14, 1757, Davies, *Letters From the Rev. Samuel Davies, &c. Shewing the State of Religion in Virginia, Particularly Among the Negroes. Likewise an Extract From a Gentleman in London to his Friend in the Country, Containing Some Observations on the Same* (London, 1757), p. 40.

[35] "Old Documents," pp. 540–541.

[36] Davies to Crutenden, March 2, 1756, *ibid.*, p. 548.

[37] These are Davies to J. F., April 1, 1755, March 2, 1756, J. Wesley, *Journal*, July 27, 1755, IV, 125–126; March 1, 1756, IV, 149–150. Wesley intimates that they were addressed to him. He apparently inserted the letters in his *Journal* on the date they were written rather than on the date they were received. These letters were originally published in Davies, *Letters*, pp. 9–11, 15–21.

who were generally neglected by their masters as not being fit subjects for religion, the letters further describe them as "poor neglected *Negroe Slaves,* who are so far from having money to purchase books, that they themselves are the property of others." "These *poor Africans,*" he concluded the first letter, "are the principal objects of [my] compassion; and, I think, the most proper objects of the SOCIETY's Charity." [38]

Davies' second letter to the Society describes the effects of the shipments of books, which the slaves had viewed "as a *Reward* of their *Industry*" in embracing religion. In it, Davies gives his reasons for educating them:

> I am told, that in almost every house in my congregation, and in sundry other places, they spend every leisure hour in trying to learn, since they expect *Books* as soon as they are capable of using them. Some of them, I doubt not, are excited to it by a sincere desire to know the Will of God, and what they shall do to be saved. Others, I am afraid, are actuated by the mean principles of curiosity, ambition, and vanity. However, be the principle what it will, I cannot but rejoice in the effect; as it renders them more capable of Instruction, in the great concerns of Religion.[39]

These two letters so impressed John Wesley that he made a personal contribution, which brought a warm reply from Davies expressing the essential unity of all aspects of the Great Awakening in both England and America. After noting their differences on minor points, the Presbyterian, speaking in behalf of the approximately one hundred and fifty adult Negroes who had been baptized, thanked the Methodist for his pious charity. Apparently, Charles Wesley also had been instrumental in this gift, for the letter closes with the note, "I desire you to communicate this to your brother, as equally intended for him." [40]

His public and private concern for Negro slaves did not mean that Davies was opposed to the institution of slavery as such. Like

---

[38] Davies to J. F., April 1, 1755, Davies, *Letters,* p. 9.

[39] Davies to J. F., March 2, 1756, *ibid.,* p. 17.

[40] Davies to J. Wesley, Jan. 28, 1757, J. Wesley, *Journal,* Jan. 28, 1757, IV, 194. This appears to have been the only letter written directly to Wesley.

most men in the colony at that time, he expressed whatever doubts he had about the institution simply by refraining from praising it. Furthermore, he himself owned slaves, on one occasion publicly referring to "my own negroes" [41] and on another asking his brother-in-law to inquire about the purchase of a "Negro Wench." [42] He never claimed, however, as did others, that slavery was a fortunate state for the Negroes because it gave them the opportunity to become Christians.

But there were certain aspects of the system of slavery that Davies deplored. Chief among these was the inconsiderate slaveholder who neglected the spiritual welfare of his property, "as though immortality were not a privilege common to them with their masters." [43] It was this evil that Davies determined to correct. He must have had some success with the reluctant owners, for he was able to comment that "Negroes in these parts are freely allowed to attend upon my ministry, and sometimes upon my private instructions, even by such masters as have no religion at all, or are bigots." [44]

There is no evidence to indicate any serious opposition to these early attempts at Negro education. Davies was in fact surprised that his efforts met with so little hostility, a condition that he considered "a very promising presage." The lack of opposition undoubtedly was due to the relatively limited number of Negroes involved and to Davies' approach, which was "not to make them dissenters, but good Christians, and good servants," a position he surely made clear to possible opponents. This spirit of moderation, so characteristic of his work, was also evident in the use he made of the books distributed to Negroes. They were employed, first of all, to teach the slaves how to read, rather than to convert them to his form of religion. He apparently did little actual instruction, "merely distributing the books and allowing the recipients to teach themselves or learn from one another." [45] In February 1757, Da-

---

[41] "On the Defeat of General Braddock Going to Fort Duquesne," *Sermons* (1845), III, 228.

[42] Davies to Holt, Feb. 10, 1749, Rush MSS.

[43] Davies to Crutenden, March 1755, "Old Documents," p. 540.

[44] Davies to Crutenden, March 2, 1756, *ibid.*, p. 548.

[45] *Ibid.*

vies wrote to the Society for Promoting Religious Knowledge among the Poor:

> Every new benefaction of Books sets hundreds upon attempting to read with fresh eagerness. Such of them as had already learned, I furnish with *Bibles, Testaments, Psalm Books, Catechisms,* &c. immediately upon their first application to me. Many come to me, who have not yet learned, but tell me, they are eager to make trial, and want books for that purpose: Among these I have divided the Spelling Books, which were sent to me from private hands, and I bid them come to me when they have learned them, and let me see they can read, and then I shall furnish them with other books.[46]

Of the various books sent by the Society and by the Wesleys, the slaves' favorite was the hymnal of Isaac Watts. Davies declared that Negroes "above all the human species I ever knew, have an ear for music, and a kind of ecstatic delight in Psalmody." [47] This delight in singing also inspired Davies, as he reported following his receipt of a number of books:

> For some time after this, the *poor Slaves,* whenever they could get an hour's leisure from their masters, would hurry away to my house; and received the Charity with all the genuine indications of passionate gratitude, which unpolished nature could give; and which affectation and grimace would mimic in vain. The books were all *very acceptable;* but none more so than the *Psalms* and Hymns, which enabled them to gratify their peculiar taste for *Psalmody.* Sundry of them have lodged all night in my kitchen; and, sometimes, when I have awaked about two or three a-clock in the morning, a torrent of sacred harmony poured into my chamber, and carried my mind away to Heaven. In this seraphic exercise, some of them spend almost the whole night.[48]

The generosity manifested by Englishmen who had no immediate interest in the welfare of slaves in America was often cited by Davies in an attempt to shame some of the slaveowners into imitating them. He met with some success, for he was able to report that a number of slaveowners had taken an interest in education to the

---

[46] Davies to J. F., Feb. 15, 1757, Davies, *Letters,* p. 38.
[47] Davies to Crutenden, March 1755, "Old Documents," p. 540.
[48] Davies to J. F., March 2, 1756, Davies, *Letters,* pp. 15–16.

extent of sending some of their slaves to school.[49] But his real desire was to aid the slaves in their own improvement and, at the same time, make them more loyal to their masters. The latter motive was never directly mentioned to the slaves, but during the French and Indian War, Davies constantly preached on the subject of patriotism, often urging the Negroes to be loyal to Virginia. He described how much worse off the Negroes would be should they fall into the hands of England's enemies because a French victory represented a threat to their religion. His natural prejudices as an English patriot are vividly revealed in the following description of the French, delivered in a sermon to his Negro communicants:

> They are a cruel, barbarous people; and if you should disobey them, they would torment you, or put you to death in the most shocking manner. . . . If you should fall into the hands of the French, you must either give up your religion, or be tied to a stake, and burnt to ashes for it. Then you must pray in Latin, a language that you do not understand one word of, you must not look into your Bible, or try to read; and instead of worshipping God through Jesus Christ, you must worship images and pictures made of stone, wood, or canvas—you must pray to men and women that were once sinners like yourselves; and instead of taking bread and wine in remembrance of Christ, you must believe that the bread is the real body of Christ, a piece of true flesh, and that the wine is changed into the real blood of Christ, by a priest muttering a few words.[50]

Davies was successful in both of these attempts: the Negroes remained loyal during the war, and many of them acquired the rudiments of education and formally entered the Presbyterian church. Letters written throughout his career in Virginia indicate a constant increase in the number of Christian Negroes.[51]

Several other aspects of Davies' attitude toward the institution of slavery are revealed in his sermons. He accused slaveowners who neglected the education of their Negroes of perpetuating one of the many sins for which Virginia was being punished by the war.

---

[49] Davies to J. F., Feb. 15, 1757, *ibid.*, p. 38.

[50] "On the Defeat of General Braddock," *Sermons* (1845), III, 228.

[51] Davies to Doddridge, Oct. 2, 1750, Perry, *Historical Collections*, I, 369; Davies to Bellamy, June 27, 1751, Gillies, *Historical Collections*, p. 432; Davies to Crutenden, March 1755, "Old Documents," p. 540.

"Thousands of poor slaves" were being neglected in a Christian country and were "almost as ignorant of Christianity as when they left the wilds of Africa." [52] One of his sermons was addressed specifically to slaveholders, outlining their duties toward their Negroes. Here he emphasized the necessity of humane treatment, constantly referring to Negroes as members of the master's family toward whom the master had the same obligation as he had toward his children. Children and slaves were mentioned in the same breath as demanding the same attention. [53]

A sermon on family religion was probably the most revealing of Davies' attitude toward the Negroes, for he referred therein to all members of a family—children, slaves, and parents—as having the same religious duties and privileges. [54] Characteristically, Davies was preaching to the entirety of his congregation. In this as in other sermons, he seldom singled out any one class, although he might close his sermons by moving from class to class, finally coming to the Negroes seated in the balcony of the church. Then, he might lift his eyes and say, "Poor negroes! Shall I find one among you that is willing to turn to God?" [55]

Or perhaps he would speak on the slaves' special problems or their misguided emphasis on the outward forms of religion. Many seemed to desire baptism because it was the proper thing to do, rather than because of any sincere religious belief. Davies considered this tendency worse than no baptism at all. "It would be more tolerable . . . if you had still continued wild heathens in the deserts of Africa," he would say. "You will say perhaps, 'other negroes are baptized; and why not I?' But, consider, some other negroes have been in great trouble about their souls; their hearts have been broken for sin; they have accepted of Christ as their only Saviour; and are Christians indeed: and when you are such, it will be time enough for you to be baptized." [56]

[52] "Religion and Patriotism the Constituents of a Good Soldier," *Sermons* (1845), III, 57.
[53] *The Duty of Christians to Propagate Their Religion Among the Heathens, Earnestly Recommended to the Masters of Negroe Slaves in Virginia* (London, 1758), *passim*.
[54] "The Necessity and Excellence of Family Religion," *Sermons* (1845), II, 42–61.
[55] "A Time of Universal Sickness and Mortality Improved," *ibid.*, III, 175–176.
[56] "Christians Solemnly Reminded of their Obligations," *ibid.*, pp. 447, 448.

Davies' work among Negroes, as with the rest of his pastoral duties, was not confined to his own particular congregation, for he took an active interest in similar efforts by his associates. They, in turn, emulated him in striving to educate the slaves in their own congregations and bring them into the Presbyterian church. Davies wrote to his English benefactors that he had given some of their books to John Wright, who was active in this work.[57] Wright told Davies, "I cannot express the pleasing expectations I have that God will do great things in these remote parts by the *diffusive Benevolence* of the Society, and other good Christians." [58] John Todd also received several of the books, for which he thanked the senders directly,[59] as did Robert Henry.[60]

In this respect, then, Davies was true to the tradition of his church in his encouragement of education among the Negroes. That he did not establish a school was no doubt due more to a lack of time than to a lack of inclination. His constant absences from home on preaching trips coupled with his involvement in the affairs of the Hanover Presbytery and the College of New Jersey left precious few hours for his own reading and writing and made it virtually impossible for him to teach these skills to others in an organized manner. It even entered his mind to write a book with the combined purpose of teaching reading and Christianity,[61] but the project was never realized.

An active interest in the conversion and education of non-Christians is also seen in Davies' efforts on behalf of the Indian missions of the Presbyterian church. This work had begun during the 1730's when the Society in Scotland for Propagating Christian Knowledge received a large bequest for the support of three missionaries among the American Indians. The Society made some attempts to carry out this function but was largely unsuccessful until, in 1741, it set up a Commission for Indian Affairs composed of prominent American preachers, several of whom later became energetic members of the

[57] Davies to Crutenden, March 2, 1756, "Old Documents," p. 548. Davies to J. F., Feb. 7, 1757, Davies, *Letters*, p. 31.
[58] Wright to Davies, Sept. 7, 1756, *ibid.*, p. 33.
[59] Todd to Crutenden, Feb. 3, 1757, *ibid.*, pp. 34–37.
[60] Davies to J. F., Feb. 15, 1757, *ibid.*, p. 39.
[61] Davies to Crutenden, March 1755, "Old Documents," p. 540.

Synod of New York. The new body was not slow in carrying out its duties. By the end of 1743, three missionaries were actively working with the Indians in America—Azariah Horton, David Brainerd, and John Sargent.

When the New Light preachers formed the Synod of New York, they also began to play a major role in assisting and converting the Indians. Their congregations were repeatedly asked to supplement the funds sent over from Scotland.[62] Davies shared the hopes of many of his contemporaries when he envisioned the future existence of a large nation of Christian Indians on the frontier. This vision contained a strong element of practicality, for he later observed that "7 or 800 Indians, Chirokees and Creeks" established on the frontier were "undoubtedly the best Barrier against the Incursions of their Brother Savages." [63]

His interest in such matters, however, does not seem to have been active until after his return from England. One of the reasons he gave for undertaking this voyage in the first place was that "the Commissioners for Indian Affairs will be glad of this Opportunity for the Propagation of the Religion of Jesus among the poor Savages; and it is likely we shall succeed in raising Contributions for that End." [64] While soliciting college funds from the General Assembly of the Church of Scotland, Davies also addressed the members concerning the American Indians,[65] as he had been requested to do by the Society for Propagating Christian Knowledge. Shortly thereafter, he talked with a William McCulloch of Glasgow, Governor Dinwiddie's brother-in-law, who spoke of donating £200 toward missionary work among the Indians.[66] Just how much money was raised in Great Britain for this purpose cannot be accurately reckoned; however, Gilbert Tennent reported to the Synod that an anonymous donor had given £200 "towards the support of a pious

---

[62] Briggs, *American Presbyterianism*, pp. 297–303.

[63] Davies to David Cowell, Feb. 20, 1758, MS in the Presbyterian Historical Society.

[64] "Oh! how transporting the Tho't, that these Barbarians may be cultivated by divine Grace in the use of the proper Means, and polished into genuine Disciples of the Blessed Jesus! For this alone, it would be worth our while to spend and be spent." *Diary*, July 2, 1753, p. 6.

[65] *Ibid.*, May 30, 1754, p. 97.

[66] *Ibid.*, July 5, 1754, p. 103. Davies apparently misdated this entry.

and well qualified missionary in preaching the gospel among the Indians in North America, or the supporting of a pious and well qualified Indian youth at the College of New Jersey." Davies, upon his return, was made a member of the synodical committee established to manage the fund [67] and assumed a more active role.

Although his interest in the Indian missions failed to bear fruit initially, he continued to promote the idea. George Whitefield noted in 1756 that Davies was proposing a mission among the Catawba Indians,[68] a mission apparently never undertaken. Two years later, however, a start had been made on a similar project, for Ebenezer Pemberton of New York wrote with a mixture of piety and practicality:

> I rejoice that a Mission is set on foot among the *Cheroquies*, that so suitable a person as Mr. Davies is at the head of it. Nothing can be more Agreeable to our Christian Character than to send the Gospel to the benighted Pagans; Nothing Mor Conducive to our Civil Interests than to bring them to a Subjection to the religion of Jesus. Had more pains been taken this way, I hardly think they would have been permitted by Providence, to be such terrible Scourges to us. I am persuaded that a few hundred pounds sterling per Annum, employed in sending Pious . . . and well Accomplished Missionaries Among them, would have a better Effect to preserve them in our Interest, than many thousands spent in making them yearly Presents.[69]

Pemberton was referring to Davies' successful petition to the Hanover Presbytery, "in the Name of the Society for promoting Christianity among the Indians," to send the Reverend William Richardson to preach among the Indians of the Virginia and North Carolina frontiers.[70] Davies was apparently a member of this group, for Richardson submitted a report to him as "Secretary of the Society for managing the Mission and Schools among the Indians." [71]

Richardson was a native of England who came to America and

---

[67] "Minutes of the Synod of New York," Oct. 7, 1755, *Records*, pp. 265, 269.

[68] Whitefield to Eleazar Wheelock, Nov. 5, 1756, Wheelock MSS, Dartmouth College Library. Davies to J. F., Feb. 15, 1757, Davies, *Letters*, p. 39.

[69] Pemberton to Wheelock, Nov. 18, 1758, Wheelock MSS.

[70] Rachal, "Early Minutes of Hanover Presbytery," Sept. 13, 1758, p. 164.

[71] Richardson, "An Account of my Proceedings since I accepted the Indian Mission in October 2d 1758. to go and exercise my office among the Cherokees or any other Indian Nation that wou'd allow me to preach to them," MS in the New York Public Library.

studied for the ministry in the Davies household while assisting
Davies with some of his duties. Here he seems to have been looked
upon, from the very beginning, as a worker among the Indians.
Davies said of him, "I hope he will be a successful missionary
among the *Indian Savages*, towards whom his heart is set." [72] In
July of 1758, he was ordained by Hanover Presbytery as a missionary,[73] and after going to Williamsburg to obtain letters of introduction from the governor,[74] he set out on his journey.

By the time Richardson returned from his trip to the frontier,
Davies had left the colony to assume the presidency of the College
of New Jersey, but Davies' concern for the work of his colleagues
among the Indians did not wane. His fellow college president,
Eleazar Wheelock, advised Davies that he longed for "an opportunity to converse With you perticularly of our Indian Affair." [75]
Wheelock referred to "the grand Design of Spreading the Salvation of the Redeeming Knowledge among the dispersed Pagans of
our American Wilderness," which both he and Davies were further-
ing by educating young men for that purpose.[76] This was the same
"grand Design" Davies had worked for in his every capacity,
whether as ordinary preacher to the Hanover dissenters, educator
of Negro slaves, college president, or visitor to England.

[72] Davies to J. F., Feb. 15, 1757, Davies, *Letters*, p. 39.
[73] Webster, *History of the Presbyterian Church*, p. 678.
[74] "An Account," Richardson MS.
[75] Wheelock to Davies, Nov. 12, 1759, Wheelock MSS.
[76] Wheelock to Davies, Nov. 16, 1759, *ibid.*

VII

Toward a Free Exercise of Religion

E VEN THE OPPONENTS of Samuel Davies paid tribute to the
vigor and legal acumen with which he pursued his fight for
religious toleration in Virginia, one of them reportedly observing,
"There goes a capital lawyer spoiled." Throughout his residence at
Hanover, and even while he was in Great Britain from mid-1753 to
mid-1755, this leader of New Light Presbyterianism struggled
continually to alleviate the religious and political restrictions placed
upon dissenters for the protection of the government-supported
Church of England. Although Davies did not fight for religious
freedom in the modern sense of the word—that is, for the separation of church and state—he did persuasively advocate a condition
of religious toleration, under which the Church of England, even
though still favored by the government, would permit Presbyterians and other dissenters to practice their own beliefs unmolested.
Separation was not to be achieved until a full decade after Davies
had left the colony, but his efforts surely provided a more fertile
soil for the statesmen of the Revolutionary period who did accom-
plish this goal.[1]

---

[1] [Rice], "Memoir," p. 118. Some nineteenth-century writers felt that Davies deserved
most of the credit for religious freedom in Virginia and the rest of the South. For examples,
see *ibid.*, p. 363, and Foote, I, 304–305. Although these claims are exaggerated, it has been

The long struggle began in 1747 at the time of Davies' first preaching visit to Virginia, even before he settled there permanently. This was the occasion on which he appeared before the governor in Williamsburg for the first time and was granted official licenses to preach in four meetinghouses.[2] In the following year, when he came to settle permanently in Hanover, he again obtained licenses for himself, but this time met his first defeat when his request for licenses for his friend John Rodgers was denied by the governor.[3] Rodgers, like two of his predecessors, Samuel Finley and Gilbert Tennent, had made the mistake of preaching before requesting a license—a mistake that Davies was careful to avoid.

For a while it seemed that the Anglican-controlled government would completely thwart the Hanover clergyman's attempts. When he sought licenses for additional meetinghouses, the Council was hesitant, even though he had the support of the governor.[4] A second effort to bring Rodgers into the colony brought a second refusal from the Council and a caustic comment from one of the members: "We have Mr. Rodgers out, and we are determined to keep him out." [5] This body even gave serious consideration to reducing the number of pulpits from which Davies could speak. It ignored his application for a permit to preach in Cumberland County and actually rescinded a license granted by the New Kent County Court.[6]

Several legal problems faced Davies, but the one that concerned him most involved a basic interpretation of the rights of dissenters under the English Toleration Act of 1689. Did it apply in the colony or not? He was especially interested in those provisions requiring the licensing of dissenting preachers and the registration of

---

noted that Patrick Henry often attended Davies' services as a youth, and it is reasonable to conclude that Thomas Jefferson was also at least well aware of the activities and pronouncements of his fellow Virginian. The more moderate view is presented in an earlier version of this chapter, "Samuel Davies and the Struggle for Religious Toleration in Colonial Virginia," *The Historian*, XXXVIII (1965), 48–71.

[2] Davies to Bellamy, June 27, 1757, Gillies, *Historical Collections*, p. 431.
[3] Foote, I, 141, 160–166.
[4] *Ibid.*, p. 170.
[5] Miller, *Memoirs*, p. 46.
[6] Foote, I, 170–171.

meetinghouses, and the extent of their application in Virginia. Davies' understanding of the situation was set forth in a statement made before the Council in 1750, when he sought licenses for three additional meetinghouses. Shrewdly arguing the dissenters' cause, Davies took the position that if this 1689 law, which Attorney General Peyton Randolph denied had any force in Virginia, did not apply in the colony then neither did the earlier Act of Uniformity; thus, all non-Anglicans were free to worship where and as they pleased without governmental interference.[7]

On this same occasion the clergyman followed the usual practice of presenting his case without aid of counsel. "A general *titter*" reportedly greeted his first attempt to speak. But his friend and traveling companion, John Morton, reported that soon "marks of surprise were manifest on every countenance [and] in a short time the lawyers began to whisper, 'The attorney-general has met with his match today.'" Davies spoke for the dissenters "with a force and ingenuity and knowledge of law perfectly astonishing, and completely victorious," giving rise to the remark by a member of the bar that he would make a "capital lawyer." Governor William Gooch and Commissary James Blair were suddenly observed to be "marked in their civilities."[8]

Davies emerged from this encounter as a respected spokesman for his cause and with a major victory. The application of the Toleration Act would never again be seriously questioned in Virginia. The crux of the matter thereafter was "the intent and meaning of this act" as Davies wrote two years after his first encounter with Randolph. The attorney general was now of the opinion that even though the law of 1689 was applicable, a dissenting preacher was not permitted to hold innumerable licenses to preach wherever he pleased simply because he had taken a number of formal oaths.

[7] [Rice], "Memoir," p. 118. Rice's somewhat biased account of this incident may not be accurate in every detail, but his overall presentation is probably correct. He reportedly heard the story from John Morton, who accompanied Davies to Williamsburg on this occasion.

[8] *Ibid.* Davies attended court days, or "public times," in Williamsburg whenever possible, lodging with his brother-in-law, John Holt. See Davies to Holt, Feb. 10, 1749; March 1750; Aug. 13, 1751; Sept. 12, 1751, Rush MSS.

There should be but one pulpit for each nonconforming minister as there was technically but one for each Anglican priest.[9] If so, just limits would be placed on the dissenters and thereby would curtail their attempts to win people away from the Church of England.[10] This attitude was expressed so firmly in Randolph's continued opposition to Presbyterian requests for new licenses that Davies later commented on his "Mortifications in the General Court [Council] in Virginia." [11]

In the mind of the New Light leader, the question was "whether a dissenting congregation, that is very much dispersed, and cannot meet at one place, may claim a right . . . to have a plurality of places licensed for the convenience of the sundry parts of the congregation?" He also asked whether the law permitted a nonconforming preacher "to divide his labours among two congregations at sundry meeting-houses when . . . each congregation cannot be furnished with one?" [12] Of course, he answered such rhetorical questions in the affirmative. He based his opinions on an act of the Virginia legislature of 1699 that specifically recognized the application of the English law in the colony, exempted all qualified Protestant dissenters from the penalties for nonattendance at Anglican services, and permitted them to hold meetings of their own.[13] If carried to their logical conclusion, the statements made by Davies would have permitted a qualified dissenting preacher to obtain licenses for any number of pulpits anywhere in the colony. Randolph, of course, believed that a dissenter was permitted the use of but one meetinghouse.

Official opposition was not Davies' only concern; he was faced with criticism from other quarters. The Virginia publication of John Caldwell's *Impartial Trial* in 1748, berating the entire New

[9] Davies to Benjamin Avery, May 21, 1752, Foote, I, 209. Randolph apparently ignored the existence of chapels of ease used by many Virginia Anglican clergymen to solve some of the problems caused by widely separated parish churches.
[10] Davies to Doddridge, Oct. 2, 1750, Perry, *Historical Collections*, I, 368.
[11] *Diary*, Jan. 22, 1754, p. 59.
[12] Davies to Avery, May 21, 1752, Foote, I, 209.
[13] *Statutes at Large, Being a Collection of All the Laws of Virginia From the First Session of Legislature in the Year 1619,* ed. William Waller Hening (13 vols., Philadelphia and Richmond, 1809–1823), III, 171.

Light movement for its excesses, was but one of many attacks of this type that afflicted Davies and prompted him to remark: "Tho' the pulpits around me, I am told, ring with exclamatory harangues, accusations, arguments, railings, warnings, etc, etc, etc., against New-Lights, Methodists, Enthusiasts, Deceivers, Itinerants, Pretenders, etc, etc, etc., yet I never design to prostitute mine to such mean purpose." He also complained of "Satires, etc," which were published throughout Virginia in attempts "to alarm the world of these dangerous animals" who were upsetting the religious composition of the colony.[14] These "satires" that he found so irritating were illustrative of the alarm spreading among the established clergy of the colony during the early 1750's. As concern increased, a constant stream of appeals and petitions flowed from groups of Anglicans to the House of Burgesses, the Anglican Commissary, and the Governor—and from the Commissary to his superior, the Bishop of London.

Although he did not use his pulpit to refute the Virginia Anglican's interpretation of the Toleration Act, Davies presented his arguments in a variety of ways. He wrote frequent letters to prominent dissenters in England, as well as to the Bishop of London; he made regular appearances in Williamsburg before the colonial authorities; he appealed to the Synod of New York for help in the form of petitions to England and for new ministers; and he undertook a dangerous ocean crossing in order to present his case in person.

Thus, both sides looked to Great Britain for direction; the Anglicans appealed to their customary leader, the Bishop of London, the Presbyterians to prominent English dissenters. With general acceptance of the extension of the Toleration Act of 1689 to Virginia, the disputants sought to solve the problem of its interpretation by observing the practice in England. The Bishop of London, when pressed for an opinion, declared that dissenters had the legal right to be issued "what we call a license of the place: for any meetinghouse they desired without specifying a particular preacher. Furthermore, any qualified nonconforming minister had "a right

---

[14] Davies, *Impartial Trial*, pp. 26–27.

indifferently to preach in any licensed place whatsoever, and every licensed place is open to every qualified minister," but only on an occasional basis. No English preacher was allowed to have more than one permanent congregation.[15]

Davies' mistake was in seeking more than one meetinghouse for his own use, thereby establishing a dangerous precedent. Benjamin Avery, one of his English correspondents, suggested: "When you certify places as designed for religious worship, you are not obliged to say who is to officiate in that place." By giving his name, Davies was providing those who refused to issue the licenses an excuse for their actions. Avery referred to the Occasional Conformity Act passed by Parliament in 1711 allowing dissenters to preach occasionally in pulpits other than their own. "The design of this proviso," he wrote, "was not either to prevent the multiplying our places for worship, or to oblige us to ascertain and specify the persons who are intended to officiate in these places." [16]

The same act was cited by the Bishop of London when he spoke specifically about the situation in Virginia. Bishop Sherlock determined that Randolph was "quite in the right, for the Act of Toleration confines the preachers to a particular place, . . . and so the practice here has been." In England, however, nonconformists had attacked the hardships stemming from a shortage of dissenting clergymen by obtaining passage of a supplementary act in 1711 that allowed "any dissenting minister to preach occasionally in any other county but that where he was licensed." The operative word in this opinion was "occasionally," and the bishop next applied himself to the matter of Samuel Davies. "I observe in one of the licenses," he wrote, that Davies "is permitted to assemble, etc., at several meeting-houses to be erected. . . . Now, the Act of Toleration requires that the places of meeting shall be certified and registered, but how houses that are not in being can be certified and registered, I can't understand." This, however, was only a prelude to his interpretation of the law as it related specifically to Davies'

---

[15] The Bishop of London to Doddridge, Dec. 25, 1750, quoted in Doddridge to Davies, 1751, Foote, I, 174–175.
[16] Avery to Davies (c. 1752), *ibid.*, p. 213.

complaints. He declared that "the Act of Toleration was intended to permit the Dissenters to worship in their own way, and to exempt them from penalties, but it never was intended to permit them to set up itinerant preachers, to gather congregations where there was none before." According to the original law, preachers were to minister in the county of their residence, "and how Davies can be said to live in five different counties, they who granted the licenses must explain." [17]

In Virginia, the government had not yet adopted the supplement to the Toleration Act. Furthermore, the actual practice in England was even more liberal than the bishop indicated. One of the leading dissenting ministers there, the Reverend Philip Doddridge, who presumably was governed by the act and thus familiar with its execution, sought to clarify the bishop's ignorance. Doddridge informed Sherlock that "I have had many opportunities of knowing the practice among us, which seems so far as I can judge very agreeable to the tenour of that act." In British practice, as the bishop had observed, "the License of the place" made no mention of being granted to any particular preacher. "On the other hand," Doddridge insisted, and here he contradicted Bishop Sherlock, "our preachers are licensed . . . without the least mention of their being designed for any one place more than another." The only cause for governmental action would be the case of a licensed clergyman preaching in an unlicensed meetinghouse or an unlicensed preacher speaking from a licensed pulpit.[18]

Bishop Sherlock, writing from London, had in mind the ideal of one preacher for each pulpit, which probably was the case within his own diocese; Doddridge, writing from Northampton, was apparently better acquainted with the situation outside of London. Presumably, conditions in England would apply to dissenters in Virginia, except that the colony had not adopted the supplementary act of 1711. The absence of adoption gave Commissary Dawson

[17] The Bishop of London to Doddridge, Dec. 25, 1750, quoted in Doddridge to Davies, 1751, *ibid.*, p. 177.

[18] Doddridge to the Bishop of London, May 14, 1751, Perry, *Historical Collections*, I, 374–375.

and other Anglican elements in the Virginia government the excuse they needed to deny Davies' requests for additional licenses.[19]

But Davies continued to use the supplementary act to justify his extended preaching. He now claimed that the colony's lack of action had no bearing on the case. The law was applicable, he noted illogically, because it was necessary. Thus he felt himself "legally qualified" to preach in any licensed meetinghouse in the colony. After quoting Sherlock's own words concerning the reasons for the law, he observed to the bishop that "since the reason for the law is at least as strong here as in England, and consequently it extends hither, my conduct is sufficiently justified by it." According to Davies, the real problem was still:

> Whether legally qualified protestant dissenters, who are dispersed through sundry counties, and cannot meet at one place, and by reason of the scarcity of ministers cannot obtain but one among them, may not legally share in the labours of that one, and have so many houses licensed for him to officiate in as that all of them may alternately attend on public worship! And were the question considered in this view, I confidently presume your Lordship would determine it in my favour, and no longer look upon me as an itinerant preacher, intent on making converts to a party.[20]

British practice as described by Doddridge seems to have exerted some moderating influence on the restrictive measures taken by the colonial government. Any diminution in the restrictions probably occurred because both George II and Bishop Sherlock were sympathetic to the dissenting cause and opposed those who would impose civil or religious restrictions on all nonconformists.[21] Further pressure was brought to bear on the Virginia government during the

---

[19] Eckenrode, *Separation of Church and State*, p. 33. "Undoubtedly dissenting ministers were granted licenses wherever desired in England, but this right was secured by an act supplementing the Toleration Act, that of 10th Queen Anne [1711]. This act had not been adopted by the Virginia Assembly and the narrower limits of the Toleration Act legally applied." *Ibid.* This statement might possibly be disputed because (1) Davies had precedent on his side since he already had more than one license and (2) the supplementary act may have legally applied in the colony since it was an amendment to a law which did.

[20] Davies to the Bishop of London, Jan. 10, 1752, Foote, I, 188–189.

[21] Doddridge to Davies, 1751, *ibid.*, p. 176.

years 1750 and 1751 by the rulers of England's commercial empire, the Lords of Trade, who asked the Council of Virginia to encourage "a free Exercise of Religion" as a means of preserving and
improving imperial trade. The Lords of Trade also advised Davies
and the dissenters not to irritate the Anglican clergy if they wished
to insure their rights and privileges.[22]

Perhaps this attitude of the Lords of Trade was largely responsible for the vacillating position of Anglican Commissary Dawson.
Much of the time he had acted in a friendly manner. At least once
he had spoken in Davies' behalf at a meeting of the Council,[23] and
the Presbyterian leader often spoke of Dawson "with sincere ven-
eration." [24] But periodically Dawson seemed to be trying to impress
the English ecclesiastical authorities with the harshness of his attitude toward Davies, as on one occasion when he brought up the
petty complaint of "his holding forth on working days to great
numbers of poor people who generally are his only followers."
Dawson found this "inconsistent with the religion of labour
whereby they are obliged to maintain themselves and their families" and contended that such a neglect of work might eventually
contribute to economic weaknesses in the colony.[25]

It is inconceivable that this was the Commissary's major reason
for complaint; and when Davies was informed of the letter, reportedly by Thomas Lee, president of the Council,[26] he was naturally concerned. Davies questioned the validity of the charge, which

---

[22] "With regard to the affair of Mr. Davies the Presbyterian, as Toleration and a free
Exercise of Religion is so valuable a branch of true liberty, and so essential to the enriching
and improving of a Trading Nation, it should ever be held sacred in His Majesty's Colonies: we must therefore earnestly recommend it to your care, that nothing be done which can
in the least affect that great point; at the same time you will do well to admonish Mr.
Davies to make proper use of that indulgence which our Laws so wisely grant to those who
differ from the Established Church, and to be cautious not to afford any just complaint to
the Clergy of the Church of England, or to the people in General." Lords of Trade to the
President of the Virginia Council, Sept. 1, 1750, quoted in William Dawson to the Bishop
of London, Aug. 16, 1751, Perry, *Historical Collections*, I, 379–380.
[23] Foote, I, 166.
[24] Davies to the Bishop of London, Jan. 10, 1752, *ibid.*, p. 197.
[25] William Dawson to the Bishop of London, July 27, 1750, Perry, *Historical Collections*, I, 366.
[26] Foote, I, 173.

he felt was expressed in contemptuous terms, and seemed unable to understand the "imaginary danger" [27] perceived by Dawson. He asked Doddridge in London to use every effort to counteract such a deceitful representation of the dissenters. At the same time he reported a major reversal at the hands of the government, which had rejected his application for an eighth meetinghouse.[28]

Thus began a new chain of correspondence involving Davies, the English dissenters, and Bishop Sherlock, in which were set forth the rights of dissenting preachers in England. Doddridge's reply to one of Davies' letters offered little consolation. It included the bishop's opinion that a dissenting minister was to be confined to one pulpit in his home county, as well as several loose and reckless comments on the general religious situation in Virginia. Sherlock proved himself ignorant of both American geography and religion when he rejected the frequent charges of unfitness among Anglican clergymen in the colonies. Supervision of the Anglican clergy was lacking, he claimed, because there was no resident bishop in the colonies. There was no American episcopate because the New England Congregational clergy were violently opposed to such an institution, and they had sent Davies "three hundred miles from home" to spread anti-episcopal propaganda throughout Virginia.[29] This charge was not only irrelevant but also entirely false. Davies, in keeping with his abhorrence of religious factionalism and his desire to see improvement in all denominations, actually favored the establishment of a bishopric in America, much to the dismay of some of his English friends: "I was not able to discover what injury the settlement of a bishop in Virginia or Maryland, where the Church of England is established, would be to the few dissenters in them; and I was not without hope it might tend to purge out the corrupt leaven from the established church, and restrain the clergy from the extravagancies, who now behave as they please, and promise

[27] Davies to the Bishop of London, Jan. 10, 1752, *ibid.*, p. 197.
[28] Davies to Doddridge, Oct. 2, 1750, Perry, *Historical Collections*, I, 370–371.
[29] The Bishop of London to Doddridge, May 11, 1751, quoted in Doddridge to Davies, 1751, Foote, I, 177, 180.

themselves impunity, as there is none to censure or depose them on this side the Atlantic." [30]

Now, in mid-summer of 1751, Davies became fully aware of the accusations brought against the dissenters and of his own status in the mind of the bishop. To rebut these charges, he composed a mammoth letter to Bishop Sherlock and sent it to Doddridge to be delivered at his discretion.

He began by describing the benefits that the settlement of dissenters had brought to the colony and claimed that very few would have come had they realized that their modes of worship would be proscribed by the government. Especially was this true on the frontier, where a severe shortage of ministers existed for those congregations serving as a buffer between the settled areas and the Indian lands. He answered the charge of itineracy by delving into the history of Virginia Presbyterianism and describing conditions as they existed prior to his arrival in Hanover. Itineracy, as Davies saw it, meant going from place to place in a deliberate attempt to win converts, something which he did not do. He traveled from place to place to speak to congregations already converted without having the "least instrumentality in the first gathering of a dissenting Church in these parts." Furthermore, he denied that his inability to live in five different counties prevented his effective preaching there after the manner of local Anglican priests who were in the habit of using "chapels of ease" to shorten the travels of their parishioners.

To the ridiculous allegation that he had come several hundred miles merely to oppose bishops and cause schism, he gave a flat denial. After noting his support of an American episcopate, Davies admitted that the ranks of the Presbyterians had grown during the few years of his residence in the colony but challenged the bishop to prove "whether the laws of England forbid men to change their opinions. . . . And whether the Act of Toleration was intended to tolerate such only as were dissenters by birth?" On the charge of

---

[30] Davies to Avery, n.d., "Davies's State of Religion Among the Protestant Dissenters in Virginia," *The Biblical Repertory and Princeton Review*, XII (1840), 197n.

schism, he defied the world to confute his claim "that in all the sermons I have preached in Virginia, I have not wasted one minute in exclaiming against the peculiarities of the established Church. . . . I have matters of infinitely greater importance to exert my zeal, and spend my time and strength upon . . . . 'tis the conversion and salvation of men I aim to promote; and genuine Christianity, under whatever form it appears, never fails to charm my heart."

The final paragraph of the letter was a reply to the bishop's linking of Davies to the Methodist party, a group with which Davies had made no extensive contact as yet. His reply is interesting both for its application to the situation at hand and as an expression of his opinion of certain contemporaries:

> Your Lordship huddles me promiscuously with the Methodists, as though I were of their party. I am not ashamed to own that I look upon Mr. Whitefield as a zealous and successful minister of Christ; and as such to countenance him. I love him, and I love your Lordship, (the profession, I hope, will not be offensive) because I hope you are both good men: and if my affection to him proves me one of his party, I hope your lordship will conclude me one of your own too: yet I am far from approving sundry steps in Mr. Whitefield's first public conduct; and I am glad to find by some of his late writings that he does not approve of them himself. The eruptions of his first zeal were, in many instances irregular; his regulating his conduct so much by impulses, etc., was enthusiastic, and his freedoms in publishing his experience to the world, in his journals were, in my opinion, very imprudent. As to the rest of the Methodists, I know but little of them; and, therefore, must suspend my judgement concerning them.[31]

At the time, this letter was seen as evidence of "the honesty and simplicity of Davies' heart rather than his worldly wisdom"[32] and apparently was never given to the bishop. Doddridge showed it to several of his colleagues who made the final decision for its suppression. Benjamin Avery wrote Davies of this decision, attributing it to the length of the letter. "In cases which these great men, whether

---

[31] Davies to the Bishop of London, Jan. 10, 1752, Foote, I, 180–212. The letter is twenty-six printed pages in length, to which was added a six-page postscript.

[32] Foote, I, 206.

in church or state, have most at heart, I have repeatedly seen," he wrote, "that they cannot bear long and minute representations." It was also felt that the author had been imprudent in his support of an American episcopate.[33] The suppression of the letter was perhaps unfortunate, for Davies' forthrightness on the matter of the extension of episcopal control might well have appealed to Sherlock who, with his superior the Archbishop of Canterbury, had campaigned strenuously for a colonial bishopric.[34] Such opinions might have served to counteract some of Dawson's charges, and it is difficult to see how the letter could have harmed the dissenting cause in Virginia. By not going directly to the Bishop of London, the Presbyterians left themselves only the choice of either petitioning a higher authority—the king—or deliberately evading the law. Eventually, they chose the latter course.

Davies apparently was privy to some of the correspondence passing between Commissary Dawson and the Bishop of London, for the Commissary noted his surprise at discovering that Davies was familiar with these letters. Davies told the Commissary of his own long letter to Sherlock,[35] and it was perhaps in part because of this information that Dawson now took a more reasonable attitude in the struggle with the dissenters.

Later writers,[36] in commenting unfavorably on the Anglicans in the colonial Virginia government, are fond of quoting Edmund Burke's stricture that "almost all the intelligent men in the colony . . . appear in the class of persecutors." [37] No doubt mid-century

---

[33] Avery to Davies, 1752, *ibid.*, pp. 211–214.

[34] See Bishop Sherlock's correspondence with the Duke of Newcastle in Arthur Lyon Cross, *The Anglican Episcopate and the American Colonies* (Cambridge, Mass., 1902), pp. 320–321. Also see *A Letter to the Right Honourable Horatio Walpole, Esq; Written Jan. 9, 1750–1751, by the Right Reverend Thomas Secker, LL.D. Lord Bishop of Oxford: Concerning Bishops in America* (London, 1769). Secker was Archbishop of Canterbury at this time. His was but one of a large number of English and American pamphlets on this question, many of which are discussed in Pilcher, "The Pamphlet War on the Proposed Virginia Anglican Episcopate, 1767–1775," *Historical Magazine of the Protestant Episcopal Church*, XXX (1961), 266–279.

[35] Dawson to the Bishop of London, Feb. 10, 1752, Perry, *Historical Collections*, I, 383.

[36] Foote, I, 166.

[37] Edmund Burke, *Works* (8 vols., London, 1803), III, 171.

Great Britain enjoyed a greater degree of religious toleration than did the Old Dominion, and there were those who would have made harassment of dissenters more severe than it was. The basic inclination of the leaders of the colony, regardless of their personal religious proclivities, was to support the Church of England in its opposition to dissent. But those in power did not necessarily fit Burke's stereotype, and Davies found the colonial authorities generally fair-minded in their actions, even though they were often influenced by the "shocking reports" of "officious malignants." [38]

Compared to the hostile Anglican clergy, the colonial government was marked in its tolerance and reluctant to accept all of the accusations against Davies at face value. One of these "shocking reports" came before Dawson in 1751. A petition from five priests of the Church of England requested "that all Novel notions, and perplexing uncertain Doctrines" might be "suitably check'd and discouraged," especially when they were spread by people like Davies, who called themelves Presbyterians though they had "no just claim to that character; as the Ringleaders of the Party were . . . excluded [from] the Presbyterian Synod of Philadelphia." [39] The authorities took no action and the Commissary merely sent the petition on to the Bishop of London without comment. The petitioners had specifically challenged Davies' contention that he could be licensed into more than a single meetinghouse. Apparently the petition was presented to the Council, for Dawson reported that no action was taken by that body because of the general opinion that to do so would be a violation of the Toleration Act, which permitted Davies to preach from more than one pulpit in his home county. [40]

After the Council refused to act on the petition from the five Anglican clergymen in the autumn of 1751, Davies began to see some improvement in the situation of the dissenters. In 1752, John Todd was licensed as his assistant, and the government considered

[38] Davies to Bellamy, June 27, 1751, Gillies, *Historical Collections*, p. 431.
[39] D. Mossom, Patrick Henry, John Brunskill, John Robertson, and Robert Barrett to the House of Burgesses, 1751, Perry, *Historical Collections*, I, 381–383.
[40] Dawson to the Bishop of London, Aug. 16, 1751, *ibid.*, pp. 379–381.

the adoption of the supplement to the Toleration Act.[41] Todd took over four of the Presbyterian meetinghouses outside of Hanover County and, as a result, charges of itineracy were heard less frequently.[42] It came to be recognized that a dissenting preacher had at least a minimal right to preach anywhere in his home county.[43]

Davies now centered his struggle on his right to cross county boundaries. This was the significance of Dawson's query when he asked the bishop: "should the clause in the 10th Queen Anne [the supplementary act of 1711] be inserted impowering a teacher to officiate in any Congregation altho' it be not in the County where he was qualified?"[44] Davies was now seeking a "license of the place" so that he could occasionally preach outside of Hanover County.

Governor Robert Dinwiddie had earlier denied such a minimal right when he told Davies that the Virginia government would interpret the Toleration Act in a liberal manner if only he would act circumspectly and generally confine his preaching to Hanover County.[45] Commissary Dawson reiterated the governor's limitations. When he requested the bishop's opinion on the adoption of the act of 1711, he said he believed it necessary to insert a proviso restricting a dissenting minister to his own county, noting that "otherwise as I apprehend, one teacher may and would ramble all over a Country." Dawson further declared that "the people, who hear a Teacher but once in 7, 8, or 10 weeks are in a greater danger of becoming Heathens, than they who hear a minister once a week, a forthnight or a Month."[46]

So matters stood when, in the spring of 1752, Davies sought a license for a new place of worship. Once again the application was rejected by the Council. He immediately wrote to his English correspondents asking for advice in the matter, stating that all he de-

---

[41] Dawson to the Bishop of London, 1752, *ibid.*, p. 384.
[42] Davies to Avery, May 21, 1752, Foote, I, 208.
[43] Dawson to the Bishop of London, 1752, Perry, *Historical Collections*, I, 384. Dinwiddie to the Bishop of London, June 5, 1752, *ibid.*, p. 396.
[44] Dawson to the Bishop of London, 1752, *ibid.*, p. 384.
[45] Dinwiddie to the Bishop of London, June 5, 1752, *ibid.*, p. 396.
[46] Dawson to the Bishop of London, 1752, *ibid.*, pp. 384–385.

sired was a system whereby "ten or fifteen families of Protestant dissenters" could establish a meetinghouse if they were too far from an existing place of worship. Davies suggested that some kind of appeal be made to the Bishop of London or, preferably, to the king.[47] Avery implied that any appeal in England would probably be unwise and unsuccessful and should not be attempted save as a last resort. He did, however, supply Davies with a recent opinion of Sir Dudley Ryder, the British attorney general, who disagreed with the Virginia Council. Ryder commented that the dissenters should receive licenses for any number of pulpits merely by asking for them.[48]

The following June, prior to his departure for Great Britain, Davies renewed his latest application and, despite his presentation of Ryder's opinion, was again refused. It is possible that his appearance before the Council at this time was simply a deliberate attempt to test the strength of the attorney general's opinion in order that he would have something definite to report to his English supporters. Perhaps such a strategy was alluded to by Thomas Dawson, brother of the Commissary, when he wrote to the Bishop of London: "Mr. Davies, I am informed, intends to go to England this Summer but with what design I know not. I thought it proper to give your Lordship notice of it." [49]

Thus ended the first phase of Samuel Davies' struggle for toleration with the Anglican government of Virginia. For the next two years the battle would be fought in Great Britain. When he returned to Hanover County in mid-1755, conditions would be markedly changed. The Old Dominion would be in the midst of a war for control of North America, and the future of the Virginia dissenters would depend upon their response to this crisis—a response led by Davies in the four years after his return.

[47] Davies to Avery, March 21, 1752, Foote, I, 210.
[48] Avery to Davies, 1752, *ibid.*, pp. 211–214.
[49] Thomas Dawson to the Bishop of London, July 23, 1753, Perry, *Historical Collections*, I, 407.

VIII

The Path of Duty: Great Britain

CHRISTMAS DAY 1753 marked the beginning of a new awareness and appreciation by the British public of the New Light movement in the American colonies. This was the date on which Samuel Davies and his venerable companion Gilbert Tennent arrived in London following lengthy preparation and a dangerous ocean crossing of more than four weeks' duration to raise funds for the fledgling College of New Jersey. During the almost fourteen months of their stay in Great Britain, traveling and preaching widely, the young Hanover minister and his older associate achieved remarkable success. Not only did they raise enough funds to insure the future of the college, but Davies himself added substantially to the lustre of his growing reputation as a pulpit orator and spokesman for the New Light cause. Subsequent support for virtually all of Davies' educational and humanitarian efforts was to reflect the success of this British mission.

The Virginia dissenter also continued his fight for religious toleration while in England, but his primary efforts were for the burgeoning Presbyterian college. Like all leaders in the New Light movement, Davies recognized the need for a well-educated ministry and preferred that this education be provided by an institution acceptable to all segments of secular and religious society. Such an institution he found in the College of New Jersey, which had been established by a group of men under the leadership of the preachers excluded from the Philadelphia Synod as well as numerous interested laymen and public officials, both Presbyterian and non-Presbyterian.

The log college at Neshaminy Creek had ceased to be a major producer of clergymen for the church because of the age of its founder and the varied activities of his sons, which prevented them from taking an active part in its operation. By then, also, the influx of ministers from Ireland and Scotland, which had supplied both segments of the church, had slowed considerably.[1]

The founders of the college were themselves the recipients of formal academic training, being alumni of either Yale College (Aaron Burr, Ebenezer Pemberton, and Jonathan Dickinson) or one of the classical academies (Samuel Blair and the Tennents). At the time of their break with the Philadelphia Synod, they found their desire for an educated ministry thwarted in a number of ways. In addition, the New England schools appeared to lack the necessary encouragement of personal piety. Thus, the dissident group had determined to establish an institution of their own equipped to emphasize both experimental religion and classical knowledge.[2]

Their plans, several years in the making, came to fruition in the autumn of 1746 when John Hamilton, the acting governor of New Jersey, chartered an institution under the control of seven trustees. In May of the following year, the college officially commenced operation at Elizabeth (then Elizabethtown), New Jersey, in the home of its first president, the Reverend Jonathan Dickinson. Upon the death of President Dickinson, the school was moved to Newark under the presidency of the Reverend Aaron Burr. The first commencement was held in November 1748.

It was about at the time of this first commencement that the original charter no longer seemed sufficient to fulfill the purposes of the founders. The recently arrived governor of New Jersey, Jonathan Belcher, was prevailed upon to recharter the college,

---

[1] Graham, *Presbyterian Church in Northern Virginia*, p. 23.

[2] For a more detailed description of the founding of the college, see Wertenbaker, *Princeton*, ch. 1.

which he did in 1748. Significantly, this second document provided for an equal number of clerical and lay trustees, and it permitted members of differing religious bodies to become members of the governing board.

Four years later, in 1752, the Synod decided to erect a permanent structure midway between the homes of the competing Synods. The future location was known as Prince-Town, on the dividing line between the provinces of East and West Jersey.[3] The decision to relocate the college in permanent quarters forced the New Lights to face the universal problem of all educators—the need for money —and the actual move from Newark was not accomplished until 1756. Prior to this decision, the college had received the proceeds from periodic collections requested by the Synod of New York, but the arrangement proved inadequate as a regular source of funds,[4] there being only £300 in the treasury in 1753.[5] In view of this situation the Synod had determined as early as 1751 to appoint an emissary "to make a voyage to Europe to solicit benefactions for the said college." A committee sent to New York by the Synod was unsuccessful in arranging for such an emissary, however,[6] and the matter was held in abeyance until the next meeting of the body, in October 1752. At that time "application was made to the Synod in behalf of the trustees of the College of New Jersey, requesting the Synod to appoint two of their members, viz. Messrs. Gilbert Tennent, and Samuel Davies, to take a voyage to Europe on the important affairs of said college." To this request the Synod gave its unanimous endorsement.[7]

It is unclear just why Davies was chosen to undertake this mission. The Board of Trustees in 1751 had specifically recommended that the emissary be the Reverend Ebenezer Pemberton of New

---

[3] The first charter, which was noted in the *Pennsylvania Gazette,* Aug. 13, 1757, is no longer extant; *The University Catalogue; 1939–1940* (Princeton, 1939), pp. xvii–xix. However, a composite charter is printed in Wertenbaker, *Princeton,* pp. 396–404. The location of the college is significant.

[4] "Minutes of the Synod of New York," Sept. 29, 1751, *Records,* p. 247.

[5] *Diary,* July 2, 1753, p. 2. The *Diary* is the chief source of information for this chapter.

[6] "Minutes of the Synod of New York," Sept. 27, 1751, *Records,* p. 246.

[7] *Ibid.,* Oct. 2, 1752, p. 251.

York.[8] Davies had previously taken little part in the major affairs of either his Synod or the college, being concerned primarily with his own problems in Virginia. He had been a member of the committee that tried to recruit Pemberton as the emissary,[9] however, and his work among the dissenters of his colony had been favorably noted by the committee in a report to its supporters in England—a report that contained, among other things, "a certificate of Mr. Davies's character." [10] It is also very likely that he was selected for his recognized moderation, which would balance Gilbert Tennent's extremism and thus influence those who might otherwise be alienated from the project.

The reasons for selecting Davies were not obvious even to himself, and he entered into one of those long personal debates that preceded all of his major decisions. He set down his thoughts in writing, for he had determined that "it will tend much to my future Satisfaction, to have the Reasons of my Procedure by me for a Review in the Hour of Perplexity; I think it expedient to state the Affair in Writing and to keep a Diary of all the remarkable Occurrences I may meet with." In a lengthy memorandum of his personal indecision he begged God "would clear up the Path of Duty before me, and make it as agreeable as obvious, whether it had me to the Ends of the Earth, or confine me to the Exercise of my Ministry at Home." He rejected this same call of the Synod on at least two previous occasions because of his youth and inexperience. But despite the reluctance of his wife, his fears for the state of his congregation, the danger of a sea voyage, and above all his profound feelings of inadequacy, Davies eventually agreed to make the trip.

His reasons for acceptance were many and indicated that his concern was not for the welfare of the college alone. When Tennent agreed to go, Davies declared that "the Expectation of so accomplished a Partner in the Embassy did in a great measure remove the

---

[8] *Ibid.*, Sept. 26, 1751, p. 243.

[9] *Ibid.*

[10] *Ibid.*, Sept. 27, 1751, p. 246. It is interesting to note that his Synod spelled his name "Davis" for several years prior to this decision, a mistake seldom made by such men as William Dawson, William Gooch, Robert Dinwiddie, and the Reverend Patrick Henry, who had reason to know him well.

Despondencies arising from my Want of Qualifications." He also looked forward to "the various Opportunities I may have of personal Improvement and that in Things which a Pedant and a Recluse is most deficient; the various Friendships that may be contracted, which may tend much to the Honour and Security of the Dissenters here; who stand so much in Need of Patronage." Indeed, Davies even rejoiced that someone else was financing the trip to plead the cause of the nonconformists and to raise money for the Indian missions that he supported: "oh! how transporting the Tho't, that these Barbarians may be cultivated by divine Grace in the use of the proper Means, and polished into genuine Disciples of the Blessed Jesus! For this alone, it would be worth our While to spend and be spent!"

Davies thus determined to make the voyage, provided the Synod met certain of his stipulations. He insisted that the college finance a minister to fill the Hanover pulpit during his absence and that his regular salary continue for the support of his family. He also reserved the right to return home immediately should his wife become seriously ill, for she was ill at that time. All of these conditions were acceded to without argument.[11]

Gilbert Tennent had severe doubts about the purpose and possible success of the mission. He had never been in complete agreement with the second charter's inclusion of lay members on the Board of Trustees, and, at one time, it was feared that he would sever relations with the school over this point.[12] He found himself in the uncomfortable position of trying to remain aloof, but after the death of his wife, he chose to undertake the mission as a means of seeking relief from his "domestic bereavements."[13] Tennent's old friend and colleague George Whitefield wrote of the impending visit with relish and anticipation: "I am glad Mr. Tennent is coming with Mr. Davies: if they come with their old fire, I trust they will be enabled to do wonders."[14]

---

[11] *Diary*, July 2, 1753, pp. 1–8. This first entry comprises some twenty manuscript pages.

[12] Jonathan Edwards to John Erskine, May 20, 1749, Edwards, *Works*, I, 347.

[13] Foote, I, 224.

[14] Whitefield quoted in Webster, *History of the Presbyterian Church*, p. 260.

By mid-summer Davies' wife appeared "considerably better," [15] and two months later he left for Philadelphia and the annual meeting of the Synod of New York where final preparations would be made for the voyage. Here again he set forth the cause of the Virginia dissenters, and the Synod formally recognized him as its spokesman in this matter.[16] The Synod then drew up letters of reference for Davies and Tennent, made arrangements to supply their pulpits, and prepared a petition to the General Assembly of the Church of Scotland in their behalf.[17]

Some time seems to have been spent in preparations, and it was during this month that Davies and Tennent, who had previously been mere acquaintances, became close friends despite their differing approaches to the problems of salvation and conversion. Davies referred to the older Tennent as his "Father and Friend" [18] and claimed in conversation that he was "much pleased with the pious Simplicity of my Spiritual Father, Mr. Tennent." [19] By this time Tennent had become somewhat more moderate and restrained in his method of preaching, for his travel partner was able to note on one occasion that he spoke in a "very judicious Manner." [20] Tennent was later to become a vocal advocate of the reunion of American Presbyterianism.[21]

After more than two months away from Hanover, Davies complained that they were still unable to sail from Philadelphia because of bad weather.[22] But finally the storm cleared and the wind died, and the two travelers left America on November 18, 1753, arriving safely in London on Christmas Day.[23] In less than a week they were hard at work on behalf of the college and the other matters en-

[15] *Diary*, July 11, 1753, p. 8.

[16] "Minutes of the Synod of New York," Oct. 6, 1753, *Records*, p. 257n.

[17] *Ibid.*, pp. 254–255, 255n, 256. The three documents drawn up at this time will be found in Appendix I.

[18] *Diary*, Oct. 20, 1754, p. 131.

[19] *Ibid.*, Sept. 16, 1754, p. 127.

[20] *Ibid.*

[21] Foote, I, 227.

[22] *Diary*, Nov. 14, 1753, p. 27.

[23] *Ibid.*, Dec. 25, 1743, pp. 42–43. It was probably a smooth voyage since Davies does not comment upon it in any way.

trusted to their care. They found numerous obstacles in their path, however, two of which seriously threatened their mission.

The first and most serious was British opposition to the New Light movement. This opposition was largely the work of William Smith, the emissary of the Old Light Synod of Philadelphia, which had been taking steps to solve its own educational problems in a manner similar to its New Light adversaries. The Old Lights had historically opposed the numerous classical academies of the Middle Colonies, but by 1744 they had come to recognize that the New England colleges were too distant to be an effective source of supply and determined to undertake some type of training program of their own. In that year, 1744, they assumed control of an academy that had been founded in 1741 by the Reverend Francis Alison at New London, Pennsylvania. Alison was made the master of the school, several tutors were appointed, and a collection for its support was ordered.[24]

But the members of the Old Light Synod were now faced with the inconsistency of their actions. Since they had manifested so great a reluctance to accept the graduates of the original log college and its successors, they could not very well be satisfied with the course of instruction in their own school, which was in no way superior to those of the New Lights and was, in fact, based on their examples. The New London school was therefore abandoned in 1749, but neither the Synod of Philadelphia nor Francis Alison abandoned their educational ideals; both became supporters of an academy in Philadelphia, which later developed into the University of Pennsylvania.[25] It was the emissary of this latter institution, the Reverend William Smith, a member of the Church of England, who awaited the New Light fund-raisers in Great Britain and who threatened the success of their mission.[26]

As was to be expected, there were many in Great Britain who opposed the idea of an American college completely dominated, as they believed, by a group of emotional and irresponsible enthusiasts.

[24] Briggs, *American Presbyterianism*, p. 305.
[25] *Ibid.*, p. 306.
[26] *Diary*, Jan. 22, 1754, p. 59.

Even though this belief was false,[27] Smith and others made capital
of it in an attempt to thwart the funding of the fledgling New Light
school. According to all reports, Tennent was almost overwhelmed
when confronted in England with copies of his highly emotional
and vitriolic Nottingham sermon [28] delivered fourteen years previously and upon learning of private letters that had been sent from
America to prejudice Englishmen against him and his cause.[29] The
Nottingham sermon was his famous intemperate charge against the
conservative elements of American Presbyterianism, which had
helped bring about the schism of 1741. The Old Lights had distributed it throughout the British Isles in anticipation of the arrival of
its author.

Smith, the instigator of these Old Light attacks on the two spokes-
men for the New Jersey college, was an American Anglican priest
who had become provost of the College, Academy, and Charitable
School of Philadelphia.[30] Because he was currently in England trying to raise money for his own institution, which had recently received the support of the Presbyterians of the Philadelphia Synod,
he considered himself in competition with his New Light counter-
parts for whatever funds were available to finance education in the
Middle Colonies. Throughout their travels in England and Scotland, Davies and Tennent constantly met the results of Smith's
handiwork and found their arguments, chief of which was the catholicity of the college, dangerously weakened. For example, when they
sought the support of the Reverend Samuel Chandler [31] of London,
he quoted Tennent's own earlier arguments against associating with

[27] The trustees at this time were Thomas Leonard, James Hude, Edward Shippen,
William Smith, Peter Van Brugh Livingston, William Peartree Smith, Samuel Hazard,
David Cowell, James Nielson, Samuel Woodruff, Joannes Frelinghuysen, Thomas Thomp-
son, John Pierson, Ebenezer Pemberton, Gilbert Tennent, William Tennent, Richard
Treat, Timothy Jones, Caleb Smith, Samuel Finley, and Elihu Spencer (*Catalogus Collegii
Neo-Cæsariensis* [Princeton, 1824], p. 6). Only the last nine were members of the New
York Synod; "Minutes of the Synod of New York," Sept. 28, 1752, *Records*, p. 246.
[28] *The Danger of an Unconverted Ministry. Consider'd in a Sermon on Mark VI. 34.
Preached at Nottingham, in Pennsylvania, March 8, Anno 1739–1740.*
[29] Foote, I, 227.
[30] Harris Elwood Starr in *Dictionary of American Biography*, s.v. "William Smith."
[31] Chandler was the nonconformist preacher at the Old Jewry in London at this time;
Leslie Stephen in *Dictionary of National Biography*, s.v. "Samuel Chandler."

the unconverted. Tennent now completely disavowed the opinions
he had formerly expressed, and Davies exerted on Chandler all his
"Powers of pathetic Address to give him a moving Representation
of the melancholy Case of the Churches" in America. Yet Chandler
noted "that the College was a Party Design." [32] After experiencing
the persuasive powers of Davies' pulpit oratory, however, he agreed
to support their cause and—what was perhaps more important—to
remain quiet about the controversial Nottingham sermon. [33]

In an effort to counter the opinion that Smith had effectively
molded (that the college was a "Party-Design" to insure the strength
of the New Light movement in America), the two revivalists wrote
a small pamphlet describing their school and the purposes it was
intended to serve. They attempted to prove that the College of New
Jersey was not designed purely for the education of Presbyterian
clergymen but rather for the instruction of all young men regardless of their denomination or their intended calling. For this reason,
they explained, "the Trustees of the said College have not made
such Regulations as may burden the Consciences of any; or confine
the Advantages of the Institution to a *Party;* nor did they desire
such a power; as is evident from the . . . Words of the Charter." [34]

Even this statement did not completely ease the way of the two
fund-raisers. In May, when they sought support before the General
Assembly of the Church of Scotland, Davies observed: "My Mind
is perplexed about the Success of our Mission here; and all appears
gloomy before me.—My Spirits are generally low, tho' I feel a Kind
of stupid Serenity of Mind." [35] Furthermore, a new obstacle now
presented itself. In his journal, Davies noted that they would very
likely have a difficult time with the General Assembly. In addition
to the unfavorable atmosphere created by their opponents' letters,

[32] *Diary,* Jan. 22, 23, 1754, pp. 59–61.
[33] *Ibid.,* Jan. 25, 1754, p. 62.
[34] Samuel Davies and Gilbert Tennent, *A General Account of the Rise and State of the College, Lately Established in New-Jersey, in America: And the End and Design of its Institution. Originally Published in America, An. 1752, by the Trustees of the said College; and Now Republished, in Pursuance of Their Order, With Some Alterations and Additions, Adapted to its Present State, For the Information of the Friends of Learning and Piety in Great Britain* (London, 1754), p. 7n.
[35] *Diary,* May 9, 1754, p. 89.

the Assembly was mindful of three successive general collections taken recently and was expecting another request for help, this one from Holland.

Davies and his companion were never able to counter effectively the efforts of the Old Lights to frustrate their mission, and the presence of Tennent in England seems to have worked to their disadvantage. About the middle of the year the situation was somewhat alleviated when Tennent took leave of Davies and journeyed to Ireland with hopes of securing help from the Presbyterians there. Commenting on the departure in his journal, Davies complained that he was left "solitary and sad to take a Tour thro' the principal Towns in England." [36] Tennent doubtless was motivated by the hostility he had encountered and the opportunity of visiting his homeland, as well as by the possibility of raising more funds.

Although it has been suggested that ill feelings developed between Davies and Tennent, perhaps because they later returned from Europe on different ships, the evidence does not seem to substantiate such a supposition. One commentator acknowledges a cause for conflict but denies its existence: "No doubt Mr. Davies carried off the Palm, as to popularity in London and other places; and if Mr. Tennent was at all susceptible of the feelings of envy, which are very natural to the human heart . . . he might have felt badly in finding himself eclipsed by a much younger man." [37] Davies himself may have been mildly irritated, for he observed that "Mr. Tennent treats me with the utmost Condescension" but at the same time noted that "my Anxieties at the Prospect of the Voyage are much mitigated by the Pleasure of his Conversation." [38]

Nevertheless, things were easier for Davies after Tennent left for Ireland, largely because he no longer found it necessary to disavow his friend's former attitudes. Tennent's departure did not entirely eliminate the difficulties, however, for Davies continued to record the animosity of the English in his journal. In Hull he was denied the use of the Presbyterian pulpit, an event that discouraged him

[36] *Ibid.*, June 15, 1754, p. 100. Tennent had left on the first of June.

[37] Alexander, *Biographical Sketches*, p. 57.

[38] *Diary*, Nov. 8, 1753, p. 23.

greatly, for he did not have time to tour the community seeking funds from individuals.[39] Similar conditions awaited the fund-raiser in Yarmouth, where he found "the Institution has been misrepresented . . . as a Calvinistic Scheme, or as in the Hands of Bigots." [40]

Meanwhile, Smith and his friends had seized on another method of frustrating the work of the New Light emissaries. They managed to cast severe doubts upon the validity of the New Jersey college's charter—questioning specifically the authority of Governor Belcher to license that college or any other corporation. In an attempt to resolve the problem, Davies presented a copy of the compact, along with a letter from the governor, to the Duke of Argyle, who advised him to have it approved by the Lords of Trade; others suggested that he obtain the approval of Prime Minister Henry Pelham or perhaps the Archbishop of Canterbury. Apparently he followed the advice, although plagued by the knowledge that Smith's charges had reached a wide audience, for he wrote: "For my Part, I am afraid of all Applications to that Quarter, lest we lose our Charter, and stir up an Opposition; and it is against my Mind that the Matter has been carried so far. . . . Went home anxious about the Fate of our Application to the Lords of Trade, and to the Court." [41] As a further effort, the two visitors used their pamphlet to play upon every British prejudice and policy:

> The Inhabitants of the Infant Colonies, dependant upon this Seminary, unable to relieve themselves, are constrained to solicit and implore the Assistance of others. And to whom shall they look, but to their tender and powerful *Parent?*—To move her Compassion, they plead their *Relation* as Children, as Fellow-Subjects, as Christian and Protestant Brethren with her Sons that still enjoy the Advantages of residing in their native Country—They plead the deplorable Circumstances of the Church, and the Exigencies of the State, for Want of such an Institution bro't to Maturity—And they beg Leave modestly to intimate their *Importance* to their Mother-Country, as they enlarge the *British* Dominions upon a vast Continent, whither the industrious Poor may transplant themselves, and find a comfortable Subsistance; as they are a check upon

[39] *Ibid.*, July 21, 1754, p. 110.
[40] *Ibid.*, Sept. 2, 1754, p. 123.
[41] *Ibid.*, Feb. 6, 1754, p. 70.

the Growth of the *French* Power in *America;* engage the *Indian* Natives to the *British* Interest; furnish various Assistance in Time of War against the common Enemy; and carry on sundry Branches of Trade, advantagious to *Great-Britain;* which will undoubtedly flourish more, in Proportion to their Improvements in the liberal Arts and Sciences; for History and Observation assure us, that Learning and *Trade* mutually promote each other.[42]

Davies' apprehension about the charter was unfounded, for no action was ever taken to have it annulled. He seldom mentioned the problem after the first two months in England. His journal indicates that he hoped to sublimate the question, thus avoiding a possible adverse decision: "I was afraid that in Case the College should be discountenanced by them [the Lords of Trade] they would find some flaw in the Charter and so overset it; and that a Refusal at Court would have a bad Influence on those that might otherwise contribute towards it." [43]

The campaign for funds continued, of course, with Davies or his colleague customarily delivering a visiting sermon in one of the English churches and receiving the day's collection as a contribution. The preaching engagements were supplemented by appointments with important and influential individuals and groups who might have an interest in the college. As a preacher Davies had few peers, and he seldom failed to obtain something from each of his many appearances, although not all appeals were as successful as had been hoped.

Less than a week elapsed after his arrival in London before Davies was at work as a guest minister,[44] and within a month he had seen at least one of the many private English groups that supported education. He had been summoned "by a Company of Lords and Gentlemen" that had been established to disburse a large amount of money donated personally by the king for the improvement of the educational facilities of the Pennsylvania Germans. Davies' petition was sent to this body by the same Samuel Chandler who had origi-

---

[42] Davies and Tennent, *General Account*, p. 7.
[43] *Diary*, Jan. 8, 1754, p. 51.
[44] *Ibid.*, Dec. 30, 1753, p. 45.

nally been so doubtful about the purpose of the college. Despite Chandler's support, however, Davies was unsuccessful in his appeal, observing on January 19 that he had no hope for success.[45]

A variety of responses was encountered in the course of the soliciting. Davies "waited upon Dr. Gill, the celebrated Baptist Minister," who agreed to support the college, but "modestly pleaded that his Name would be of little service, and that the Baptists in general were unhappily ignorant of the Importance of Learning." Quite often Davies enlivened his journal with descriptions of those upon whom he waited or to whom he preached. Gill, he said, "is a serious, grave little Man, and looks young and hearty, tho' I suppose near 60."[46] The Reverend Samuel Savage was "doubtful whether he would give any Thing towards our College" because he appeared to be "insensible of the Necessity of Learning in a Minister." Further, Savage did not approve of Davies and Tennent associating so much with the "Rich and Great, and Persons of all Denominations" and felt that they did not publicly associate enough with Whitefield.[47] On another occasion Davies told of a visit, this time pleasantly, with John Patrick, a Scottish Presbyterian minister in London, "who seems to have a tender Sense of the declining State of Religion."[48] When Davies preached for Thomas Gibbons in London, "Sundry of the Hearers were tenderly affected, particularly Mr. Cromwell, great grandson of the famous Oliver; who gave Mr. Gibbons 3 Guineas for the College after Sermon and thanked me for my Discourse with Tears in his Eyes."[49]

Within a few months Davies was so busy with his constant preaching and traveling that he found little time to record the details of these activities. The entries in his journal became shorter and shorter, sometimes covering the events of an entire week in one brief para-

[45] *Ibid.*, Jan. 19, 1754, pp. 57–58.
[46] *Ibid.*, Jan. 30, 1754, p. 65. This was the Reverend John Gill, who was the Baptist minister at Horselydown, Southwark, at this time; Thomas Hamilton in *Dictionary of National Biography*, s.v. "John Gill."
[47] *Diary*, Jan. 30, 1754, p. 65. Samuel Morton Savage was co-pastor of the independent congregation at Duke's Place, Bury Street, St. Mary Axe, Isaac Watts' old pulpit (Alexander Gordon in *Dictionary of National Biography*, s.v. "Samuel Savage").
[48] *Diary*, March 7, 1754, p. 81.
[49] *Ibid.*, March 16, 1754, p. 81.

graph. "My Hurries will not allow me an Hour in a Week to write my Journal," he lamented, "and therefore I must content myself with a general Account." [50] Nevertheless, he never became so busy as to abandon the continual self-examinations: "I think my Heart rises in Sincere Gratitude to God for advancing me from a mean Family and utter Obscurity, into some Importance in the World, and giving me so many Advantages of public usefulness." [51]

In London, Davies found his fellow Presbyterians "generally very shy and unsociable" and even suspicious of the motives behind the establishment of the college.[52] In Scotland he observed that there "appears but little of the Spirit of serious Christianity among the young Clergy." [53] But he achieved some of his greatest successes in Scotland, where he made many friends among the Presbyterians. "I have scarcely felt such strong Emotions of Friendship since I left Home," [54] he wrote, describing his stay in the North. Another time he declared: "I find I begin to grow popular here, especially among the Religious." [55]

It was in Scotland, it will be remembered, that Davies and Tennent most feared the adverse effects of the efforts that had been made on behalf of the Old Light college in Philadelphia.[56] Despite all such influences, however, Davies was able to persuade the General Assembly to come to the assistance of the College of New Jersey. Responding to his arguments, the Assembly in a moving appeal proclaimed that "the Young Daughter of the Church of Scotland, helpless and exposed in this foreign Land, Cries to her tender and powerful Mother for Relief." The Assembly ordered a collection at every church door in the kingdom and urged that all members be generous.[57] This success gave Davies a somewhat higher opinion of his Scottish brethren. While in Edinburgh he observed that he en-

[50] *Ibid.*
[51] *Ibid.*, March 19, 1754, p. 84.
[52] *Ibid.*
[53] *Ibid.*, May 16, 1754, p. 91.
[54] *Ibid.*, July 1, 1754, p. 104.
[55] *Ibid.*, June 10, 1754, p. 58.
[56] *Ibid.*, May 9, 10, 1754, pp. 89–90.
[57] "Act For A Collection For The College of New Jersey," May 31, 1754, Briggs, *American Presbyterianism,* pp. ci–civ.

countered more Christian friendship there than anywhere else in Great Britain.[58]

On his return to England, Davies visited some of the major English towns, daily recording his success or failure as a fund-raiser. In Morpeth he was successful, obtaining the assurance that the dissenting minister there would take a collection for the college.[59] But in Leeds he again met with Presbyterians of differing theological beliefs and found himself confronted by a moral dilemma: "In Conversation with the Gentlemen of the new Scheme, I am generally upon the Reserve about my own Principles, lest it should prejudice them against the Business of my Mission. But when I reflect upon it, I seem to despise myself as a Coward. My Conscience indeed does not generally accuse me of Guilt in this Respect; but a Sense of Honour or Pride or I know not what to call it, makes me look mean and sneaking to Myself." [60]

Encounters with those unsympathetic to his mission, however, occurred infrequently compared to those with persons who favored the cause and agreed with his principles. In Norwich he was able to raise £20,[61] and he found another £6 awaiting him at Chelmsford.[62] At Sudbury he contacted several individuals who were "very friendly" both to himself and to his mission,[63] one of them even donating the munificent sum of £50 to the college.[64]

One of the tasks facing Davies, related only indirectly to the College of New Jersey, was his self-imposed mission of seeking relief for the Virginia dissenters. He was determined to help his followers if at all possible and appeared often before various non-Presbyterian congregations and committees, especially the Baptists, to plead the dissenters' cause.

His chief concern was to resolve the dispute over multiple meetinghouses, desiring the removal of all limitations upon him and his

[58] *Diary*, June 15, 1754, p. 99.
[59] *Ibid.*, July 5, 1754, pp. 105–106.
[60] *Ibid.*, July 28, 1754, pp. 113–114.
[61] *Ibid.*, Sept. 15, 1754, p. 126.
[62] *Ibid.*, Sept. 30, 1754, p. 131.
[63] *Ibid.*, Sept. 20, 1754, p. 128.
[64] *Ibid.*, Sept. 30, 1754, p. 131.

associates. Even before he left the colonies, an English group devoted to promoting the interests of the nonconformists had assured
him that the Act of Toleration entitled dissenting preachers to as
many pulpits as they desired. It was the view of this group that the
necessary licenses were to be issued automatically upon proper application, whether in England or America.[65] Unfortunately for the
Virginia dissenters, this opinion was not shared by the Bishop of
London or the government of the colony.

Not long after his arrival in Great Britain, Davies wrote that he
and Tennent had appeared before an informal committee of dissenters, headed by Benjamin Avery, to seek advice about how to
pursue their goal of toleration in the face of opposition from the
Bishop of London and the colonial government.[66] They received
no assistance but were advised to return later. Several weeks passed
before Davies again had the opportunity of presenting his case, but
once more he was unsuccessful. The committee now advised him
that the Toleration Act was not written in such a way that it could
apply to Virginia. Reportedly, the only part of the law operative in
the colony was that which exempted dissenters from attendance at
Anglican services. It was therefore suggested that the frontier nonconformists petition the king for redress, especially since they oc-
cupied territory of strategic importance.[67]

Without prospects of securing immediate redress, Davies nevertheless drew up a petition in behalf of the Virginia dissenters. In
his journal he lamented the recent events that seemed to mitigate
against the future of this phase of his mission: "The Death of Mr.
Pelham, the Project of Sending a Bishop over to America, the Con-
fusions between the Governour and Assembly in Virginia, and Mr.
Randolph, my old Adversary being now in London, are all great
obstructions at present to the Relief of my oppressed People." [68]
He did find one who was sympathetic to the cause of the noncon-

[65] Avery to Davies [1752], Foote, I, 211–214.
[66] *Diary*, Jan. 30, 1754, p. 65.
[67] *Ibid.*, Feb. 27, 1754.
[68] *Ibid.*, March 16, 1754, pp. 82–83.

formists, the Reverend Samuel Stennett,[69] a Baptist minister, and to him gave "a particular Account of the Rise and Progress of the Dissenting Interest in Virginia, and the Restraints and Embarrassments the People laboured under from the Government." [70]

The ultimate fate of Davies' petition is unknown. It probably never reached those for whom it was intended. Eventually, he was forced to discontinue active work on behalf of the dissenters when he discovered that most of those upon whom he was depending were somewhat out of sympathy with the New Light movement. According to Davies, the members of Avery's committee could not "look upon the dissenting Interest in Virginia as a religious Interest because founded upon Principles which they disapprove; and therefore they can only espouse it as the Cause of Liberty: but a Zeal for it in this View, is not so vigorous a Principle, as in the other." Moreover, Davies decided that the Courtiers, upon whom would rest any final resolution of the problem, were "so regardless of Religion, abstracted from Politics, that it will be difficult to carry such a Point with them especially as the whole Weight of the Government in Virginia will be on the other side." [71] He was further handicapped by the weight of his fund-raising duties and his prolonged absences from London, which made it impossible to arrange meetings with important governmental officials or keep in close touch with his advisers. As a result, Davies left Stennett and Avery [72] to press the case upon the government. He seems to have realized that the battle would necessarily be fought and won in Virginia rather than in Great Britain.[73]

The mission to England was not completely devoid of results for Virginia's non-Anglicans, however. Large bodies of English dis-

---

[69] There were two Baptist ministers of this name, father and son. The elder (1692–1758) was the preacher at Little Wild Street Church, Lincoln's Inn Fields, London. The younger (1728–1795) was his assistant and successor. Alexander Gordon in *Dictionary of National Biography*, s.v. "Samuel Stennett."

[70] *Diary*, March 16, 1754, p. 83.

[71] *Ibid.*, Nov. 18, 1754, p. 134.

[72] *Ibid.*

[73] See above, ch. VII.

senters adhered to Davies' view of the problem, and he made a number of influential acquaintances who shared his concern. Even while he was at sea returning home, friends in England were working in his behalf. Although Avery's committee of nonconformists deemed it inadvisable to present one of his petitions to the king, they did recommend "that when any house or place for religious worship is wanted, that you apply first to the County Court for a license thereof,—if refused there, then apply to the Governor alone for a license,—and if he refuses, then use such house or place for religious worship, as if it had been licensed,—and if prosecuted for so doing acquaint the Committee therewith, and they will then send you further directions how to act." [74] But this was only advice, not official sanction, and the interests of the college had to take precedence over those of his fellow Virginia Presbyterians.

As has been noted previously, one of the important by-products of Davies' fund-raising trip was the considerable personal prestige he gained as a preacher, a reputation that lingered in both England and Scotland until long after his death. Some of his preaching so impressed his hearers that Davies was urged to publish a collection of the sermons, a project he seriously considered.[75] Perhaps the greatest compliment was paid him by Londoners, of whom he remarked: "I observe a Set of Hearers that generally attend me wherever I preach, particularly the young Students." [76]

Davies' powers of observation, seen so vividly in his poetry and description of individuals, make his comments as a tourist both valuable and entertaining. He took great delight in knowing some of the near-greats of British religious society, yet he never let this friendship dull his descriptive powers. Comments resulting from the first meeting with John and Charles Wesley, though not unfavorable, would probably not have endeared him to the Methodist brothers:

[74] Nathaniel Sheffield, for the Committee of the Deputation of Protestant Dissenters, to Davies, Feb. 5, 1755, Foote, I, 296–297.
[75] Diary, Sept. 28, 1754, p. 130; Nov. 18, 1754, p. 133.
[76] Ibid., Oct. 27, 1754, p. 132.

We waited on Messrs. John and Ch. Westley. Notwithstanding all their wild Notions, they appear very benevolent, devout and zealous Men, that are labouring with all their Might to awaken the secure World to a Sense of Religion; and they are honoured with Success. But I am afraid their encouraging so many illiterate Men to preach the Gospel, will have bad Consequences. I heard one of them last Tuesd. Night but he explained Nothing at all. His Sermon was a meer Huddle of pathetic Confusion, and I was uneasy, as it might bring a Reproach upon experimental Religion. The despised Methodists, with all their Foibles, seem to me to have more of the Spirit of Religion than any Set of People in this Island.[77]

After listening to one of Whitefield's sermons, he observed succinctly that "the Discourse was incoherent." [78] Not always so critical, however, he "was pleasingly entertained with a Sermon on the Parable of the unjust Steward" delivered by Chandler, "a most ingenious, accurate Gentleman." [79]

Davies purchased a map of London for the rather large sum of five guineas [80] and used it to find his way around the city. Among other places, he visited the tomb of John Locke, where he transcribed the entire Latin epitaph for his journal.[81] It was a source of regret that he was not able to do the same at the grave of his late friend and correspondent Philip Doddridge,[82] who had influenced him so greatly in his hymn writing. This interest in hymn writing also led him to the home of Isaac Watts, where he admired Watts' original manuscripts. Especially interesting to Davies were "the pictures of sundry great men, ranged in the order the Dr. has left them" and "the turret, and the venerable oaks and elms, etc.," [83] that had provided Watts' inspiration. The account of another diversion from the pressures of the trip indicates both his interests and his sense of propriety: "When I came to N. Castle in the Evening, I found a

[77] *Ibid.*, pp. 132–133.
[78] *Ibid.*, Jan. 1, 1754, p. 47.
[79] *Ibid.*, p. 46.
[80] *Ibid.*, Jan. 5, 1754, p. 49.
[81] *Ibid.*, Oct. 27, 1754, p. 133.
[82] Davies to Mrs. Philip Doddridge, April 28, 1755, MS in Princeton University Library.
[83] *Diary*, Feb. 25, 1754, p. 77.

Comedy called the Careless Husband was to be acted: and as I apprehended I should not be known and consequently could give no Offence, I went to gratifie my Curiosity. But the Entertainment was short of my Expectations." [84]

The tourism, however, was no more than a momentary respite from the purpose of his mission, and Davies engaged in it only when one of his associates was unable to keep an appointment or while he was awaiting the return of his partner from Ireland. By early November of 1754 Tennent had returned to London, and the two prepared to embark for America. Tennent wished to sail to Philadelphia, which was near his home, whereas Davies did not relish the thought of riding some three hundred miles on horseback after a year and a half away from home. Thus, they separated, Davies sailing directly for Virginia and taking leave of Great Britain at Gravesend on November 18, 1754, aboard the *Charming Anne*. He did not look forward to the trip, as indicated by a foreboding entry in his journal: "now when I am about to encounter the Terrors of a Winter-Passage over the tumultuous Ocean, I would solemnly commit myself to the God of my Life, and the Ruler of Sea and Land." [85]

After the eastward crossing of five weeks—which must have been particularly uneventful, judging by the lack of comment in the journal—Davies was unprepared for the long return voyage. For three months the *Charming Anne* was intermittently buffeted by foul weather, and during this time he was plagued with seasickness. In late December, about half way through the voyage he moaned: "For this Week past, we have had the usual Vicissitudes of Sailors, sometimes foul, and sometimes fair . . . . I was so disordered with Sea-Sickness, that I was not able [to preach]. Alas! I lead a most useless Life." [86] Early in January the situation became even more grave:

> For above a Fortnight, we have had but very little fair Wind; Some Days have been very sually, and others quite calm, with very high Swells: which is extremely disagreeable. Two Days ago, we had no Wind, and

[84] *Ibid.*, July 5, 1754, p. 106.
[85] *Ibid.*, Nov. 18, 1754, p. 133.
[86] *Ibid.*, Dec. 28, 1754, p. 138.

the Seas run very high; and the Ship got between two large Swells, and we were in the greatest Danger of sinking, the Capt. as pale as Death, cryed out to get the Boats loose, that in them we might commit ourselves to the Ocean, and endeavour to get to a Ship in Sight, but it pleased God that the Vessel righted, and we were safe beyond all Expectation.[87]

While suffering the "Vicissitudes of Sailors," Davies studied some of the books he had purchased in Great Britain. His chief source of pleasure was Gilbert Burnet's *History of My Own Time*, portions of which he carefully outlined in the journal with his customary insight:

When I am able, I read in Bp. Burnet's Hystory of his own Life and Times; in which is a more full Account of the strange Intrigues of Courts than can we meet with in most of Hystories. He is always fond of searching into the Springs and Causes of Actions: and no doubt he often discovers the true ones: but sometimes this Temper betrays him into censorious Conjectures about the Hearts of others, of which he was no Judge. The Spirit of Moderation and Piety that breathes thro' his Writings, is quite charming.[88]

Unfortunately, the traveler found such opportunities for study and self-improvement to be rare interludes in the hazardous crossing. The storms of early January gave way to the even more terrifying storms of February:

Sund. Feb. 2. It is a remarkable Mercy that I am now alive, and capable to take Memorials of any Thing that happens in the Regions of Mortality. About 10 o'clock the Night before last, a violent Storm blew up from the N.E. which continued near 36 Hours; and I never was more apprehensive of Danger. The Waves beat with such Violence against the Ship, that one could hardly expect but she would have been dashed to Pieces or overset; and the Capt. and the most veteran Sailors were full of alarming Apprehensions. Alas! how helpless are we, on this boisterous Element all our Dependence upon one feeble Bottom; and no other Way of Safety or Deliverance. I think there is no Phenomenon in Nature so terrible, as a Storm at Sea, especially in the Night. It requires no small Fortitude to stand upon Deck, and take a view of it.[89]

[87] *Ibid.*, Jan. 9, 1755, p. 139.
[88] *Ibid.*, Dec. 28, 1754, p. 138.
[89] *Ibid.*, Feb. 2, 1755, p. 143.

But the beauty and power of these wintry blasts whetted Davies' poetic imagination; this last storm before reaching Virginia inspired one of his better and most secular poetic efforts:

> What Horrors crowd around! Destruction frowns
> In all its frightful shapes. The lowering Clouds
> Spread out their solid Glooms, and not a Star
> Emits a Ray of cheering Light. The Winds
> Discharge their whole Artillery; rear vast Piles
> Of Waves on Waves, and watry Pyramids,
> Capt with white Foam, that lash'd to fiery Rage,
> Sparkles and burns: betwixt conflicting Seas,
> Toss'd like a Cork, alas! our feeble Barque,
> Our sole Defence, denies us Hope; the Waves
> In Deluges break o'er her, dash her Sides,
> And threaten to o'erwhelm her. Hark! the Roar
> Of breaking Precipices, and the Howl
> Of furious Winds, that from the Bottom turn
> The Wild, fermenting Ocean; while the Night
> Spreads her thick Glooms o'er all the dreadful Scene.[90]

By the middle of February the Hanover pastor was back at home and was soon preparing to set off for a meeting of the Synod. His wife and family were found in good health and receptive to the tales of his travels.[91] As soon as a report could be made to the Synod he could once again devote himself to the problems of the Virginia dissenters.

The total amount of money raised by Davies and Tennent during the course of their year in Great Britain is impossible to determine, for donations ranging from a few shillings to a hundred pounds or more were mentioned in the journal. Furthermore, the two travelers were expected to meet all of their expenses out of the contributions, and the collection ordered by the General Assembly in Scotland was not completed until long after the two men had returned to America. In fact, donations continued to come from the British Isles up until the time of the Revolution, although how many of these were inspired by lingering memories of Tennent and

[90] *Ibid.*
[91] Davies to Mrs. Doddridge, April 28, 1755, MS in Princeton University Library.

Davies is not clear. The difficulty of arriving at a reliable total hinges on the incompleteness of official records and the differing estimates provided by other sources. According to minutes of the Synod of New York, the two men raised almost £300 for a scholarship fund, which, by the time they reported to the Synod, had become £600.[92] The same sources record that another £200 was collected for the education of Indians, to be used either for scholarships or for missionary efforts of those trained at the college.[93] A later commentator on this campaign asserts that the two men raised a total of more than £3,000: the sum of £1,700 in England, more than £1,000 in Scotland, and about £500 in Ireland.[94] This may well be short of actuality, for by August of 1755, President Burr was informed that the collection for the New Jersey college amounted to more than a thousand pounds and that there were still many parishes in Scotland whose ministers had not collected or sent in their collections.[95]

Whatever the total, there can be little doubt that it was quite large, probably larger than had been expected. The infant institution was placed on a sound financial basis. Perhaps even more important, the emissaries had firmly committed the college to a program of liberal education for young men of all faiths.[96] Certainly, when Davies traveled back to Virginia to work for the dissenters, he himself was committed more firmly than ever to the Presbyterian ideals of education. His interest in the affairs of the College of New Jersey continued, and eventually the college became the major object of his labor.

[92] "Minutes of the Synod of New York," Oct. 3, 1755, *Records*, pp. 264–265.
[93] *Ibid.*, p. 265.
[94] Briggs, *American Presbyterianism*, p. 309.
[95] ———— Hogg to Aaron Burr, Aug. 28, 1755, "Catalogus Collegii. Neo-Cæsariensis. Princetonæ," *The Biblical Repertory and Princeton Review*, XII (1840), 378.
[96] Briggs, *American Presbyterianism*, pp. 308–309.

IX

Religion and Patriotism

WHILE DAVIES PLEADED the Virginia dissenters' cause in England, the struggle at home was at a stalemate. With their champion away, the dissenters made no progress; on the other hand, the government took no precipitate action either. The law to supplement the Toleration Act was not passed, and the leaders of the government continued to write to the Bishop of London for advice. Fortunately for the dissenters, the bishop maintained a discreet silence, consistently failing to give the requested advice.

In 1752, prior to Davies' trip to England, William Dawson had asked Bishop Secker's opinion about confining dissenting preachers to their home counties but apparently received no reply. When Dawson's brother wrote a note of warning the following year, he also sought guidance, mentioning that the proposed supplement was still under consideration. In the spring of 1754, two years after the first request, they were still waiting, and the Anglican Commissary complained to his superior: "Last July I writ your Lordship a long letter relating to . . . the unreasonable application of the dissenting teachers for greater indulgences, but I have not as yet had the honor of an answer." [1] Governor Dinwiddie had an equal lack of success in his correspondence with the bishop.[2]

---

[1] William Dawson to the Bishop of London, March 11, 1754, Perry, *Historical Collections*, I, 409.

[2] Dinwiddie to the Bishop of London, June 5, 1752, *ibid.*, p. 396.

William Dawson died early in 1755 and was succeeded by his brother Thomas, who proved to be less tolerant. In time, the attitude of Thomas Dawson might have become troublesome for Davies and the Presbyterians had not other events intervened in favor of the dissenters. England was experiencing troubles in America. The French were inciting the Indians along the frontier, posing a threat to the British colonies. As these incidents developed into the French and Indian War, government officials quickly realized that the increasing number of dissenters on the frontier provided an excellent buffer against the Indians. The government also was acutely conscious of the morale and recruiting support being provided by such New Light leaders as Samuel Davies.

With the colony's security threatened, the government gradually eased its restrictive measures, and the Presbyterians found themselves increasingly free to ignore the former restraints on their conduct. As a result, greater and greater numbers of New Light preachers poured into the colony. These men, characterized by high personal standards and excellent education, found a ready following wherever they went. When Davies returned from England in 1755, he found five other New Light preachers active in the colony: John Todd, Robert Henry, Alexander Craighead, John Wright, and John Brown. The presence of these men made the formation of a separate Presbytery a logical and necessary step, and Davies became the chief promoter of such a plan.

At the same meeting of the Synod of New York (October 1755) to which he reported his successes in Great Britain, he also presented a petition for a new Presbytery in Virginia. There was no opposition to this move, for the request was granted on the same day, and the Virginian was chosen to preach the opening sermon.[3] The new Hanover Presbytery was established at Pole Green Church in Hanover County on December 3, 1755, and Davies was immediately chosen moderator.[4] Petitions from congregations without ministers were presented at once to the new organization seeking his services as a preacher.[5] As a result of his efforts and those of

---

[3] "Minutes of the Synod of New York," Oct. 3, 1755, *Records*, p. 263.
[4] Rachal, "Early Minutes of Hanover Presbytery," p. 54.
[5] *Ibid., passim.*

his associates to fill such requests, "this frontier Presbytery became a centre of evangelistic work which extended into South Carolina, Georgia, and Tennessee." [6] In fact, the Hanover Presbytery, oldest in the South, is generally regarded as the mother Presbytery of the Presbyterian Church in the region.[7]

The increased vitality of the Virginia revival movement following Davies' return in 1755, reinforced by the visit of George Whitefield in the same year, caused the new Anglican Commissary to comment that "the new Lights seemed to be in a declining Condition during the Absence of Mr. Davies, but upon his Return they revived,—at least they make much Noise." [8] More meetinghouses were petitioned for, and licenses were granted by the courts of Lancaster and Northumberland counties.[9] A similar request was refused by the Westmoreland County authorities, but the dissenters continued to preach there and were not molested by the government.[10] The requests for Davies' services as a preacher continued to flood into the new Presbytery from all over Virginia, many from areas where he had preached.[11] The traveling engagements became so extensive that at one point he wrote: "In about two months I rode about five hundred miles, and preached about forty Sermons." [12] In fact, by 1758 the absences had become so frequent that the elders of his own congregation asked the Presbytery to relieve him of all duties except those in Hanover.[13]

Events in Virginia's Northern Neck vividly illustrate the ever-widening influence of the Hanover leaders. Davies and Todd were chiefly responsible for the establishment of organized Presbyterianism in this region. They made it possible for the Presbytery to supply visiting preachers to new congregations in these counties on a fairly regular basis until after Davies' departure from Virginia.

---

[6] Briggs, *American Presbyterianism*, p. 328.

[7] Morton, *Colonial Virginia*, II, 595.

[8] Thomas Dawson to the Bishop of London, Aug. 13, 1755, Dawson MSS. This is evidently a first draft.

[9] David Currie and John Leland to [Thomas Dawson], April 12, 1758, *ibid.*

[10] Gewehr, *Great Awakening*, p. 94.

[11] Gaines, *Cub Creek Church*, p. 21.

[12] Davies to Gibbons, Sept. 12, 1757, *Sermons* (1766), I, lxxi.

[13] Rachal, "Early Minutes of Hanover Presbytery," April 28, 1758, pp. 72–74.

Action was forthcoming, but its result was scarcely comforting to the people of Virginia, for on July 10, 1755, General Edward Braddock was crushed by a force of French and Indians. The colony was panic-stricken. Indian activity increased, and survivors spread harrowing stories of savage brutality. Ten days later, Davies made Braddock's defeat the basis for another patriotic sermon, comparing Virginia to an ancient Israel that had become "sunk in security" and had neglected to call upon God for help. Again he called for repentance because Virginia was being punished for her sins. As a first requisite for victory the people must "cry aloud to God for help," but they must also arm themselves and prepare for defense, for "Christians should be patriots. What is that religion good for that leaves men cowards upon the appearance of danger?" He proclaimed his own determination not to move from Hanover until the danger was over.

During the war, Davies cautioned dissenters that their right to dissent was contingent upon loyalty to their country. "Let us," he said, "show ourselves worthy of protection and encouragement, by our conduct on this occasion." [22] A minister's duty was to inform his people of the important issues at stake, to inspire them with a public spirit and love of country, and to encourage them by teaching and example to risk their lives and property in its defense,[23] and this Davies tried to do in all his wartime sermons.

Like many of England's wars, this one was characterized by a series of initial blunders and defeats that seriously affected the spirits of those close to the area of combat. Davies found it necessary to preach several sermons aimed at raising morale even though his

---

[22] "On the Defeat of General Braddock," *ibid.*, pp. 215–232. Davies "became famous for the powerful eloquence with which he stirred up the hearts of the Virginians in the war against the French and Indians, when they were panic-stricken by the defeat and death of General Braddock" (James S. M. Anderson, *The History of the Church of England, in the Colonies and Foreign Dependencies of the British Empire* [3 vols., London, 1856], III, 134). "The influence of his war sermons appears to have been irresistible: and an examination of them might be advantageous to those who may be called to address soldiers" (Foote, I, 295).

[23] Davies and Todd to the Earl of Loudon, Aug. 10, 1756, Rachal, "Early Minutes of Hanover Presbytery," p. 61.

hearers might not be immediately threatened. Of his extant sermons, eight, all of which presumably were preached more than once, dealt specifically with the war, and numerous others touched upon it.

Several of these sermons were first intended for the benefit of the Virginia militia rather than for Davies' own congregations. In fact, the first company of volunteers to be recruited in the colony after Braddock's defeat was raised in Hanover County, and its commander, Captain Samuel Overton, asked Davies to speak to his unit. In complying on August 17, 1755, Davies preached a sermon titled "Religion and Patriotism, the Constituents of a Good Soldier," calling for courage in battle and picturing the recruits as the flames of the martial fire that God sought to kindle throughout America. When Davies later prepared this sermon for publication, he added a famous footnote, which has often been cited as proof of his powers of perception and his ability to judge human character: "As a remarkable instance . . . I may point out to the public, that heroic youth, Col. Washington, whom I cannot but hope Providence has hitherto preserved in so signal a manner, for some important service to his country." [24]

As the war progressed, more volunteers were needed, and Davies delivered a public sermon on May 8, 1758, with the purpose of raising a company for Captain Samuel Meredith. This, perhaps his most militant call to arms, was so successful that the enlistment was oversubscribed. Titling the sermon "The Curse of Cowardice," Davies exhorted:

> May I not reasonably insist upon it, that the company be made up this very day before we leave this place? Methinks your king, your country, nay your own interest command me: and therefore I insist upon it. Oh! for the all pervading force of Demosthenes' oratory—but I recall my wish that I may correct it. Oh! for the influence of the Lord of armies, the God of battles, the Author of true courage, and every heroic virtue, to fire you into patriots and soldiers this moment! Ye young and hardy men, whose very faces seem to speak that God and nature formed you for

[24] "Religion and Patriotism, the Constituents of a Good Soldier," *Sermons* (1845), III, 41–62, 47*n*.

soldiers, who are free from the incumbrance of families depending upon you for subsistence, and who perhaps are of but little service to society while at home, may I not speak for you and declare as your mouth, "Here we are, all ready to abandon our ease, and rush into the glorious dangers of the field, in defence of our country?" Ye that love your country, enlist. . . . I seriously make the proposal to you, not only as a subject of the best of kings, and a friend to your country, but as *a servant of the Most High God:* for I am fully persuaded, what I am recommending in his will; and disobedience to it may expose you to his curse.[25]

When he finished, his listeners are said to have followed him to the tavern where he had tethered his horse and there urged him to continue. This he did until exhausted.[26]

Many years later, John Holt Rice, a prominent religious writer, was to report on his conversations with some "aged friends" who had been present several times when Davies spoke. These witnesses "represented in lively terms, the dejection and gloom depicted on every countenance" facing Davies as he began to speak. Then, they recalled, "as the preacher poured forth the strains of his eloquence, his own spirit was transfused into his hearers, the cheek that was blanched with fear reddened, and the drooping eyes kindled with martial fires." [27]

Davies' inspirational recruiting sermons had a wide circulation in pamphlet form. *Religion and Patriotism* was published before the end of 1755 and was reprinted at least twice the following year.[28] *The Curse of Cowardice* went through at least four printings.[29] Thus, it is not surprising that Davies and his fellow dissenters were allowed to work without interference, for, as one later commentator observes, "the Attorney General could scarcely venture to throw

[25] "Curse of Cowardice," *ibid.*, pp. 91–92.

[26] [Rice], "Memoir," p. 360.

[27] *Ibid.*, pp. 359–360.

[28] *Religion and Patriotism, the Constituents of a Good Soldier. A Sermon Preached to Captain Overton's Independent Company of Volunteers, Raised in Hanover County, Virginia, August 17, 1755* (Philadelphia, 1755; London, Belfast, 1756).

[29] *The Curse of Cowardice: A Sermon Preached to the Militia of Hanover County, Virginia, at a General Muster, May 8, 1758. With a View to Raise a Company for Captain Samuel Meredith* (London, 1758; Woodbridge, Philadelphia, Boston, New York, 1759).

impediments in the path of the best recruiting officer in the province." [30]

The colonial governors were quick to recognize this asset. Governor Robert Dinwiddie was one of the first Virginia government officials to perceive the value of the dissenters in defending the colony. Since replacing the tactful and popular Sir William Gooch as lieutenant-governor in 1751, Dinwiddie had managed to antagonize practically all of the powerful first families who made up the House of Burgesses. His one-pistole tax on land patents created one of the most heated controversies before the Revolution, and his failure to support William Stith, grandson of William Randolph of Turkey Island, for the post of Anglican Commissary further antagonized one of Virginia's most influential families. Dinwiddie's sharp tongue and his habit of being first and always a Briton contrasted sharply with his predecessor's diplomacy and constant concern for the rights of Virginia citizens.[31] Now, faced with opposition and delay in his prosecution of the war, he was no doubt glad to receive support from any quarter. At least he does not seem to have hindered Davies in any way after the outbreak of hostilities.

In 1758, Dinwiddie was replaced by Francis Fauquier. Upon his settlement in Virginia, Fauquier was visited by Davies and his colleague John Wright, who carried a letter from the Presbytery of Hanover, assuring the new governor of their loyalty and their desire to see a vigorous prosecution of the war. The new administrator was also petitioned to "secure and continue to them all the peaceable and unmolested enjoyment of the Liberties and Immunities of the Act of Toleration." [32] Governor Fauquier expressed pleasure at the Presbytery's action and promised his cooperation. "The Presbytery may be assured," he said, "that I shall always ex-

[30] Foote, I, 296.

[31] See Richard Beale Davis, ed., *The Colonial Virginia Satirist: Mid-Eighteenth-Century Commentaries on Politics, Religion, and Society* in *Transactions* of the American Philosophical Society, N.S., Vol. 57, Pt. 1 (1967).

[32] Hanover Presbytery to Francis Fauquier, July 12, 1758, Rachal, "Early Minutes of Hanover Presbytery," p. 162.

ert myself to support the Act of Toleration, and secure the peaceful Enjoyment of all its Immunities to all his Majesty's Subjects who conform thereto." [33] The reply offered the dissenters nothing new, but it did demonstrate the new governor's tolerant attitude, which apparently never changed during his subsequent relations with the Presbyterians.

Thus it was that a generally relaxed attitude toward the dissenters had come to prevail in the colony during the latter part of Samuel Davies' residence in Hanover. In reality, the dissenters acquired more freedom than they asked for, some of them being allowed to preach unmolested wherever they desired until the Revolution.[34] In fact, as early as 1755, more than three years before Davies left Hanover, John Wright reported that he could even then "preach any where, being so distant from the metropolis, and the time being so dangerous and shocking." [35] This relative freedom, fostered so effectively by Davies, was to continue even through the Revolution and the chaotic days immediately following independence. Once the new state legislature was established, it was besieged with petitions and memorials signed by dissenters of all denominations, opposing the continuance of a government-supported church. The Hanover Presbytery persisted in its leadership of this opposition throughout the period. Its ablest spokesman, the Reverend John B. Smith, president of Hampden-Sydney College, addressed a legislative committee for three full days, arguing against a bill for government support of religion. Furthermore, Smith was instrumental in winning the eventual passage of the act establishing religious freedom in Virginia, an act that served the framers of the Constitution in guaranteeing freedom of worship. An early nineteenth-century historian maintained that "It is owning to the exertions made by Davies, and the public discussions on this subject, in which a man of his powers engaged, that sentiments, so just and

---

[33] Fauquier to Hanover Presbytery, Sept. 27, 1758, *ibid.*, p. 165.

[34] The Reverend Patrick Henry complained of both Todd and Wright in this respect; Henry to Thomas Dawson, n.d., quoted in Gewehr, *Great Awakening*, p. 98*n*.

[35] Wright to ———, Aug. 18, 1755, Foote, I, 308.

liberal respecting religious liberty have pervaded the population of Virginia." [36]

[36] [Rice], "Memoir," p. 363. Although overstated, this comment is typical of early nineteenth-century opinions of Davies. Foote bears this out: "His residence in the State is an era in its history . . . . The Virginia creed in politics acknowledges his principles of religious freedom and civil liberty. His influence on politics was indirect, but not the less sure. The sole supremacy of Chirst in the Church,——the authority of the Word of God,——the equality of the ministers of religion,——and individual rights of conscience, in defence of which he encountered such men as Pendleton, Wythe, Randolph, and the whole host of the aristocracy, are now a part and parcel of the religious and political creed of an overwhelming majority of the citizens of the 'Ancient Dominion.' He demonstrated the capability of the Church of Christ to sustain itself, not only without the fostering aid of the State, but under its oppressive laws." Foote, I, 304–305.

X

The Path of Duty: Nassau Hall

AFTER YEARS OF PLANNING AND HOPING, including four years of actual negotiations, the two competing Synods of the colonial Presbyterian church came together as the Synod of Philadelphia and New York on May 29, 1758. It was proclaimed "that all former differences and disputes are laid aside and buried; and that no future inquiry or vote shall be proposed in this Synod concerning these things; but if any member seeks a Synodical inquiry, or declaration about any of the matters of our past differences, it shall be deemed a censurable breach of this agreement, and he be rebuked accordingly." [1] American Presbyterianism was now reunited, but it immediately faced, among other problems, the task of finding a president for the College of New Jersey. President Aaron Burr had died, in September of 1757, as had his successor, Jonathan Edwards, in January of the following year, less than four months after his inauguration.[2] Those concerned with the future of the infant institution were in a turmoil. When the Board of Trustees met in

---

[1] "Minutes of the Synod of Philadelphia and New York," May 29, 1758, *Records*, pp. 285–288.
[2] Wertenbaker, *Princeton*, pp. 41–42.

April 1758, they offered the Reverend James Lockwood of Wethersfield, Connecticut, the presidency. Just four months later they were back in session and still in a state of confusion; Lockwood had refused the offer.[3] The trustees now looked to Virginia for a leader for the college, and they elected Samuel Davies to the position.[4] Their problems were not over, however, for their latest selection was unwilling to leave his home and pulpit in Hanover.

Davies had always been extremely reluctant to make any decision that would force him to alter the course of his life. Since the presidency would mean leaving Virginia permanently, he was even more uncertain about how to answer, particularly when he heard that some members of the Board of Trustees had preferred the Reverend Samuel Finley to himself. This concern was largely unfounded, however, for even though Finley had been considered at both the April and August elections, Davies was the clear choice because of his superior reputation as a preacher.[5]

Never had Davies been "cast into such anxious perplexities." Never had he felt himself "so much in need of divine direction, and so destitute of it." As he told his congregation when taking leave of them, "My difficulty was not to find out my own inclination which was, pre-engaged to Hanover, but the path of duty; and the fear of mistaking it, in so important a turn of life, kept me uneasy night and day."[6] To resolve the conflicting claims upon his loyalty, Davies decided to present his dilemma to the Presbytery of Hanover for a final decision.

In his capacity as moderator of the Presbytery, Davies summoned his fellow members to a special meeting at his home on September 13, 1758. Here, in the presence of two messengers from Princeton, his associates and friends made clear their idea of his path of duty by requesting that he remain in Virginia:

---

[3] "Minutes of the Board of Trustees of New Jersey College," April 19, 1758, Green, *Discourses*, p. 327. Lockwood was consistent in his actions and rejected the presidency of Yale College in 1766 (John Rogers Williams, *The Handbook of Princeton* [New York, 1905], p. 11).

[4] "Minutes of the Board of Trustees," Aug. 16, 1758, Green, *Discourses*, p. 327.

[5] Wertenbaker, *Princeton*, p. 44.

[6] "Apostolic Valediction," *Sermons* (1845), III, 481.

The Presbytery readily own, and are deeply sensible of the vast Importance of the College of New Jersey; its present unsettled State, and its Need of a Skilful healing Hand at the Head of it: They are also sensible of Mr. Davies' Influence, Popularity, Moderation, and in many Respects his Literary Accomplishments for so great a Trust. But the Presbytery being best acquainted with the State of Religion in Virginia, and best knowing Mr. Davies' Importance here, can by no means agree to his Removal, as they foresee Consequences very dangerous to the important Interests of Religion among us; and therefore cannot deliberately agree so sensibly to weaken our own Hands, and so deeply wound that Cause we desire above all things to promote.[7]

The two messengers returned to the Board of Trustees with their second refusal in as many months, presenting the statement of the Presbyters and Davies' personal letter of rejection.[8] But Davies immediately began to entertain painful second thoughts. He had always manifested an interest in the college and in the future of Presbyterian education in general. In fact, the very next day after the meeting of the Presbytery, he wrote to his Old Light friend on the Board of Trustees, the Reverend David Cowell of Trenton, New Jersey, expressing a definite change of mind. "The very suspicion that I may have done it an Injury, by not accepting the Honour the Trustees were pleased to confer upon me, causes me to appear almost an impardonable Criminal to myself," he said. Then he observed that he would "rejoice" and be "perfectly satisfied" if the trustees saw fit to elect his friend Finley. But Davies also offered an alternative. If agreement could not be reached on Finley, "I shall think it my Duty to accept the offer, if the Trustees judge it proper to continue or renew my Election." In summation, Davies stated his view of his mission: "My life, Sir, I should look upon as secured to God and the Public: and the Service of God and Mankind is not a *local* Thing in my View: Wherever it appears to me I may perform it to the greatest Advantage, There, I hope, I should chuse to fix my Residence, whether in Hanover, Princeton, or even Lapland or Japan."[9]

[7] Rachal, "Early Minutes of Hanover Presbytery," Sept. 13, 1758, p. 164.
[8] "Apostolic Valediction," *Sermons* (1845), III, 481.
[9] Davies to Cowell, Sept. 14, 1758, MS in Presbyterian Historical Society.

Although he left the way open for his own service, Davies continued to advocate the selection of Finley. If the Board of Trustees considered Davies fit to be the president of the college, then the Hanover pastor considered himself fit "to judge of the proper Qualifications" necessary for that office. His long and intimate acquaintance with Samuel Finley since their days together at Blair's academy in Fagg's Manor had led him to conclude that his friend was "the best qualified Person in the Compass of my Knowledge in America." It was only a matter of time, Davies felt, before Finley would emerge from his relative obscurity in Maryland and "blaze out, to the Satisfaction, and even Astonishment, of all candid Men." [10]

Davies was convinced that the Board of Trustees would take his advice and fully expected to hear no more about it. During the winter, however, he received a request to act as temporary vice-president until the trustees could meet for another election. This time, he unequivocally refused, and in very strong terms. But the members of the board were still determined to obtain his services, and at the beginning of the new year a letter arrived from Cowell containing the following statement: "1. That you will be elected next May; 2. That if you are not, Mr. Finley will not be." Cowell concluded with the argument, "I am sensible your leaving Virginia is attended with very great difficulties, but I can not think your affairs are of equal importance with the College of New Jersey." [11]

In March of 1759 came "a third application in more importunate terms than ever!" Again Davies refused, but finally he gave the Board of Trustees some official hope of his eventual acceptance: "I came to this conclusion—To mention at large, all my difficulties and objections—to insist that my first election should be null, because my electors were not then apprised of my objections—and to leave it to the trustees, after hearing all that could be said against it, whether to re-elect me at their next meeting." But selection by this body alone would not suffice, for Davies further insisted that "in

[10] Davies to Cowell, Oct. 18, 1758, *ibid.*

[11] Cowell to Davies, Dec. 25, 1758, John Hall, *History of the Presbyterian Church in Trenton, N. J. From the First Settlement of the Town* (New York, 1859), p. 132.

case they should re-elect me, it should be referred to the synod of New York and Philadelphia, whether I should accept the place." [12]

On May 9, 1759, the Board of Trustees met after a long winter of frustration and again proceeded to the election of a president for their college. The minutes of their meeting state that "the Rev. Mr. Samuel Davies was proposed as a candidate for the Presidency of the college, and admitted Nem: Cont: and also the Rev. Mr. Samuel Finley, was admitted a candidate in the same manner." After a period of "mature deliberation," they again chose Davies, and this time ordered several emissaries to present the case for the college at the next meeting of the Synod.[13]

Exactly one week later, the recently formed Synod of Philadelphia and New York was presented with opposing pleas: "An application . . . for the liberation of Mr. Davies from his pastoral charge" and "A Supplication . . . from Mr. Davies' congregation, earnestly requesting his continuation with them." [14] The case for Hanover was presented in moving terms in a lengthy petition, which had previously been submitted to the Presbytery of Hanover on the occasion of the first election and which described both Davies' work in Virginia and his worth in the minds of those he served.[15] The Synod no doubt found it difficult to reject such an emotional appeal from the leading congregation in the South, but it was forced to decide in favor of the greater good of the church. "After solemn prayer to God for direction," the members of the body judged "that the arguments in favor of said liberation do preponderate, and agree that Mr. Davies pastoral relation to his congregation be dissolved in order to his removal to the college, and do accordingly hereby dissolve it." [16]

All conditions having been fulfilled, the College of New Jersey

[12] "Apostolic Valediction," *Sermons* (1845), III, 481–482. Davies to Cowell, March 12, 1759, MS in Presbyterian Historical Society.

[13] "Minutes of the Board of Trustees," May 9, 1759, Green, *Discourses*, p. 329.

[14] "Minutes of the Synod of Philadelphia and New York," May 16, 1759, *Records*, p. 292.

[15] "New Jersey College and President Davies," *The Biblical Repertory and Princeton Review*, XII (1840), 382–383. For this petition see Appendix II.

[16] "Minutes of the Synod of Philadelphia and New York," May 16, 1759, *Records*, p. 292.

now had a president-elect after more than a year without leadership. For Davies, the agonies of leave-taking were even more severe
than the agonies of decision-making. For more than a decade he had
been the leader of Virginia Presbyterianism in all its struggles, and
he had become closely attached to his congregation in Hanover.
Yet the force of circumstances was uprooting him—painfully, even
though he was assuming the foremost position his church could convey. Thus he spoke of his own personal preferences: "Had interest
been my motive, I should undoubtedly have preferred two hundred
a year, before a scanty hundred, Had honor been my motive, I
should have chose to have sat in the president's chair in Nassau Hall,
rather than continued a despised and calumniated new-light parson
in Virginia. Or had ease been my motive, I should have preferred a
college life, before that of a hurried, fatigued itinerant." [17] But no
longer could he refuse, as he had done so many times before,[18] the
call to another station.

In July of 1759, Davies reluctantly took leave of the people he
had guided for so many years and bade farewell to the Presbytery
he had helped to establish.[19] On the first of that month he preached
his farewell sermon, "The Apostolic Valediction Considered and
Applied," based on a text from Corinthians, which reads, "finally,
brethren, farewell. Be perfect, be of good comfort, be of one mind,
live in peace: and the God of love and peace shall be with you." [20]
Soon thereafter he left the colony, arriving in Princeton on July 26.[21]

As the new president rode into the small college town, he must
have observed a sight similar to that described by a later traveler,
the Marquis de Chastellux:

[17] "The Guilt and Doom of Impenitent Hearers," *Sermons* (1845), III, 467.

[18] For example, the following comment was made by a leader of New York's First
Presbyterian Church: "We have been refused Mr. Davies." Samuel Lowden to Bellamy,
Oct. 7, 1754, K. H., "An Original Letter About Church Affairs in New York," *The Pres-
byterian Magazine*, III (1853), 337–338.

[19] Rachal, "Early Minutes of Hanover Presbytery," July 19, 1759, p. 174.

[20] *Sermons* (1845), III, 478–493. A footnote says that the original title was "A Farewell Sermon, addressed to the Presbyterian Congregation in Hanover, Virginia, July 1,
1759, on the Authors removal to the College in New Jersey," *ibid.*, p. 478n. The Biblical
text was II Corinthians 13:2.

[21] "Minutes of the Board of Trustees," Sept. 26, 1759, Green, *Discourses*, p. 334.

Beyond Kingston, the country begins to open, and continues so to Prince-
Town. This town is situated on a sort of plateau not much elevated, but
which commands on all sides: it has only one street formed by the high
road; there are about sixty or eighty houses, all tolerably well built, but
little attention is paid them, for that is immediately attracted by an
immense building, which is visible at a considerable distance. It is a college built by the state of Jersey . . . on the left of the road going to
Philadelphia, that is situated towards the middle of the town, on a distinct spot of ground, and . . . the entrance to it is by a large square
court surrounded with lofty palisades.[22]

Nassau Hall, the main building of the college which was to attract the Frenchman's eye, had been completed in 1756 with the
funds Davies had collected in Great Britain. At about that time an
unknown writer, referring to the structure as "nearly finished,"
claimed it was capable of housing almost a hundred and fifty
students in its forty-nine dormitory rooms, each of which was approximately twenty feet square. There was also "an elegant hall of
genteel workmanship," about forty feet square, containing "a small,
though exceeding good organ" and a stage "for the use of the students in their public exhibitions." On opposite sides of the hall
were portraits of George I [23] and Governor Jonathan Belcher. The
library on the second floor was "a spacious room, furnished . . .
with about 1,200 volumes, all of which have been the gifts of the
patrons and friends of the institution, both in *Europe* and *America*."
On the first floor was to be found "a commodious dining hall . . .
together with a large kitchen, steward's apartments, etc." The
building was made of stone and was crowned with "a neat cupola."
It was generally "esteemed to be the most conveniently planned
for the purpose of a college, of any in *North America*." [24] The
president's large house stood just to the south of Nassau Hall.

These were the physical surroundings for Davies as he entered

[22] François Jean Chastellux, *Voyages de M. le Marquis de Chastellux dans l'Amérique
Septentrionale dans les Années 1780, 1781, & 1782* (2 vols., Paris, 1786), I, 138–139.
[23] When the British sacked the college library during the Revolution, they stole the
portrait of George I: "A loss for which the Americans easily consoled themselves" (*ibid.*,
p. 141).
[24] Quoted in George R. Wallace, *Princeton Sketches, The Story of Nassau Hall* (New
York, 1894), pp. 10–13.

into his new duties as a college president. In deference to his position, students reportedly treated him with the utmost respect, being required to doff their hats at least ten rods before meeting him and to stand whenever he entered the room.[25]

Davies began his duties with the same energy and thoroughness that had characterized his work in Virginia. His exact salary is not known, but he presumably shared the financial straits of most men of his profession, for the trustees' minutes indicate that his income had to be supplemented by a number of perquisites, among which were the income from the grammar school conducted in conjunction with the college and free tuition for his three sons should they choose to attend the institution.[26]

The first official task undertaken by the new president was an examination of the library, with a view to publishing a list of its contents. This was done at the behest of the Board of Trustees,[27] who probably intended to use it to attract prospective students to Princeton as well as to encourage the donation of more volumes. The project gave Davies the opportunity to set forth his ideas concerning the place of books in education and also to describe what he considered to be the weaknesses in the school's collections. He stated the position of every serious educator when he claimed that "a *Large* and well-sorted Collection of Books on the various Branches of Literature, is the most ornamental and useful Furniture of a College, and the proper and valuable Fund with which it can be endowed." In Davies' view, a library was "one of the best Helps to enrich the Minds both of the Officers and Students with Knowledge; to give them an extensive Acquaintance with Authors; and to lead them beyond the narrow Limits of the Books to which they are confined in their stated Studies and Recitations."

Since it was designed in part as a fund-raising venture, the report stressed the weaknesses of the college's collections more than its strong points:

[25] *Ibid.*, p. 25.
[26] "Minutes of the Board of Trustees," Sept. 26, 1759, Green, *Discourses*, p. 334.
[27] *Ibid.*, Sept. 27, 1759.

A Survey of its *literary* Wealth . . . will soon convince the Friends of Learning and *Nassau-Hall*, how poor it still is in this important Article; to which no additions can be made from the Treasury, which is far from being equal to other unavoidable and more indispensable Exigences. But few modern Authors, who have unquestionably some Advantages above the immortal Ancients, adorn the Shelves. This Defect is most sensibly felt in the Study of Mathematics, and the *Newtonian* Philosophy, in which the Students have but very imperfect Helps, either from Books or Instruments.[28]

Such an interest in the development of the college library was illustrative of the pattern of Davies' administration. He made few alterations in the actual course of instruction, but rather tried to improve those things that had fallen into neglect during the long period when the president's chair was vacant. Chief among these improvements was the general raising of academic qualifications by means of a more rigorous system of examinations. After his first year at the college, the trustees accepted his proposal to end the automatic advancement from class to class that had formerly prevailed. It was decided that "the President and tutors, in conjunction with any other gentlemen of liberal education who shall choose to be present . . . examine the several classes, and that such as are found to be unqualified shall not be allowed to rise in the usual course." [29] More rigid residence requirements were also adopted for the degree of master of arts. These new regulations were never applied during Davies' short presidency, but they were indicative of his desire to elevate the standard of scholarship among those attending the institution.[30]

Davies also required the members of the senior class to deliver monthly orations on subjects of their own choosing, purportedly to give them a taste for the activities that he himself most enjoyed,

[28] [Samuel Davies, comp.], *A Catalogue of Books in the Library of the College of New-Jersey, January 29, 1760* (Woodbridge, N. J., 1760), pp. iii, iv. More than a thousand different titles were listed, many of which had been donated to Davies and Tennent while they were in Great Britain.

[29] "Minutes of the Board of Trustees," Sept. 24, 1760, Green, *Discourses*, p. 337.

[30] John MacLean, *History of the College of New Jersey From its Origin in 1746 to the Commencement of 1854* (2 vols., Philadelphia, 1877), I, 212.

composition and public speaking. The speakers were expected to "compose a popular harangue to be delivered publicly in the College-Hall before the Masters and Students, and as many of the inhabitants of the town as chose to attend." The president personally supervised and corrected the written texts and criticized their delivery. One of Davies' successors described this practice as follows: "About six of the young Gentlemen usually delivered their Orations in the afternoon of the first *Wednesday* in every Month to crowded audiences; and it is hard to say, whether the entertainment of the hearers, or the improvement of the students, was the greater." [31]

Davies apparently met little opposition to the changes that he tried to institute during his administration, and his relations with the tutors and students seem to have been uneventful. Shortly after his settlement at Princeton, he wrote that the college was "a peaceable manageable Society," [32] and four months later he commented that "affairs at College go on Smooth and easy; and we seem at least to have so much Goodness as to love one another." [33] The absence of internal problems must have made the position easier than it might have been, and it did leave Davies a certain amount of leisure time.

He used his spare moments in the same manner he had used them in Virginia, for his own self-improvement. It was reported that he often worked in his study until the early hours of the morning, yet always arose at five when the horn sounded to awaken the students.[34] It was this habit, coupled with the continuous confinement of his office, that weakened his already precarious health. In typical manner, however, Davies used his own recurrent ill health and the constant outbreaks of disease among the students to promote medical education, even though the college could not offer a proper course of study to this end. As an example of this interest in

[31] Finley, "The Dis-interested and Devoted Christian," *Sermons* (1766), I, liii–liv.

[32] Davies to Peter Van Brugh Livingston, Aug. 18, 1759, "Three Letters from Samuel Davies, D.D. President of Princeton College, to Mr. P. V. B. Livingston of New York, the Originals of Which are in the Rutherford Collection," *Proceedings of the New Jersey Historical Society*, series one, I, (1845), 77.

[33] Davies to Livingston, Dec. 6, 1759, *ibid.*

[34] Finley, "The Dis-interested and Devoted Christian," *Sermons* (1766), I, lii.

medical matters, he wrote to Peter Livingston of New York, a member of the Board of Trustees, asking him to "Present my Compliments to your Friend the Doctor, and inform him that the most promising Time to apply to College for young Gentlemen for his Purpose [i.e., as an apprentice] is at the Commencement and he may frequently have an opportunity of being supplied." [35] To Cowell, who was a physician as well as a preacher, he wrote to inquire about one of his former students: "I long to hear from my promising Pupil under your Care." [36]

The new president also found time to improve upon his already considerable reputation as a pulpit orator. In addition to his college duties, he was the regular pastor of the Presbyterian congregation at Princeton, attracting a wide following throughout the area. Large crowds filled the main hall of the college, which was used for want of a regular meetinghouse, to hear him preach on Sundays.[37] He was now able to devote all of his pastoral labors to one congregation, seldom preaching elsewhere except on some special occasion, such as the funeral of his friend David Cowell.[38] An observer noted that on occasions such as commencement when Davies invited one of the attending clergymen to share his pulpit, "it was scarcely possible to prevent the manifestation of the disappointment and regret which were universally felt." [39]

Commencement, of course, was the major event in the college year, drawing dignitaries from throughout the colonies of Delaware, Pennsylvania, New York, and New Jersey. If the college was particularly fortunate, the governor would journey over from Trenton to lend his dignity and prestige to the occasion. Such was the case in September of 1760 when the *Pennsylvania Gazette* reported that Thomas Boone, the newly appointed chief executive of the colony, joined the procession that paraded from the president's house to Nassau Hall. With the ringing of the college bell, "pre-

[35] Davies to Livingston, Jan. 18, 1760, "Three Letters," p. 78.
[36] Davies to Cowell, Feb. 15, 1760, MS in Presbyterian Historical Society.
[37] Green, *Discourses*, p. 328.
[38] Hall, *Presbyterian Church in Trenton*, pp. 137–144. This was never published with his other sermons but is extensively excerpted here.
[39] Green, *Discourses*, p. 351.

cisely at 10 o'clock in the forenoon," the festivities began. First came the candidates for the degree of bachelor of arts "two and two, uncovered," followed by candidates for the degree of master of arts. Next came the members of the Board of Trustees according to their seniority, the youngest first, the governor and president last. When the graduates arrived at the middle entrance of the building, they halted, "and the whole Procession divided itself equally on each side of the gravel Walk, and entered in an inverted Order."

Now the festivities began in earnest. First, there was "a handsome Salutatory Oration in Latin" followed by "a Latin Syllogistick Dispute." After this, Davies' most famous student, Benjamin Rush, arose and "in a very sprightly and entertaining Manner delivered an ingenious English Harangue in Praise of Oratory." There was then a "Forensick Dispute in English," a "Latin Dispute in a Socratick Way," and "a well-composed Valedictory Oration," also in English, after which the morning part of the exercises was concluded with "the Singing of an Ode on Science, composed by the President of the College."

But commencement at a colonial college was an all-day affair. "The Entertainment in the Afternoon" began with an address to his Excellency the Governor, followed by another Latin disputation, this time by the candidates for the master's degree. Next came the highlight of the day, the presentation of degrees by President Davies. Following this central event, "an elegant, pathetic Valedictory Oration in English" was delivered, and "the Singing of an Ode on Peace" then concluded the day's festivities "to the Universal Pleasure and Satisfaction of a numerous Auditory." [40]

The large number of orations, harangues, odes, and disputations indicates, to a certain extent, the influence that Davies' stress on public speaking exerted upon the life of the college. No mention is made of the number of students participating in the 1760 commencement, but a list of graduates of the college indicates that about seventy were under Davies' supervision at the time of his

---

[40] *Pennsylvania Gazette*, Oct. 9, 1760; the commencement was held on Sept. 25, 1760. The "Ode on Science" and the "Ode on Peace" are reprinted in *Collected Poems*, pp. 210–211, 215.

death the following year.[41] Several of these were to rise to positions of considerable prominence in public life and service. Among them were John Archer, who served three terms in the United States House of Representatives; Samuel Blair, Jr., who became a well-known educator and later declined the presidency of the college; Jonathan Bayard Smith, who served two years in the Continental Congress; and of course, Benjamin Rush, the prominent Philadelphia physician and professor who signed the Declaration of Independence.[42]

As busy as Davies was in conducting the affairs of the College of New Jersey, in ministering to the local Presbyterian congregation, and in continuing his own private studies, he still managed to take an active part in the larger work of American Presbyterianism. Although he apparently did not regularly attend the meetings of the Presbytery of New Brunswick, he did attend the meeting of his Synod in May of 1760. Here he was again honored, this time by his election as moderator, and given an opportunity to pursue another of his major interests—the Indian missions. The Synod instructed him to correspond with his friends and former associates who had charge of the missions in Virginia and North Carolina, telling them of the plight of the New Jersey Indians, and asking for advice and help.[43]

At this time, Davies also became embroiled in an unfortunate incident involving the Anglicans of Philadelphia. It seems that the Reverend William McClenachan, though a member of the Church of England, was preaching the doctrines of the New Light to the congregation of Christ Church, where he served as assistant to the rector. Many of his listeners were favorably impressed with his preaching, but others were critical of his position and sought his exclusion from the pulpit. As could have been expected, this became a topic of conversation among the assembled Presbyterian clergymen, many of whom sought to help McClenachan in some way. A letter, written by Gilbert Tennent and bearing the signatures of eighteen

---

[41] *Catalogus Collegii Neo-Cæsariensis*, pp. 16–17.

[42] MacLean, *College of New Jersey*, I, 217–218.

[43] "Minutes of the Synod of Philadelphia and New York," May 22, 1760, *Records*, p. 300.

members of the Synod, including Davies, was dispatched to the Archbishop of Canterbury seeking his intervention and assuring him of McClenachan's fitness and piety. Even though this was not a synodical act, it brought loud protests from the Philadelphia Anglicans and also from those of the Synod who were still firm in their Old Light beliefs. To the latter, this was open interference in the affairs of another congregation, similar to that which had caused the former schism in the Presbyterian church.[44]

Although nothing seems to have come of this controversy, except for some ridicule aimed at the signers of the letter,[45] it represented one of the few times Davies acted foolishly and in a manner possibly harmful to the interests of his church. After his death, the other signers of the letter had second thoughts about their action, and the Synod formally denied it as an official act. The denial not only contained an implied apology but also the hope "that the same good understanding which has hitherto happily subsisted between us and the Reverend Gentlemen of the Church of England, may still continue." [46]

If Davies did not neglect the work of the Synod of Philadelphia and New York, neither did he neglect the people of his former congregation in Hanover, from whom he had parted so reluctantly in 1759. Immediately after the commencement exercises of 1760, he made a brief visit to his former home in Virginia. Three entries in the diary of his friend, Colonel James Gordon of Lancaster County, the only record of this visit, report Davies' arrival and the disappoint-

---

[44] A discussion of this incident can be found in Horace Wemyss Smith, *Life and Correspondence of the Rev. William Smith, D.D., First Provost of the College and Academy of Philadelphia. First President of Washington College, Maryland. President of the St. Andrew's Society of Philadelphia. President of the Corporation For the Relief of the Widows and Children of Clergymen in the Communion of the Church of England in America. Secretary of the American Philosophical Society, etc., etc. With Copious Extracts From His Writings* (2 vols., Philadelphia, 1879–80), I, 214–275. Also John W. Christie, "Presbyterians and Episcopalians in 1761," *Proceedings of the Ohio Presbyterian Historical Society*, II (1940), 15–29.

[45] When the Synod met in 1761, the letter was reportedly being circulated in printed form by hawkers who went about the city crying, "*Eighteen Presbyterian Ministers* for a groat," Miller, *Memoirs*, p. 107.

[46] "Minutes of the Synod of Philadelphia and New York," May 21, 1761, *Records*, p. 306.

ment of the people in the Northern Neck when they heard that he could not come to preach to them.[47]

This was his last appearance among those he had served for so many years. On his return to Princeton he once again resumed his taxing schedule, studying far into the night and continuing his total involvement in college affairs. According to his contemporaries, the intense application to college business, coupled with his lack of physical exercise, further weakened his health. Whatever the cause, Davies appears to have been ill during most of late 1760, although still endeavoring to preach regularly to his congregation. When informed toward the end of the year that he would be expected to deliver a New Year's Day sermon, Davies readily complied. At this time also, he was told "that the late President *Burr*, on the first day of the year wherein he died, preached a Sermon on *Jer*. xxvii. 16. *Thus saith the Lord, This year thou shalt die;* and that after his death, the people took occasion to say it was premonitory." Davies reportedly thought this occurrence remarkable, even though he scoffed at the popular interpretation of the event.[48]

For some reason, possibly to allay what he believed to be a misconception of the circumstances surrounding Burr's death, Davies chose to speak from the same text.[49] Only a few days after giving this sermon, the popular young preacher contracted a severe cold for which he was improperly bled, but from which he appeared to recover. He was able to preach twice more to his Princeton congregation and was well enough to prepare personally a manuscript sermon on the death of King George II, which he intended for publication. Furthermore, he had sufficiently recovered to add a postscript in his own hand to his last letter to his brother-in-law, John Holt.[50] But

---

[47] "Journal of Col. James Gordon," Oct. 10, 11, 19, 1760, p. 203.

[48] Finley, "The Dis-interested and Devoted Christian," *Sermons* (1766), I, lv.

[49] "A Sermon on the New Year," *Sermons* (1845), II, 139–153. "Doctor Witherspoon was in the practice of preaching on New Year's day: And the writer remembers to have heard him tell, that it had been remarked to him that he *avoided this text;* and that his reply was, that he avoided it, not because he feared that preaching on it would prove the precursor of his death, but because he considered it, in its connexion, as not affording a fit subject for the occasion" (Green, *Discourses*, p. 352*n*).

[50] Davies to Holt, Jan. 21, 1761, Rush MSS. The postscript in Davies' hand is dated Jan. 22, 1761.

his condition worsened; his right arm, which had been bled, became inflamed, and he was "seized with a violent chilly fit, which was succeeded by an inflammatory fever." On February 4, less than two weeks after his last letter, Davies died.[51]

The death of Samuel Davies at the youthful age of thirty-seven shocked and saddened Presbyterians throughout the world. Funeral sermons were preached in the major churches of London, New York, and Philadelphia, not to mention the countless places where he had spoken in the course of his brief but brilliant career. Collections were made in several American cities for the support and education of his children.[52] His wife returned to Hanover where she reportedly lived with her mother in relative obscurity for the remainder of her life.[53] His mother, Martha David, who had figured so prominently in his entrance into the ministry, spent her remaining years in the household of her son's friend and companion, the Reverend John Rodgers of New York.[54]

That so short a life should have left so rich a legacy is a phenomenon difficult to appreciate until his accomplishments are surveyed. Davies' sermons, in addition to earning a worldwide reputation for the young minister during his lifetime, were printed and reprinted and still used for more than a century after his death; their content and organization provided a source of instruction for several succeeding generations of preachers. First of the truly original American hymn writers, this New Light leader composed works that are still being sung in some churches in the twentieth century.[55] His poetry, which was widely distributed, distinguished Davies in his own age and, further, was of a genre profitably studied even today.

---

[51] All contemporary accounts of Davies' death are in general agreement, although Green, *Discourses*, p. 339, erroneously gives the date as Feb. 4, 1762. All other accounts— and his tombstone—give the date as 1761. His epitaph can be found in *ibid*. pp. 355–356.

[52] "The people of Philadelphia have collected £95 per annum for five years to support his three sons at College, and Philadelphia and New York have raised between four and five hundred pounds for the widow and two daughters, for he left little estate"; David Bostwick to Bellamy, March 17, 1761 (MacLean, *College of New Jersey*, I, 246).

[53] Todd to Gibbons, n.d., *Sermons* (1766), I, cxvi*n*.

[54] Miller, *Memoirs*, p. 25*n*.

[55] "Lord, I am Thine, entirely Thine" is included in the still widely used *Methodist Hymnal* (Nashville, 1939), no. 224.

As pulpit orator, this Virginia preacher had few peers among his contemporaries either in Great Britain or in America; his oratory exerted a profound influence on later preachers and perhaps had a significant effect on Southern secular oratory of the Revolutionary period. He pioneered in the education of Negro slaves in Virginia, contributed measurably to the education of Indians, and came to be recognized as the foremost educator of his denomination. Finally, as the champion of Virginia Presbyterians and the leading spokesman for religious toleration, Samuel Davies helped lay a firm base for the ultimate separation of church and state in Virginia.

All of this developed from a life that displayed a remarkable unity of inward belief and outward action, the very ideal that he tried to encourage in others. The extent to which Davies had achieved his goal was well expressed by his friend and successor, Samuel Finley, who delivered his funeral sermon. "He plainly intimated," said Finley, "that the audience should be entertained, not with an ornamental funeral Oration, but with such an instructive discourse as the text itself naturally suggests." Because Davies himself had chosen the text, Finley was of the opinion that the "friendly audience will the more closely and seriously attend, as conceiving him, *though dead, yet speaking* to them the solemn truths it contains. For having been admitted into full knowledge of his religious principles, I may presume on speaking many of the sentiments he intended from this text. . . ." [56] The text that Davies had chosen was Romans 14:7–8. It expressed the belief that had governed his life:

> For none of us liveth to himself, and no man dieth to himself. For whether we live, we live unto the Lord; and whether we die, we die unto the Lord: whether we live therefore, or die, we are the Lord's.

[56] Finley, "The Dis-interested and Devoted Christian," *Sermons* (1766), I, xix–xx, xvi.

Appendix 1

A Certificate On Behalf Of The Dissenters in Virginia

Whereas, the Protestant dissenters of the Presbyterian denomination in the colony of Virginia lie under some restraints, particularly with regard to the number of their meeting-houses, which is not at all equal to what their circumstances require, though they have taken all legal measures to have a sufficient number registered according to the act of toleration. And whereas, the Rev. Mr. Samuel Davies has been appointed to take a voyage to Great Britain in behalf of the college of New Jersey, and may have an opportunity of using proper means to secure a redress of said grievance, this Synod do humbly and earnestly request the concurrence and assistance of their friends there, for the relief of an helpless and oppressed people in a point of so great consequence, in which their religious liberties are so nearly concerned.

We do therefore cheerfully recommend the said Mr. Davies, who is settled in Virginia and the Rev. Mr. John Todd, his colleague, as

---

[1] "Minutes of the Synod of New York," Oct. 6, 1753, *Records*, pp. 254–257, 255n, 265n.

regular and worthy members of their body, zealously and prudently engaged in advancing the Redeemer's kingdom.

A Certificate For Messrs. Gilbert Tennent And Samuel Davies

The Rev. Messrs. Gilbert Tennent and Samuel Davies, the bearers hereof, undertaking a voyage to Europe, by the appointment of this Synod, in concurrence with the trustees of the college of New Jersey, for the service of said college; the Synod do hereby certify, that the above reverend gentlemen are worthy and well approved members of their body, and do recommend them to the acceptance of the church of God, and the work of their mission, wheresoever Divine Providence may call them, imploring the Divine Presence with them and success to their important undertaking.

SIGNED BY ORDER OF THE SYNOD.

An Address to the General Assembly of the Church of Scotland

To the very venerable and honourable the moderator and other members of the General Assembly of the Church of Scotland, to meet at Edinburgh, May, 1754. The petition of the Synod of New York, convened at Philadelphia, October 3, 1753, humbly showeth:

That a college has been lately erected in the province of New Jersey by his majesty's royal charter, in which a number of youth has been already educated, who are now the instruments of service to the church of God; and which would be far more extensively beneficial were it brought to maturity. That after all the contributions that have been made to the said college, or can be raised in these parts, the fund is far from being sufficient for the erection of proper buildings, supporting the president and tutors, furnishing a library, and defraying other necessary expenses; that the trustees of said college, who are zealous and active to promote it for the public good, have already sent their humble petition to this venerable house for some assistance in carrying on so important a design; and also petitioned this Synod to appoint two of their members, the Rev. Messrs. Gilbert Tennent and Samuel Davies, to undertake a voyage to Europe in behalf of said college.

And as your petitioners apprehend the design of said petition to be of the utmost importance to the interests of learning and religion in this infant country, and are confident of the zeal of so pious and learned a body as the General Assembly of the Church of Scotland, to promote such a design; they beg leave to lay before this venerable house, a general representation of the deplorable circumstances of the churches under their Synodical care, leaving it to the commissioners to descend to particulars.

In the colonies of New York, New Jersey, Pennsylvania, Maryland, Virginia, and Carolina, a great number of congregations have been formed upon the Presbyterian plan, which have put themselves under the Synodical care of your petitioners, who conform to the constitution of the Church of Scotland, and have adopted her standards of doctrine, worship, and discipline. There are also large settlements lately planted in various parts, particularly in North and South Carolina, where multitudes are extremely desirous of the ministrations of the gospel; but they are not yet formed into congregations, and regularly organized for want of ministers.

These numerous bodies of people, dispersed so wide through so many colonies, have repeatedly made the most importunate applications to your petitioners, for ministers to be sent among them; and your petitioners have exerted themselves to the utmost for their relief, both by sending their members and candidates to officiate some time among them, and using all practicable measures for the education of pious youths for the ministry.

But alas! notwithstanding these painful endeavours, your petitioners have been utterly incapable to make sufficient provision for so many shepherdless flocks; and those that come hundreds of miles crying to them for some to break the bread of life among them, are often obliged to return in tears, with little or no relief, by reason of the scarcity of ministers.

Though every practicable expedient, which the most urgent necessity could suggest, has been used to prepare labourers for this extensive and growing harvest; yet the number of ministers in this Synod is far from being equal to that of the congregations under their care. Though sundry of them have taken the pastoral charge of two or three congregations for a time, in order to lessen the number of vacancies; and though sundry youth have lately been licensed, ordained, and settled in congregations, that were before destitute; yet there are no less than forty vacant congregations at present under the care of this Synod, besides many more which are incapable at present to support ministers; and the whole colony of North Carolina, where numerous congregations of Presbyterians are forming, and where there is not one Presbyterian minister settled.

The great number of vacancies in the bounds of this Synod, is owing partly, to the new settlements lately made in various parts of this continent, partly to the death of sundry ministers belonging to this Synod, but principally to the small numbers of youth educated for the ministry, so vastly disproportionate to the numerous vacancies; and unless some effectual measures can be taken for the education of proper persons for the sacred character, the churches of Christ in these parts must continue in the most destitute circumstances, wandering shepherdless and forlorn through this wilderness, thousands perishing for lack of knowledge, the children of God hungry and unfed, and the rising age growing up in a state little better than that of heathenism, with regard to the public ministration of the gospel.

The numerous inconveniences of a private, and the many important advantages of a public education are so evident, that we need not inform this venerable assembly of them, who cannot but be sensible from happy experience, of the many extensive benefits of convenient colleges.

The difficulty, (and in some cases impossibility,) of sending youth two, three, four, or five hundred miles or more, to the colleges in New England, is also evident at first sight. Now it is from the College of New Jersey only, that we can expect a remedy of these inconveniences; it is to *that* your petitioners look for the increase of their number; it is on *that* the Presbyterian churches, through the six colonies above mentioned, principally depend for a supply of accomplished ministers; from *that* has been obtained considerable relief already, notwithstanding the many disadvantages that unavoidably attend it in its present infant state; and from *that* may be expected a sufficient supply when brought to maturity.

Your petitioners, therefore, most earnestly pray, that this very reverend Assembly would afford the said college all the countenance and assistance in their power. The Young Daughter of the Church of Scotland, helpless and exposed in this foreign land, cries to her tender and powerful Mother for relief. The cries of ministers oppressed with labours, and of congregations famishing for want of the sincere milk of the word, implore assistance. And were the poor Indian savages sensible of their own case, they would join in the cry, and beg for more missionaries to be sent to propagate the religion of Jesus among them.

Now as the college of New Jersey appears the most promising expedient to redress these grievances, and to promote religion and learning in these provinces, your petitioners most heartily concur with the trustees, and humbly pray, that an act may be passed by this venerable and honourable Assembly, for a national collection in favour of said college.

Appendix II

A LETTER TO HANOVER PRESBYTERY AND
THE SYNOD OF NEW YORK [1]

To the Reverend Presbytery of Hanover

The Petition of the people under the ministerial care of the Rev. Samuel Davies, in and about Hanover.

Humbly sheweth, that we are not able to support [ourselves] under the mighty torrent of overwhelming grief that rushes upon us, since we have learned that the trustees of the College of New Jersey, desire the removal of our dear pastor from us. We make no doubt that your wisdom, in conjunction with our reverend pastor, will proceed in this weighty affair with the utmost caution and integrity; yet we feel so much interested in it, that we beg leave to lay these conditions before you. It was, gentlemen, a peculiar, kind providence that first gave him to us. He has relieved us from numberless distresses as our spiritual father and guide to eternal life; defended us from the formidable confederacy of our numerous enemies, and has been mighty through God, to conquer all who oppose us, and to defend the cause of the Redeemer in this degenerate land.

---

[1] "New Jersey College and President Davies," pp. 382–383.

Out of weakness we are now become strong in some good degree. After a long night of gloomy darkness, agreeable prospects begin to dawn or open upon us, and we hope to live and enjoy the most important blessings, for which only we can be willing to live, and to see the religion of our Redeemer in its purity and power among us; nay, that he is a public blessing to our land, and even to barbarous nations. In short, there is no great and good work to be conducted in our country in general, and among us in particular, but our pastor is engaged, some way or other, in it; and the eyes of almost all are directed to him as a leader.

But, dear Sirs, should our reverend pastor be removed from us, overwhelming thought! our hopes are blasted; our light becomes darkness, and our fairest prospects are fled with him. Then the crumbling materials which compose this congregation will fall to ruins, when the band that now holds it is broken; and we shall never be gathered together, we fear, and united in another minister. Our enemies will rush upon us like hungry lions to devour, and enjoy a malignant triumph over us in our loss. We are already wounded to hear them say, Ah, he will go, no doubt, when he has a good bait laid to catch him. But we are assured our reverend pastor is animated by nobler motives, and that nothing but a conviction of duty would ever remove him from us. Yet we are persuaded that many will stumble and fall before the powerful torrent of temptation, that will pour upon them from every quarter, and we shall forever be exposed to the scorn and reproach of our enemies, and become a most ruined, broken and undone people with a breach that cannot be healed. Our hearts, gentlemen, bleed at the prospect, to see multitudes turn their backs and contribute nothing to the support of the gospel among us, and throw an unsupportable burden on a few weaklings, who must sink under the weight; the cause of presbyterians dwindle away, and this poor church fall a helpless prey to its devouring enemies.

Your petitioners most humbly pray, we beseech and intreat your wisdoms, in conjunction with our dear pastor, that you will consult, and fall upon some other expedient for the relief of the college, that will not rob us of the greatest blessing we enjoy under God, and leave us a people forever undone.

And your petitioners shall ever pray, &c.

Signed by the representatives of the congregation in the name of the whole, September 13th, 1758.

SAMUEL MORRIS	DAVID WHITLOCKS
ROGER SHACKELFORD	WM. SMITH
JOHN WHITE	EDWARD CURD
BENJAMIN FAULKNER	MELCH BRAME
JAMES ALLEN	JOHN SHORE
TURNER RICHARDSON	WILLIAM CRAGHEAD

Bibliography

The Writings of Samuel Davies

An Account of a Remarkable Work of Grace, or the Great Success of the Gospel in Virginia. In a Letter . . . to the Rev. Mr. Bellamy. London, 1752.

This is the same as his *The State of Religion . . .* (Boston, 1751).

An Appendix Proving the Right of the Synod of New York to the Religious Liberties and Immunities Allowed to Protestant Dissenters by the Act of Toleration. Williamsburg, 1748.

Apparently this was appended to his *Impartial Trial . . .* (Williamsburg, 1748).

(comp.). *A Catalogue of Books in the Library of the College of New-Jersey, January 29, 1760.* Woodbridge, N. J., 1760.

"Charity and Truth United or the Way of the Multitude exposed in Six Letters to the Rev. Mr. William Stith, A.M., President of William and Mary College. In Answer to Some Passages in William Stith's Sermon Entitled the Nature & Extent of Christ's Redemption, Preached Before the General Assembly of Virginia, Nov. 11, 1753," edited by Thomas Clinton Pears. *Journal of the Presbyterian Historical Society,* XIX (1940–1941), 193–323.

Christ Precious to All True Believers. New York, n.d.; Philadelphia, n.d.

Collected Poems of Samuel Davies, 1723–1761. Edited, with an introduction, by Richard Beale Davis. Gainesville, 1968.

"The Compassion of Christ to Weak Believers." *History and Repository of Pulpit Eloquence* . . . , edited by Henry Clay Fish (New York, 1857), II, 410–424.

"Copy of an Original Letter from the Rev. S. Davies to the Rev. Joseph Bellamy." *The Virginia Evangelical and Literary Magazine,* VI (1823), 567–569.

The Crisis: or, the Uncertain Doom of Kingdoms, at Particular Times, Considered with Reference to Great-Britain and Her Colonies in Their Present Circumstances. A Sermon Preached in Hanover, Virginia, Oct. 28, 1756; a Day Appointed by the Synod of New-York, to be Observed as a General Fast, on Account of the Present War with France. With a Preface by the Reverend Mr. Thomas Gibbons. London, 1757.

The Curse of Cowardice: A Sermon Preached to the Militia of Hanover County, Virginia, at a General Muster, May 8, 1758. With a View to Raise a Company for Captain Samuel Meredith. London, 1758; rpt. Boston, 1759; rpt. New York, 1759; rpt. Philadelphia, 1759; rpt. Woodbridge, N. J., 1759.

The Duties, Difficulties and Rewards of the Faithful Minister. A Sermon Preached at the Installation of the Revd. Mr. John Todd . . . Into the Pastoral Charge of the Presbyterian Congregation, In and About the Upper Part of Hanover County in Virginia, Nov. 12, 1752. With an Appendix, Containing the Form of Installation, etc. Glasgow, 1754.

The Duty of Christians to Propagate Their Religion Among the Heathens, Earnestly Recommended to the Masters of Negroe Slaves in Virginia. A Sermon Preached in Hanover, January 8, 1757. London, 1758.

The Good Soldier. Extracted From a Sermon Preached to a Company of Volunteers, Raised in Virginia, August 17, 1755. London, 1756.

A series of extracts from his *Religion and Patriotism* . . .
(Philadelphia, 1755).

"The Hymns of President Davies." Edited by Louis Fitzgerald
Benson. *Journal of the Presbyterian Historical Society,* II
(1903), 343–373.

The Impartial Trial Impartially Tried and Convicted of Partiality.
Williamsburg, 1748.

   Appended to this was his *Appendix Proving the Right of the
Synod* . . . (Williamsburg, 1748).

Letter to Joseph Bellamy, July 4, 1751. *The Presbyterian Magazine,* IV (1854), 513.

*Letters From the Rev. Samuel Davies, and Others; Shewing the
State of Religion in Virginia, South Carolina, etc., Particularly
Among the Negroes.* London, 1761.

*Letters From the Rev. Samuel Davies, etc., Shewing the State of
Religion in Virginia, Particularly Among the Negroes. Likewise
an Extract From a Gentleman in London to his Friend in the
Country, Containing Some Observations on the Same.* London,
1757.

   This should not be confused with his *Letters From* . . . *South
Carolina* . . . (London, 1761).

"Letters of Samuel Davies." *The Virginia Evangelical and Literary
Magazine,* II (1819), 537–543.

*Little Children Invited to Jesus Christ. A Sermon Preached in Han-
over County, Virginia; With an Account of the Late Remarkable
Religious Impressions Among the Students in the College of
New-Jersey.* London, 1758; rpt. Boston, 1759; rpt. London,
1763; rpt. Boston, 1764; rpt. Boston, 1765; rpt. Hartford, 1766;
rpt. Boston, 1770; rpt. Boston, 1791; rpt. Boston, 1798; rpt.
Northampton, 1798.

*The Method of Salvation Through Jesus Christ. A Sermon, By
the Late Reverend and Pious Samuel Davies, A.M. President
of the College in New-Jersey.* Providence, 1793.

*The Military Glory of Great Britain, An Entertainment, Given by
the Late Candidates for the Bachelor's Degree, at the Close of*

the Anniversary Commencement, Held in Nassau-Hall, New-Jersey, September 29, 1762. Philadelphia, 1762.

  The words, but not the music, are generally attributed to Samuel Davies.

"The Military Glory of Great Britain, An Entertainment." *The Magazine of History,* XXIX, extra number 114 (1925), 19–34.

Miscellaneous Poems, Chiefly on Divine Subjects. In Two Books. Published for the Religious Entertainment of CHRISTIANS in General. Williamsburg, 1752.

"An Ode on the Prospect of Peace." Philadelphia, 1761.

  A broadside of the ode originally presented at the commencement of 1760.

"Old Documents." *The Virginia Evangelical and Literary Magazine,* IV (1821), 538–552.

  Five letters from Samuel Davies to Richard Crutenden and John Gillies.

Pregeth ar yr Adgyfodiad Cyffredinol; Oddiworth Ioan v. 28, 29. Yn Saesonaeg gan y Parchedig Samuel Davies, A.M. yn Princetown Jersey Newydd, America. Wedi ei Throi i'r Cymraeg gan y Parchedig M. Jones. Caerfryddin, 1798.

Pregeth ar yr Adgyfodiad Cyffredinol, yn Saesonaeg, gan y Parch. Samuel Davies, Diweddar Olygwr ar y Colledge Princeton, yn Jersey Newydd, yn America. Wedi ei Chyfieithu i'r Gymraeg gan y Parch. M. Jones. Nghaerfryddin, 1789.

"A Recovered Tract of President Davies: Now First Published." *The Biblical Repertory and Princeton Review,* IX (1837), 349–364.

  Davies called it "Remarks on . . . Bolingbroke."

Religion and Patriotism, the Constituents of a Good Soldier. A Sermon Preached to Captain Overton's Independent Company of Volunteers, Raised in Hanover County, Virginia, August 17, 1755. Philadelphia, 1755; rpt. Belfast, 1756; rpt. Glasgow, 1756; rpt. London, 1756.

  Extracts were printed as *The Good Soldier . . .* (London, 1756).

Religion and Public Spirit. A Valedictory Address to the Senior

Class, Delivered in Nassau-Hall, September 21, 1760, the Sunday Before Commencement. Philadelphia, 1761; rpt. New York, 1761; rpt. Portsmouth, N. H., 1762.

"Remarks on the Philosophical Works of Lord Bolingbroke." *The Biblical Repertory and Princeton Review*, IX (1837), 349–364. A letter from Samuel Davies to —— Donald, April 5, 1757, published under the title "A Recovered Tract . . . ."

The Reverend Samuel Davies Abroad: The Diary of a Journey to England and Scotland, 1753–55. Edited, with an Introduction, by George William Pilcher. Urbana, Ill., 1967.

A Sermon Delivered at Nassau-Hall, January 14, 1761. on the Death of His Late Majesty King George II. Published by Request. To Which is Prefixed a Brief Account of the Life, Character, and Death of the Author. By David Bostwick, A.M., Minister of the Presbyterian Congregation in New-York. Boston, 1761; rpt. Philadelphia, 1761; rpt. New York, 1761; rpt. Boston, n.d.

A Sermon on Man's Primitive State; and the First Covenant. Delivered Before the Reverend Presbytery of New-Castle, April 13th 1748. Philadelphia, 1748.

A Sermon Preached at Henrico, 29th April, 1753, and at Canonsgate, 26th May, 1753. Edinburgh, 1754.

A Sermon Preached Before the Reverend Presbytery of New-castle, October 11, 1752. Published at the Desire of the Presbytery and Congregation. Philadelphia, 1753.

Sermons and Tracts, Separately Published at Boston, Philadelphia, etc. Edinburgh, 1793.

Sermons on the Most Useful and Important Subjects, Adapted to the Family and Closet. By the Rev. Samuel Davies, A.M. Late President of the College at Princeton in New Jersey. To Which are Prefixed, a Sermon on the Death of Mr. Davies, by Samuel Finley, D.D. And Another Discourse on the Same Elegiac Occasion, Together with an Elegiac Poem to the Memory of Mr. Davies, by Thomas Gibbons, D.D. Edited by Thomas Gibbons. 5 vols., London, 1766–1771; 3 vols., New York, 1766; 3 vols., London, 1777; 4 vols., London, 1779; 3 vols., London, 1792;

3 vols., New York, 1792; 2 vols., Philadelphia, 1794; 3 vols., London, 1804–1806; 4 vols., London, 1804; 1 vol., Boston, 1810; 3 vols., Boston, 1811; 4 vols., London, 1815; 5 vols., Baltimore, 1816; 4 vols., London, 1824; 3 vols., New York, 1828.

The three-volume, New York, 1766 edition is no longer extant and may never have been published. It is listed in Charles Evans, *American Bibliography,* number 10277.

Sermons on Important Subjects . . . . Edited by Albert Barnes. 3 vols., New York, 1841; 3 vols., New York, 1842; 3 vols., New York, 1844; 3 vols., New York and Pittsburgh, 1845; 3 vols., New York, 1846; 3 vols., New York, 1849; 3 vols., New York, 1851; 3 vols., New York, 1854; 3 vols., New York, 1862; 2 vols., Edinburgh, 1867.

Sermons on Important Subjects . . . . Edited by William Buell Sprague. 3 vols., Philadelphia, 1864.

The State of Religion Among the Protestant Dissenters in Virginia; in a Letter to the Reverend Mr. Joseph Bellamy of Bethlem, in New England: From the Reverend Mr. Samuel Davies, V.D.M., in Hanover County, Virginia. Boston, 1751.

Substance of Sermons, by Samuel Davies . . . Given in His Own Words. By the Compiler of the Sailor's Companion. Designed for Gratuitous Circulation. Edited by J. K. Davis. New York, 1851.

"Three Letters from Samuel Davies, D.D. President of Princeton College, to Mr. P. V. B. Livingston of New York, the Originals of Which are in the Rutherford Collection." *Proceedings of the New Jersey Historical Society,* series one, I (1845), 77–78.

Verses Composed by a Pious Clergyman in Virginia. Printed broadside, in University of Virginia Library, Charlottesville.

The Vessels of Mercy, and the Vessels of Wrath, Delineated, in a New, Uncontroverted, and Practical Light. A Sermon First Preached in New-Kent, Virginia, August 22, 1756. London, 1758.

Virginia's Danger and Remedy. Two Discourses, Occasioned by the Severe Drought in Sundry Parts of the Country; and the

Defeat of General Braddock. Glasgow, 1756; rpt. Williamsburg, 1756.

"VIRO PRÆCLARISSIMO Ingenius Artibus, Atque Humanitate Perpolito, THOMÆ BOONE Armerigo, Provinciæ *Novæ-Cæsariæ* GUBERNATORI, Cancellario, marisque contermini VICE-ADMIRALLO perquam illustri, nostre quoque, Academiæ Mæcenati, nec non Curatorum Præsidi, summo Honore dignando; Reverendo æque ac honorando D. SAMUEL DAVIES, Collegii Neo-Cæsariensis Præsidi . . . ." Philadelphia, 1760.

A broadside schedule of the events at the commencement of New Jersey College in 1760.

(with Philip Doddridge, and Anon.) *A System of Family Duty, Containing the Duty Which Husbands, Wives, Parents, and Children, Owe to Each Other, In Their Respective Situations. With an Appendix: Containing I. An Address to Husbands and Wives.—II. An Address to Parents.—III. An Address to Children. To Which is Now Added, a Sermon to Children. By Samuel Davies, A.M. and a Plain and Serious Address to the Master of a Family. On the Important Subject of Family Religion. By Philip Doddridge, D.D.* Hartford, 1814.

(with Gilbert Tennent) *A General Account of the Rise and State of the College, Lately Established in New-Jersey, in America: And the End and Design of its Institution. Originally Published in America, An. 1752, by the Trustees of the said College; and Now Republished, in Pursuance of Their Order, With Some Alterations and Additions, Adapted to its Present State, For the Information of the Friends of Learning and Piety in Great Britain.* London, 1754; Edinburgh, 1754.

Gilbert Tennent was the sole author of the 1752 edition.

UNPUBLISHED MATERIALS

Manuscripts

Dartmouth College Library
Eleazar Wheelock MSS.
Four letters to and from Wheelock concerning Samuel Davies and the Indian missions.

Library Company of Philadelphia—Historical Society of Pennsylvania

Benjamin Rush MSS.
"Remarks on the VII ch of Dr. Sherlock's Discourse on Judgements" by Samuel Davies.
"Synoptical Tables of the Humane Passions" by Samuel Davies.
Seventeen letters from Samuel Davies to John Holt.
Ebenezer Hazard MSS.
Two letters from Davies to Hazard.

Library of Congress

William and Thomas Dawson MSS.
Two volumes of letters and papers concerning religious affairs in Virginia.

New York Public Library

William Richardson MS.
"An Account of my Proceedings since I accepted the Indian Mission in October 2d. 1758. to go & exercise my office among the Cherokees or any other Indian Nation that wou'd allow me to preach to them" by William Richardson.

Princeton University Library

Samuel Davies MSS.
Forty-six pages of undeciphered abbreviated writing.
MS Journal, July 2, 1753–February 13, 1755.
MS Sermon on Luke 14:27.
Miscellaneous letters.

Presbyterian Historical Society, Philadelphia

Samuel Davies MSS.
Five letters to David Cowell.

Virginia Historical Society, Richmond

Samuel Davies MS.
MS page from Samuel Davies' Old Testament.

Theses and Dissertations

Alley, Robert Sutherland. "The Reverend Mr. Samuel Davies: A Study in Religion and Politics, 1747–1759." Diss. Princeton University, 1962.

Bost, George Henry. "Samuel Davies, Colonial Revivalist and Champion of Religious Toleration." Diss. Chicago, 1942.

Gilborn, Craig A. "The Literary Work of the Reverend Samuel Davies." Thesis. University of Delaware, 1961.

OTHER PRIMARY WORKS

Blair, John. "Diary of John Blair." Edited by Lyon G. Tyler. *William and Mary Quarterly*, series one, VII (1898), 133–153; VIII (1899), 1–17.

Burke, Edmund. *Works*. 8 vols., London, 1803.

Caldwell, John. *An Impartial Trial of the Spirit Operating in this Part of the World; by Comparing the Nature, Effects and Evidences, of the Present Supposed Conversion With the Word of God. A Sermon Preached at New Londonderry, October 14th, 1741.* Boston, 1742; rpt. Williamsburg, 1748.

Chastellux, François Jean. *Voyages de M. le Marquis de Chastellux dans l'Amérique Septentrionale dans les années 1780, 1781, & 1782.* 2 vols., Paris, 1786.

College of New Jersey. *Catalogus Collegii Neo-Cæsariensis.* Princeton, 1824.

Edwards, Jonathan. *Sinners in the Hands of an Angry God. A Sermon Preached at Enfield, July 8th, 1741. At a Time of Great Awakenings; and Attended With Remarkable Impressions on Many of the Hearers.* Boston, 1741.

——. *The Works of President Edwards: With a Memoir of His Life.* Edited by Sereno Edwards Dwight. 10 vols., Boston, 1830.

Finley, Samuel. "The Dis-interested and Devoted Christian: A Sermon Preached at Nassau-Hall, Princeton, May 28, 1761. Occasioned by the Death of the Rev. Samuel Davies, A.M. Late President of the College of New Jersey" in Samuel Davies,

Sermons on the Most Useful and Important Subjects . . . , edited by Thomas Gibbons (London, 1766), I, xvi–lv.

Fish, Henry Clay (ed.). *History and Repository of Pulpit Eloquence, (Deceased Divines,) Containing the Masterpieces of Bossuet, Bourdalogue, Massillon, Flechier, Abbadie, Taylor, Barrow, Hall, Watson, M'Laurin, Chalmers, Evans, Edwards, Davies, John M. Mason, Etc., Etc., With Discourses From Chrysostom, Basil, Gregory Nazienzen, Augustine, Athanasius, and Others Among the "Fathers," and From Wickliffe, Luther, Calvin, Melancthon, Knox, Latimer, Etc. of the "Reformers." Also, Sixty Other Celebrated Sermons, From as Many Eminent Divines in the Greek and Latin, English, German, Irish, French, Scottish, and Welsh Churches; a Large Number of Which Have Now, For the First Time, Been Translated. The Whole Arranged in Their Proper Order, and Accompanied With Historical Sketches of Preaching in the Different Countries Represented, and Biographical and Critical Notices of the Several Preachers and Their Discourses.* 2 vols., New York, 1857.

This contains "The Compassion of Christ . . ." by Samuel Davies.

Fisher, George. "Narrative of George Fisher. Commencing With a Voyage From London, May, 1750, for Yorktown in Virginia and Ending in August, 1755, on His Return From Philadelphia to Williamsburg." *William and Mary Quarterly,* series one, XVII (1908), 100–139, 147–176.

Gibbons, Thomas. *"Divine Conduct Vindicated, or the Operations of* God *Shown to be the Operations of Wisdom:* In the Substance of Two Discourses, Preached at Haberdashers-Hall, London, March 29, 1761; Occasioned by the Decease of the Rev. Samuel Davies, A.M. and President of the College of *Nassau-Hall* in *New Jersey."* Samuel Davies, *Sermons on the Most Useful and Important Subjects . . . ,* edited by Thomas Gibbons (London, 1766), I, lxii–xcviii.

This was originally published separately in London, 1761.

———. *Hymns Adapted to Divine Worship.* London, 1769.

Gordon, James. "Journal of Col. James Gordon, of Lancaster

County, Va." *William and Mary Quarterly*, series one, XI (1902), 98–112, 217–236; XII (1903), 1–12.

Hartwell, Henry, James Blair, and Edward Chilton. *The Present State of Virginia and the College*. Edited by Hunter Dickinson Farish. Williamsburg, 1940.
  A reprint of the original 1727 edition.

Hawks, Francis Lister (ed.). *Contributions to the Ecclesiastical History of the United States of America*. 2 vols., New York, 1836.

Hening, William Waller (ed.). *The Statutes at Large, Being a Collection of All the Laws of Virginia From the First Session of Legislature in the Year 1619*. 13 vols., Philadelphia and Richmond, 1809–1823.

H——, K—— (ed.). "An Original Letter About Church Affairs in New York." *The Presbyterian Magazine, III* (1853), 337–338.

James, Charles F. (ed.). *Documentary History of the Struggle for Religious Liberty in Virginia*. Lynchburg, Va., 1900.

McIlwaine, Henry Read, and J. P. Kennedy (eds.). *Journals of the House of Burgesses of Virginia, 1619–1776*. 13 vols., Richmond, 1905–1915.

——, Wilmer L. Hall, and Benjamin J. Hillman. *Executive Journals of the Council of Colonial Virginia*. 6 vols., Richmond, 1925–1966.

Miller, Samuel. *Memoirs of the Rev. John Rodgers, D.D. Late Pastor of the Wall-Street and Brick Churches in the City of New York*. New York, 1813.

Nutter, Charles S. (ed.). *Hymn Studies: An Illustrated and Annotated Edition of the Hymnal of the Methodist Episcopal Church*. New York and Cincinnati, 1884.

Perry, William Stevens (comp.). *Historical Collections Relating to the American Colonial Church*. 4 vols., Hartford, 1870.

Rachal, William M. E. (ed.). "Early Minutes of Hanover Presbytery." *Virginia Magazine of History and Biography*, LXIII (1945), 53–75, 161–185.

"Records of Old Londonderry Congregation, Now Faggs Manor,

Chester Co., Pa." *Journal of the Presbyterian Society*, VIII (1917), 343–379.

Records of the Presbyterian Church in the United States of America: Embracing the Minutes of the Presbytery of Philadelphia, From A.D. 1706 to 1716: Minutes of the Synod of Philadelphia, From A.D. 1717 to 1758: Minutes of the Synod of New York, From A.D. 1745 to 1758: Minutes of the Synod of Philadelphia and New York, From A.D. 1758 to 1788. Philadelphia, 1841.

"The Records of the Presbytery of New Castle Upon Delaware." *Journal of the Presbyterian Historical Society*, XIV (1930–1931), 289–308; XV (1932–1933), 73–120, 174–207.

Records of the Welsh Tract Baptist Meeting, Pencader Hundred, New Castle County, Delaware, 1701 to 1828. Papers of the Historical Society of Delaware, V, no. xlii, pt. 1. Wilmington, 1904.

Secker, Thomas. *A Letter to the Right Honourable Horatio Walpole, Esq; Written Jan. 9, 1750–1751, by the Right Reverend Thomas Secker, LL.D. Lord Bishop of Oxford: Concerning Bishops in America.* London, 1769.

Tennent, Gilbert. *The Danger of an Unconverted Ministry. Consider'd in a Sermon on Mark VI. 34. Preached at Nottingham, in Pennsylvania, March 8, Anno 1739–1740.* Philadelphia, 1740.

Thompson, John. *The Doctrine of Conviction Set in a Clear Light, or an Examination and Confutation of Several Errors Relating to Conversion. Being the Substance of a Sermon Preached by the Author to His Own and a Neighbouring Congregation, With Some Enlargements.* Philadelphia, 1741.

———. *The Government of the Church of Christ, and the Authority of Church Judicatories Established on a Scriptural Foundation, and the Spirit of Rash Judging Arraigned and Condemned; or the Matter of Difference Between the Synod of Philadelphia and the Protesting Brethren Justly and Fairly Stated. Being an Examination of Two Papers Brought in by Two of the Protesting Brethren, and Read Publickly in Open Synod in May 1740: And Also an Apology Brought in, Subscribed by the Protesting Brethren, and Read Also in Open Synod in May 1739.* Philadelphia, 1741.

Wesley, John. *The Journal of the Rev. John Wesley, A.M. Sometime Fellow of Lincoln College, Oxford, Enlarged From Original MSS., With Notes From Unpublished Diaries, Annotations, Maps, and Illustrations.* Edited by Nehemiah Curnock. 8 vols., London [1909–1916].

Woolman, John. *Considerations on the True Harmony of Mankind; and How it is to be Maintained.* Philadelphia, 1770.

SECONDARY WORKS

A——, R. W. "Review of Samuel Davies, *Sermons on Important Subjects* . . . , ed. Albert Barnes (New York, 1842)." *The Methodist Quarterly Review,* XXVIII (1846), 138–146.

Alexander, Archibald. *Biographical Sketches of the Founder and Principal Alumni of the Log College. Together With an Account of the Revivals of Religion Under Their Ministry.* Philadelphia, 1851.

Alexander, James Waddel. *The Life of Archibald Alexander, D.D., First Professor in the Theological Seminary, at Princeton, New Jersey.* New York, 1845; New York and Philadelphia, 1846.

"Aliquis." "Biographical Sketch of President Davies." *The Presbyterian Magazine,* III (1853), 570–574.

Anderson, James S. M. *The History of the Church of England, in the Colonies and Foreign Dependencies of the British Empire.* 3 vols., London, 1856.

Beam, Jacob N. "Dr. Robert Smith's Academy at Pequea, Pennsylvania." *Journal of the Presbyterian Historical Society,* VIII (1915), 145–161.

Benson, Louis Fitzgerald. *The English Hymn: Its Development and Use in Worship.* Richmond, 1962.

——. "President Davies as a Hymn Writer." *Journal of the Presbyterian Historical Society,* II (1903), 277–286.

Bishop, Robert H. *An Outline History of the Church in the State of Kentucky, Containing the Memoirs of the Rev. David Rice.* Lexington, 1824.

Bost, George Henry. "Samuel Davies, Preacher of the Great Awakening." *Journal of the Presbyterian Historical Society*, XXVI (1948), 65–86.

———. "Samuel Davies as President of Princeton." *Journal of the Presbyterian Historical Society*, XXVI (1948), 165–181.

Briggs, Charles Augustus. *American Presbyterianism; its Origin and Early History, Together With an Appendix of Letters and Documents, Many of which have Recently Been Discovered.* New York, 1885.

Bruce, Philip Alexander, Lyon G. Tyler, Richard L. Morton, *et al. History of Virginia: Colonial Period, 1607–1763.* 3 vols., Chicago and New York, 1924.

Brydon, George MacLaren. *Virginia's Mother Church and the Political Conditions Under Which it Grew.* 2 vols.: vol. I, Richmond, 1947; vol. II, Philadelphia, 1952.

Campbell, Charles. *History of the Colony and Ancient Dominion of Virginia.* Philadelphia, 1860.

"Catalogus Collegii. Neo-Cæsariensis. Princetonæ." *The Biblical Repertory and Princeton Review*, XII (1840), 378.

Christie, John W. "Presbyterians and Episcopalians in 1761." *Proceedings of the Ohio Presbyterian Historical Society*, II (1940), 15–29.

Collins, Varnum Lansing. *Princeton, Past and Present.* Princeton, 1945.

Covey, Cyclone. *The American Pilgrimage; the Roots of American History, Religion and Culture.* New York, 1961.

Cross, Arthur Lyon. *The Anglican Episcopate and the American Colonies.* Cambridge, Mass., 1902; rpt. Hamden, Conn., 1964.

Davidson, Robert. *History of the State of Kentucky; With a Preliminary Sketch of the Churches in the Valley of Virginia.* New York, 1847.

"Davies's State of Religion Among the Protestant Dissenters in Virginia." *The Biblical Repertory and Princeton Review*, XII (1840), 169–205.

Davis, Harry Alexander. *The Davis Family in Wales and America (Davies and David), Genealogy of Morgan David of Pennsylvania.* Washington, D. C., 1927.

Dictionary of American Biography. Edited by Dumas Malone. New York, 1928–1937.

Dictionary of National Biography. Edited by Leslie Stephen and Sidney Lee. London, 1917.

Duffield, Samuel Willoughby. *English Hymns: Their Authors and History*. New York, 1886.

Eckenrode, H. J. *Separation of Church and State in Virginia: A Study in the Development of the Revolution*. Special report of the Department of Archives and History, Virginia State Library. Richmond, 1910.

Faris, John T. *Old Churches and Meeting Houses in and Around Philadelphia*. Philadelphia and London, 1926.

Foote, Henry Wilder. *Three Centuries of American Hymnody*. Cambridge, Mass., 1940.

Foote, William Henry. *Sketches of Virginia: Historical and Biographical*. Series one. Philadelphia, 1850; rpt. Richmond, 1966.

———. *Sketches of Virginia: Historical and Biographical*. Series two. Philadelphia, 1856.

Ford, Henry Jones. *The Scotch-Irish in America*. Princeton, 1915.

Gaines, Elizabeth Venable. *Cub Creek Church and Congregation, 1738–1838*. Richmond and Texarkana, 1931.

Gewehr, Wesley Marsh. *The Great Awakening in Virginia: 1740–1790*. Durham, 1930.

Gilborn, Craig A. "Samuel Davies' Sacred Muse." *Journal of Presbyterian History*, XLI (1963), 63–79.

Gillies, John. *Historical Collections Relating to Remarkable Periods of the Success of the Gospel, and Eminent Instruments Employed in Promoting it*. 2 vols., Glasgow, 1754.

———. *Historical Collections . . . .* 2 vols. in one. Kelso, Va., 1845.

Graham, James R. *The Planting of the Presbyterian Church in Northern Virginia Prior to the Organization of Winchester Presbytery, December 4, 1794*. Winchester, 1904.

Green, Ashbel. *Discourses Delivered in the College of New Jersey; Addressed Chiefly to Candidates for the First Degree in the Arts; With Notes and Illustrations, Including a Historical Sketch of the College, From its Origin to the Accession of President Wither-spoon.* Philadelphia, New York, and Trenton, 1822.

Gummere, Richard M. *Seven Wise Men of Colonial America.* Cambridge, Mass., 1967.

Hall, John. *History of the Presbyterian Church in Trenton, N.J. From the First Settlement of the Town.* New York, 1859.

Heimert, Alan. *Religion and the American Mind from the Great Awakening to the Revolution.* Cambridge, Mass., 1966.

—— and Perry Miller. *The Great Awakening.* Indianapolis, 1967.

Henry, William Wirt. *Patrick Henry; Life, Correspondence and Speeches.* 3 vols., New York, 1891.

Hodge, Charles. *The Constitutional History of the Presbyterian Church in the United States of America.* 2 vols. in one. Philadelphia, 1851.

Howison, Robert Reid. *A History of Virginia, From its Discovery and Settlement by Europeans to the Present Time.* 2 vols., Philadelphia, 1846.

Hughes, John G. "Samuel Davies." *The John P. Branch Historical Papers of Randolph-Macon College,* IV (1941), 65–79.

Johnson, Thomas Cary. *Virginia Presbyterianism and Religious Liberty in Colonial and Revolutionary Times.* Richmond, 1907.

Julian, John (ed.). *A Dictionary of Hymnology Setting Forth the Origin and History of Christian Hymns of all Ages and Nations With Special Reference to Those Contained in the Hymn Books of English-Speaking Countries, and Now in Common Use. Together With Biographical and Critical Notices of Their Authors and Translators and Historical Articles on National and Denominational Hymnody, Breviaries, Missals, Psalters, Sequences, &C. &C. &C.* New York, 1892.

Kenney, William Howland, 3d. "George Whitefield, Dissenter Priest of the Great Awakening, 1739–1741." *William and Mary Quarterly,* third series, XXVI (1969), 75–93.

Klett, Guy Souillard. *Presbyterians in Colonial Pennsylvania.* Philadelphia, 1937.

Love, W. DeLoss. *Samson Occum and the Christian Indians of New England*. Boston, 1899.

MacLean, John. *History of the College of New Jersey From its Origin in 1746 to the Commencement of 1854*. 2 vols., Philadelphia, 1877.

Martz, Louis L. "Foreword" to *The Poetry of Edward Taylor*. Edited by Donald E. Stanford. New Haven, 1960.

Maxson, Charles Hartshorn. *The Great Awakening in the Middle Colonies*. Chicago, 1920.

Meade, Robert Douthat. *Patrick Henry, Patriot in the Making*. Philadelphia, 1957.

Miller, Perry. *Jonathan Edwards*. New York, 1949.

Morton, Richard L. *Colonial Virginia*. 3 vols., Chapel Hill, 1960.

Murphy, Thomas. *The Presbytery of the Log College; or Cradle of the Presbyterian Church in America*. Philadelphia, 1889.

Nevin, Alfred (ed.). *Encyclopedia of the Presbyterian Church in the United States of America: Including the Northern and Southern Assemblies*. Philadelphia, 1884.

"New Jersey College and President Davies." *The Biblical Repertory and Princeton Review*, XII (1840), 377–393.

Patton, Jacob Harris. *A Popular History of the Presbyterian Church in the United States of America*. New York, 1900.

Pears, Thomas Clinton, and Guy Souillard Klett (eds.). *Documentary History of William Tennent and the Log College*. Philadelphia, 1940.

Pilcher, George William. "The Pamphlet War on the Proposed Virginia Anglican Episcopate, 1767–1775." *Historical Magazine of the Protestant Episcopal Church*, XXX (1961), 266–279.

———. "Samuel Davies and the struggle for Religious Toleration in Colonial Virginia." *The Historian*, XXVIII (1965), 48–71.

———. "Samuel Davies and the Conversion of Negroes in Early Virginia," *Virginia Magazine of History and Biography*, LXXIV (1966), 293–300.

———. "Virginia Newspapers and the Dispute Over the Proposed Colonial Episcopate." *The Historian*, XXIII (1960), 98–113.

"Review of Charles C. Jones, *The Religious Instruction of the*

Negroes in the United States (n.p., 1842)." *The Biblical Repertory and Princeton Review,* XV (1843), 22–41.

"Review of Samuel Davies, *Sermons on Important Subjects* . . . , ed. Albert Barnes (New York, 1841)." *The Biblical Repertory and Princeton Review,* IV (1842), 142–169.

[Rice, John Holt]. "Memoir of the Rev. Samuel Davies." *The Virginia Evangelical and Literary Magazine,* I (1819), 112–119, 186–188, 201–217, 329–335, 353–363, 474–479, 560–567.

[————]. "The Origin of Presbyterianism in Virginia." *The Virginia Evangelical and Literary Magazine,* II (1819), 345–353.

Smith, Horace Wemyss. *Life and Correspondence of the Rev. William Smith, D.D., First Provost of the College and Academy of Philadelphia. First President of Washington College, Maryland. President of the St. Andrew's Society of Philadelphia. President of the Corporation For the Relief of the Widows and Children of Clergymen in the Communion of the Church of England in America. Secretary of the American Philosophical Society, etc., etc. With Copious Extracts From His Writings.* 2 vols., Philadelphia, 1879–1880.

Smyth, Charles. *The Art of Preaching. A Practical Survey of Preaching in the Church of England; 747–1939.* London, 1940.

Spotswood, John Boswell. *An Historical Sketch of the Presbyterian Church in New Castle, Delaware.* Philadelphia, 1859.

Sprague, William Buell. *Annals of the American Pulpit or Commemorative Notices of Distinguished American Clergymen of Various Denominations, From the Early Settlement of the Country to the Close of the Year Eighteen Hundred and Fifty-Five. With Historical Introductions.* 9 vols., New York, 1859–1869.

Sweet, William Warren. *Makers of Christianity; From John Cotton to Lyman Abbott.* New York, 1937.

————. *Revivalism in America, its Origin, Growth, and Decline.* New York, 1944.

————. *The Story of Religion in America.* New York and London, 1930.

Tenney, Mary McWhorter. *Communion Tokens, Their Origin, History and Use, With a Treatise on the Relation of the Sacra-*

ment to the Vitality and Revivals of the Church. Grand Rapids, 1936.

Thompson, Ernest Trice. *Presbyterians in the South, 1607–1861.* Richmond, 1963.

Tracy, Joseph. *The Great Awakening: A History of the Revival of Religion in the Time of Edwards and Whitefield.* Boston, 1842.

Trinterud, Leonard J. *The Forming of an American Tradition; a Re-examination of Colonial Presbyterianism.* Philadelphia, 1949.

[Tyler, Lyon G.], "The Holt Family." *Tyler's Quarterly Magazine of History and Genealogy,* VII (1926), 277–285.

Vallandigham, James Laird, and Samuel A. Gayley. *History of the Presbytery of New Castle From its Organization, March 13, 1717, to 1888.* Philadelphia [1889].

Wallace, George R. *Princeton Sketches, The Story of Nassau Hall.* New York, 1894.

Webster, Richard. *A History of the Presbyterian Church in America, From its Origin Until the Year 1760, with Biographical Sketches of its Early Ministers.* Philadelphia, 1857.

Wertenbaker, Thomas Jefferson. *The Founding of American Civilization: The Middle Colonies.* New York, 1938.

———. *Princeton: 1746–1896.* Princeton, 1946.

Whitsitt, William Heth. *Genealogy of Jefferson Davis and Samuel Davies.* New York and Washington, D. C., 1910.

Williams, John Rogers. *The Handbook of Princeton.* New York, 1905.

Winslow, Ola Elizabeth. *Jonathan Edwards, 1703–1758.* New York, 1940 and 1961.

Wirt, William. *Sketches of the Life and Character of Patrick Henry.* Philadelphia, 1817.

Index

Davies, Rev. Samuel, Publications
(*cont.*)
Danger and Remedy, 76; *The
Curse of Cowardice*, 76, 167;
Catalogue of Books, 178–179. *See
also* Davies, Poetry, *and* Davies,
Sermons
———— Sermons: excerpted, 58–59,
73, 77–78, 79, 80, 81; impor-
tance of, 68, 70, 186; published
collections, 69–70; in Welsh, 69,
69n; to Presbytery of New Castle,
72; urged to publish, 152; on
Braddock's defeat, 165, 165n;
funeral sermon for David Cowell,
181; on death of George II, 185.
See also Davies, Preaching, *and*
Davies, Publications
Davies, Samuel, Jr.: birth, 39
Davies, Sarah Kirkpatrick: marries
Samuel Davies, 13; dies, 13
Davies, William: birth, 39
Davis, Harry Alexander: cited, 3n,
4n, 5n, 6n
Davis, Richard Beale: on Davies' poe-
try, 47n, 52–53; on Davies'
preaching, 70; cited, 44n, 48n,
52n, 168n
Davis, William: land grant to, 4
Dawson, Rev. Thomas, Commissary
of Virginia: on Davies' trip to
Great Britain, 134; appointed
Commissary, 159; on return of
Davies to Va., 160
Dawson, Rev. William, Commissary
of Virginia: correspondence with
Davies, 58; correspondence with
Bishop of London, 87–88, 131,
158; on Davies, 87–88, 127; on
Toleration Act, 125–126, 132;
on dissent, 127; petitioned to sup-
press Davies, 132; on Occasional
Conformity Act, 133; death, 159
Denham, John: Davies visits, 55
Dews, Rev. Samuel: Davies preaches
for, 56

Dickinson, Rev. Jonathan: secedes
from Synod of New York, 27;
president of College of New Jersey, 136; and Yale College, 136;
death, 136
Dickinson, Sarah: marries David
Davies, 4; death, 4
Dinwiddie, Robert, Governor of
Virginia: compared to William
Gooch, 96; Davies' opinion of,
96–97; Davies' relations with,
96–97; opinion of John Todd,
96–97; aids Davies in Great Britain, 97; correspondence with
Bishop of London, 97; on Occasional Conformity Act, 133; on
Toleration Act, 133; opinion of
Davies, 168; recognizes dissenter
military import, 168; replaced by
Francis Fauquier, 168; men-
tioned, 93n, 116n, 158n
Dodd, William E.: cited, 83
Doddridge, Philip: hymns of, 48; on
Toleration Act, 125, 128; correspondence with Davies, 128; influence on Davies, 153
Donegal, Presbytery of: and Alexander Craighead, 100
Dutch Reformed Church: in N. J.,
21

Eckenrode, H. J.: on Toleration Act,
126n; cited, 64
Edinburgh, University of: Lord Provost subscribes to Davies' sermons,
69n
Edwards, Rev. Jonathan: and revival
in Mass., 22; concept of "divine,"
48; letter from Davies, 54; as
preacher, 68; compared to Davies,
76; attempt to bring to Va., 95;
Davies characterizes, 95; settles at
Stockbridge, Mass., 95; on John
Todd, 96; as president of College
of New Jersey, 171; death, 171
England, Church of: in Va., 14, 27;
Davies on, 14–15; attacked by

Shippen, Edward: trustee of College of New Jersey, 142n

Shore, John: petitions Hanover Presbytery, 195

Smith, Rev. Caleb: trustee of College of New Jersey, 142n

Smith, Horace Wemyss: cited, 184n

Smith, Rev. John B., President of Hampden-Sydney College: and religious freedom, 169

Smith, Jonathan Bayard: at College of New Jersey, 183

Smith, Rev. Robert: founds school, 9–10, 101n

Smith, Rev. William (of Philadelphia): hostility to College of New Jersey, 141, 142, 145; Davies' reaction to, 145

Smith, William (of Hanover, Va.): petitions Hanover Presbytery, 195

Smith, William (of New York City): trustee of College of New Jersey, 142n

Smith, William Peartree: trustee of College of New Jersey, 142n

Smyth, Rev. Charles: cited, 63n, 64n

Society for managing the Mission and Schools among the Indians: Daives as secretary of, 117

Society in London for Promoting Religious Knowledge among the Poor: Davies meets, 105; sends books to Va., 105, 108, 112; correspondence with Davies, 109–110, 112

Society in Scotland for Propagating Christian Knowledge: and Davies, 115–116; establishes Commission for Indian Affairs, 115

Spencer, Rev. Elihu: trustee of College of New Jersey, 142n

Spener, Philip Jacob: organizes devotional groups, 20

Sprague, William Buell: on Davies as preacher, 68, 69

Starr, Harris Elwood: cited, 142n

Stennett, Rev. Samuel: Davies meets, 151

Stephen, Sir Leslie: cited, 142n

Stith, Rev. William: attacks Davies, 61n; seeks Commissary position, 168

Sweet, William Warren: on Davies as preacher, 68; cited, 46n

Synod of ———. *See* individual listings under New York, Philadelphia, *and* Philadelphia and New York

Taylor, Rev. Edward: poetry, 151

Tennent, Rev. Gilbert: education, 21; influence of Frelinghuysen, 21; preaching, 21–22, 138; follows Whitefield, 23; *Danger of an Unconverted Ministry*, 25n; and New Brunswick Presbytery, 26; preaches in Va., 33, 120; reports to Synod of New York, 116–117; extremism of, 138; on College of New Jersey, 139; character of, 140; sails for Great Britain, 140; arrives in London, 140; trustee of College of New Jersey, 142n; opposition of William Smith, 142; meets Samuel Chandler, 142–143; goes to Ireland, 144; meets with Avery committee, 150; returns from Ireland, 154; sails for Philadelphia, 154; supports William McClenachan, 183–184; petition on behalf of, 189–192

Tennent, Rev. William: founds "Log College," 8, 21, 101n; trustee of College of New Jersey, 142n; mentioned, 9

Tennent, William, Jr.: and New Brunswick Presbytery, 26

Tennent family: and Presbyterian Church, 23; and education, 136

Tenney, Mary McWhorter: on communion tokens, 93n

Thomas, Ann: marries Shionn David, 4

SAMUEL DAVIES

Apostle of Dissent in Colonial Virginia

was manually set on the Linotype in 11½ point Caslon Old Face
with two-point line spacing. Monotype Caslon Old Style No. 337
was selected for display. The optional italic swash characters, available in both faces, were used to demonstrate the versatility of classic
Caslon, uncommon among contemporary book faces.

The book was designed by Jim Billingsley and composed,
printed, and bound by Kingsport Press, Inc., Kingsport, Tennessee.
The paper on which the book is printed is designed for an effective
life of at least three hundred years.

THE UNIVERSITY OF TENNESSEE PRESS
Knoxville